The Hidden Enterprise Culture

The Hidden Enterprise Culture

Entrepreneurship in the Underground Economy

Colin C. Williams

Professor of Work Organization, University of Leicester Management Centre

Edward Elgar

Cheltenham, UK • Northampton, MA, USA

Published by
Edward Elgar Publishing Limited
Glensanda House
Montpellier Parade
Cheltenham
Glos GL50 1UA
UK

Edward Elgar Publishing, Inc.
136 West Street
Suite 202
Northampton
Massachusetts 01060
USA

A catalogue record for this book
is available from the British Library

Library of Congress Cataloging in Publication Data
Williams, Colin C., 1961–
    The hidden enterprise culture : entrepreneurship in the underground
economy / Colin C. Williams.
        p. cm.
    Includes bibliographical references and index.
    1. Informal sector (Economics) 2. Entrepreneurship. 3. New business
enterprises. I. Title.
    HD2341.W483 2006
    338'.04—dc22

2006005603

ISBN-13:   978 1 84542 520 3 (cased)
ISBN-10:   1 84542 520 0 (cased)

Printed and bound in Great Britain by MPG Books Ltd, Bodmin, Cornwall

Contents

List of figures and tables

FIGURES

TABLES

Acknowledgements

This book is no different to any other in the sense that the author is indebted to many people who have given their time and energy to discuss the matters contained herein. As such, there are a long list of people and organizations to be acknowledged.

To commence, a number of organizations funded research projects out of which the ideas in this book directly arise. First, several organizations funded the collection of the empirical data for the English Localities Survey discussed herein, namely the Joseph Rowntree Foundation, Countryside Agency and the European Commission via its Targeted Socio-Economic Research (TSER) programme. Besides acknowledging the financial support of these organizations, I would like to take this opportunity to thank Theresa Aldridge, Jo Cooke, Stephen Hughes and Richard White for providing the research assistance and all of the respondents for taking the time to help us understand the role of underground transactions in their lives.

Second, the Office of the Deputy Prime Minister (ODPM) in the UK provided funding to write a synthesis report on the relationship between the underground sector and deprived neighbourhoods. In this regard, I would like to express my gratitude not only to the ODPM for giving me the opportunity to think through policy approaches towards the underground sector in deprived neighbourhoods, but also my co-workers, Stephen Syrett and Mel Evans.

Third, the Small Business Service (SBS) and Small Business Council (SBC) provided financial support to investigate small businesses in the informal economy and what should be done about them. In relation to this project, I am grateful to both members of the SBC Steering Group, especially Paul Harrod, Monder Ram and Simon Topman for their insights, as well as the friendly and encouraging support for my ideas offered by numerous SBS officials, but particularly Sheena O'Sullivan and Caroline Berry, along with the officials from other Government Departments who participated in the resultant discussions and focus groups.

Fourth and finally, I would like to express my gratitude to the Office of National Statistics (ONS) for funding an evaluation of data sources on entrepreneurship and the underground economy so as to explore possible future avenues for mapping this relationship. With regard to this project, I owe a debt to my collaborators for being so good-natured and stimulating, namely Rebecca Harding of London Business School (now at Deloitte), Simon King of Hedra PLC and Angela Zvesper of Social Research Associates.

I am also deeply grateful to a host of other organizations and individuals that have played a vital role in helping the ideas contained in this book come to fruition. First, I would like to thank all members of the cross-government Informal Economy Steering Group (IESG) for inviting me to attend their discussions and gain an insight into policy formulation and implementation in this realm. I am particularly grateful to those senior officials in Her Majesty's Revenue and Customs (HMRC), Department of Food and Rural Affairs (DeFRA), Home Office, Department of Work and Pensions (DWP), Department of Trade and Industry (DTI), HM Treasury and Small Business Service (SBS) who entrusted me with such privileged access to their discussions. Let them rest assured that I do not here break the 'Chatham House extra' promises of confidentiality I made.

Second, I would like to show my appreciation to members of the Formal and Informal Work in Europe (FIWE) research programme funded by the European Commission, especially the co-ordinator, Professor Birgit Pfau-Effinger, for giving me the opportunity to discuss some of the ideas contained in this book and providing valuable feedback, as well as for so warmly welcoming me on my sojourn in Hamburg. Third, I am grateful to those who participated in the Public Administration Committee (PAC) Conference stream on the 'shadow economy and public administration' in September 2005 for providing further valuable feedback on some of the ideas discussed here. Finally, I am indebted to a number of senior civil servants within Her Majesty's Revenue and Customs (HMRC) crosscutting policy team who have so openly shared their knowledge and ideas with me on both the availability of evidence and the feasibility of various policy options.

There are also a multitude of additional academic colleagues who have over the past few years provided advice on various ideas raised in this book, notably Peter Armstrong, Liliana Bàculo, Danny Burns, Jenny Cameron, Julie Gibson, Katherine Graham, Bill Jordan, Enrico Marcelli, Sue Marlow, Pete North, Monder Ram, Piet Renooy, John Round, Michael Samers, Jim Thomas and Richard White. As always, however, I owe by far the largest debt to my long-time research collaborator, Jan Windebank. As she knows so well, and continuously reminds me, it is actions on my part and not mere words of gratitude that are required. Hopefully, by the time she reads these words, I will have started to make some inroads into my massive debt to her.

Last but not least, I would like to thank my colleagues at the University of Leicester School of Management (ULSM) for providing such a friendly, supportive and inspiring environment in which to work. I could not wish for a better and more stimulating group of colleagues. Mindful of some of their reactions to my expressions of gratitude in a previous book, I will not here repeat what it means to me to have such a wonderful work environment. They should already know.

The usual disclaimers of course apply. The ideas and recommendations in this book are those of the author and do not necessarily represent the position of any of the above individuals, organizations or institutions.

1. Introduction

INTRODUCTION

How many enterprises and entrepreneurs start up in business conducting a portion or all of their trade on an off-the-books basis? And how many continue to conduct a portion of their trade in such a manner once they become more established? What should be done about them? Should governments adopt ever more punitive measures to eradicate this form of risk-taking enterprise and entrepreneur from the economic landscape? Should a laissez-faire approach be adopted towards them? Or should these underground entrepreneurs be recognized as a hidden enterprise culture and policies pursued to help them legitimize their business ventures? If so, how might this be achieved? What can be done to help those currently working on an underground basis to move towards formalizing their business operations? And what preventive measures can be taken to ensure that in future, enterprises start up in a legitimate manner?

This book seeks answers to these questions. For a long time, academic commentators, the media and governments predominantly represented the underground economy in western nations as a 'sweatshop' realm where off-the-books employees work for low pay under exploitative conditions for unscrupulous employers. The picture painted was of back-street garment manufacturers in deprived neighbourhoods, vulnerable people standing on street corners waiting to be hired as 'cash-in-hand' day-labourers, ruthless and unprincipled gang-masters who employ (illegal) immigrant groups as labour in the agricultural sector, and of shady and corrupt employers who exploit weak and unprotected immigrant groups as cockle-pickers under lethal conditions on dangerous tidal beaches. The underground economy, in other words, was depicted as an exemplar of what occurs when unbridled profit-motivated capitalism is allowed to let rip.

It is consequently of no surprise that academic, media and government discourses throughout the western world have called for its eradication. Indeed, improving the ability of governments to detect this endeavour and developing tougher punishments to deter employers and employees has been widely pursued, in order that this apparently objectionable and undesirable toil can be eradicated from the economic landscape of the western world. If all underground labourers were indeed working as off-the-books employees for low pay under exploitative sweatshop-like conditions, then there would be perhaps little need for this book. After all, there is little doubt that underground sweatshops need to be eradicated and stringent deterrents appear to be just the tonic required. In this book, however, I wish to evaluate critically the validity of this representation of the underground economy and in doing so, to question whether deterrence really is the appropriate way forward.

In an earlier book written as the first in what is intended to be a trilogy on the underground economy (Williams, 2004a), a significant portion of the underground economy in the western world, especially in lower-income populations, was revealed to be comprised of friends, neighbours and acquaintances engaging in 'paid favours' for each other, conducted not for the purpose of financial gain but in order to help each other out. The resulting argument was that if governments continue with their deterrence approach towards the underground economy, the social capital and active citizenship that governments are elsewhere in public policy seeking to nurture will be destroyed since paid favours now constitute a large portion of all mutual aid in contemporary society, especially in deprived populations. A call was therefore made for a new public policy approach to legitimize this hidden economy of paid favours (rather than eradicate it), in order that a more joined-up public policy approach towards underground work and developing social capital can be achieved, spheres so far considered as separate and unconnected.

In this second volume in the intended trilogy, the dominant representation of the underground economy as exploitative sweatshop-like employment and the deterrence approach is again put under the spotlight but this time, the focus of attention is on that large portion of underground work carried out under work relations akin to formal employment and for profit-motivated purposes, rather than as paid favours. My intention is to reveal first, that the vast majority of underground employment conducted for financial gain is not undertaken by off-the-books employees under sweatshop conditions but by people working on a self-employed basis and, second, that many of these self-employed engaged in off-the-books transactions display entrepreneurial qualities and can thus be seen as constituting a 'hidden enterprise culture'. Indeed, the argument of this book will be that unless this underground entrepreneurship is recognized, then western governments with their deterrence approach will destroy precisely the entrepreneurship and enterprise culture that they are otherwise so ardently seeking to foster.[1]

To display the urgent need for this re-representation of underground enterprise as a hidden enterprise culture, as well as for a root and branch rethinking of how governments tackle this sphere, let me introduce Justin, a young man in his early 20s whom I met while conducting interviews for this book. Justin is self-employed running his own rapidly growing car valet business with a number of employees and is a shining example of the sort of entrepreneurial person that western governments are seeking to nurture through their enterprise culture policies. How, therefore, did he become what he is today? As he recounted during our conversation, as a young boy, he had washed cars one Saturday morning at a charity event with his local scout group and following this, having seen the demand for such a service, had decided to continue to do so at weekends for people in his neighbourhood in order to earn some extra cash.

Knocking on doors and offering his services, he had quickly built up a regular clientele and had carried on doing this throughout his school years. By the time he reached 16 years old, he had a well-formulated plan of what he was going to do for a living. Rather than continue on to further education, he therefore left school and set about implementing it. He used the money accumulated from his weekend work to purchase a van and equipment to set up as a car valet and then set about building upon his existing client base. Today, five years after starting up, he employs three people and is currently seeking to reduce the share of his turnover from domestic customers and expand the proportion from the more commercial side of his operation, such as used car dealers and car maintenance garages for whom he provides a valet service. Although he continues to conduct a portion of his work for domestic customers on an off-the-books basis, especially for long-standing customers, he has over the years slowly transferred a greater share of his business into the legitimate realm and is intending to be in his words 'more or less fully legit' within the next year or so.

This book is about all of the Justins of this world. It is about those who engage in off-the-books work on a self-employed basis either when they are starting up their business ventures and/or more serially once they have established their enterprises. For some readers, these characters might be considered a rather minor group, some insignificant and superfluous backwater of the contemporary business world of little or no relevance or importance. In this book, however, these underground entrepreneurs will be shown to be far from being some trivial and inconsequential faction in commercial life. Indeed, and as will be later revealed, if they were a business, on most counts, Underground Entrepreneurs PLC would be by far most western countries' biggest corporation. In the USA, it would certainly eclipse General Motors or any of the other conglomerates that sit at the top of the Fortune 500. Likewise, Underground Entrepreneurs UK PLC would be larger than any of the FTSE 100 companies, and the same applies across all other western nations.

In bringing this hidden enterprise culture out into the open, the intentions in this book are twofold. On the one hand, the objective is to significantly advance understanding of the underground economy in western societies. By transcending the conventional negative depiction of this sphere as sweatshop-like exploitative work and revealing how off-the-books work is chiefly conducted by the self-employed who display entrepreneurial characteristics, not only will this book reconfigure how the underground economy is represented but also will display the need for a fundamental overhaul of how western governments deal with this sphere. Until now, tackling underground work and nurturing an enterprise culture have been treated as separate policy realms, resulting in western governments deterring through their policies towards underground work precisely the enterprise and entrepreneurship that other policies are seeking to develop. By here exposing the extent and character of this hidden enterprise culture and investigating what can be done about it, how this troubling contradiction can be overcome will be explored.

On the other hand, the aim in this book is to significantly advance understandings of entrepreneurship and enterprise culture. Until now, the entrepreneur has been predominantly represented by academic textbooks, the media and government as some sort of superhero figure and ideal-type that lesser mortals can only dream of emulating while enterprise culture has been depicted as a risk-taking society that always plays by the rules. Here, however, I will expose how such an uncontaminated, wholesome and legitimate representation of entrepreneurship and enterprise culture is wholly out of keeping with the lived experience, as the practices of the Justins of this world so clearly display. In other words, this book somewhat tarnishes, discredits and despoils the textbook ideal-type of the entrepreneur as some risk-taking superhero by exposing how trading on an underground basis is often deeply implicated in their practices. Similarly, it also blemishes the concomitant depiction of enterprise culture as always legitimate and above board by displaying how the glistening whiter-than-white legitimate enterprise culture that most commentators portray represents just the tip of the iceberg and that below the metaphorical waterline and so far ignored is a vast hidden enterprise culture of underground entrepreneurs. This, of course, has major implications for how public policy in future seeks to foster enterprise culture and entrepreneurship that are dealt with throughout this book.

Before going any further, however, it is necessary to be clear about what is here being discussed. After all, some new to the study of the underground economy might think that this book is seeking to represent drug dealers and those selling stolen or counterfeit goods on market stalls and in back-street public houses as entrepreneurs and part of some hidden enterprise culture.

Let me be clear at the outset that even if such endeavour might be interpreted as entrepreneurial (see Friman 2004; VanderBeken 2004; Vanduyne, 1993), this type of criminal activity is not the subject of this book.

Underground workers are here defined as those engaged in the production and sale of goods and services that are unregistered by, or hidden from, the state for tax, social security and/or labour law purposes but which are legal in all other respects. Importantly, therefore, for those who might assume that drug dealers, those selling stolen goods and so forth are being discussed, this definition explicitly denotes that the only criminality about underground work is the fact that the production and sale of the goods and services are not registered for tax, social security and/or labour law purposes (for example, Feige, 1990; Leonard, 1998a, b; Pahl, 1984; Portes, 1994; Thomas, 1992). The underground economy, that is, covers only work where the means are illegitimate, not the ends (goods and services) themselves. As such, underground workers are engaged in either: the evasion of direct (that is income tax) and/or indirect (for example VAT, excise duties) taxes; benefit fraud where the officially registered unemployed work while claiming benefits; or the avoidance of labour legislation, including employers' insurance contributions, minimum wage agreements or certain safety and other standards in the workplace.

This definition of what is included and excluded in the underground economy conforms in its entirety to nearly all other definitions found in the academic literature (for example, Feige, 1990; Leonard, 1998a, b; Marcelli *et al.*, 1999; Pahl, 1984; Portes, 1994; Thomas, 1992; Williams and Windebank, 1998). Importantly, it also mirrors the definition of the underground economy adopted by most western governments (for example, ACOSS, 2003; European Commission, 1998; Grabiner, 2000; ILO, 2002; OECD, 2000a, b, 2002).

This strong consensus across both governments and academic commentators concerning how to define the underground economy, however, is not apparent when it comes to denoting such work. Over the years, a multitude of adjectives and nouns have been used to symbolize such work (see Table 1.1). Some of the more popular include the 'black economy' (now redundant because of its racist connotations when contrasted to the formal 'white economy'), 'cash-in-hand work' (even though cheques are often used) and the 'informal economy' (which often causes confusion since unpaid work is also frequently included under this banner).

In this book, any permutation of the multiplicity of adjectives and nouns listed in Table 1.1 could have been hypothetically used to denote this sphere, even if some are perhaps more accurate than others (for example, to call this a 'ghetto' economy is to imply a socio-spatial concentration of such work that is far from evident). It is important to state, therefore, that the term 'underground economy' has been chosen for one straightforward reason. This is the most popular phrase used to denote such work, particularly in North America, so is most likely to generate instant recognition of what is being discussed among the widest number of readers. No other rationales underpin the decision to use this phrase. As such, readers should not assume any other rationales underpinning this choice of name. More important to understand is what is here being asserted about the nature of this work and what is to be done about it. In the rest of this introductory chapter, therefore, attention turns towards outlining the arguments being made.

Table 1.1   Adjectives and nouns used to denote underground enterprise

Adjectives			
Black	Cash-in-hand	Clandestine	Concealed
Dual	Everyday	Ghetto	Grey
Hidden	Invisible	Irregular	Marginal
Moonlight	Non-observed	Non-official	Occult
Off-the-books	Other	Parallel	Peripheral
Precarious	Second	Shadow	Submerged
Subterranean	Twilight	Underground	Unexposed
Unobserved	Unofficial	Unorganized	Unrecorded
Unregulated	Untaxed	Underwater	
Nouns			
Activity	Business	Economic activity	Economy
Employment	Enterprise	Firms	Industry
Sector	Work		

Source: extension of Williams (2004a, Table 1.1)

ARGUMENT OF THE BOOK

This book reveals that pervading western economies is a hidden enterprise culture that has so far received little attention. Part I highlights how studies of entrepreneurship and enterprise culture have on the whole failed to recognize this hidden enterprise culture while studies of the underground economy have similarly largely neglected the entrepreneurship of underground workers, at least in advanced economies. This sets the scene for the rest of the book that seeks to bring together these disparate fields of enquiry. Part II documents the extent and nature of the underground economy so as to reveal the relative magnitude of this hidden enterprise culture and provide a portrait of those involved while Part III evaluates the various options available to public policy with regard to this endeavour. Arguing that western governments are currently destroying through their punitive approach towards the underground economy precisely the enterprise culture that they wish to foster, Part IV then sets out a new public policy approach that treats this hidden enterprise culture as an asset to be harnessed and details initiatives both to help enterprise in future start-up in a proper manner and to enable fledgling entrepreneurs and more established enterprises currently embedded in the underground economy to legitimize their operations. The outcome is not only a re-representation of the underground economy but also the provision of a guide as to how western governments can bring this hidden culture of enterprise into the legitimate realm.

Part I, in consequence, sets the scene for the rest of the book by revealing how the study of entrepreneurship and the study of the underground economy have both so far neglected the linkages between enterprise culture and underground workers. Chapter 2 will reveal how the literature on entrepreneurship and enterprise culture, although depicting entrepreneurs as risk-taking heroes and enterprise cultures as risk societies, seldom if ever questions whether this means that they always play the game by the rulebook. Notable by its absence from nearly all accounts of entrepreneurship and enterprise cultures will be shown to be the notion that risk-takers and risk societies might weigh up the costs of being caught and the level of punishments and decide to do business on an underground basis. As this chapter begins to intimate, however, such a clean and legitimate representation does not seem to dovetail with the lived experience of entrepreneurship and enterprise culture in the contemporary business world.

Chapter 3 then charts how until very recently, the literature on the underground economy in western societies largely failed to consider whether underground workers display entrepreneurial characteristics. Mapping the broad trajectories in the evolution of thought on the underground economy over the past three decades, this chapter will display how an ongoing tendency has been to focus upon its negative attributes and as such, represent it as a form of work that needs to be eradicated using deterrence measures. This chapter will display, however, that in recent years there has slowly begun to emerge a new stream of thought that is beginning to represent this sphere as a potential asset and how this is leading to a rethinking of whether deterrence is always the appropriate public policy response. This emerging view of the underground economy as a potential asset, it will be here shown, is very different to the much earlier strand, encapsulated in the writing of Hernando de Soto and other neo-liberals (for example, De Soto, 1989; Rosanvallon, 1980), which viewed underground workers (mostly in the third world) as entrepreneurs and argued that the solution was to deregulate the formal economy to set all workers free from the shackles of state intervention. Instead, and in stark contrast, this new perspective that recognizes the presence of entrepreneurship in the underground economy will be here revealed to be exploring how this entrepreneurial endeavour can be transferred from the underground sphere into the formal economy and as such, resonates strongly with the current view of most western governments.

Having set the scene by displaying how entrepreneurship and the underground economy have been largely treated as separate and unrelated matters, Part II then begins to explicate the relationship by mapping the extent and nature of the underground economy to reveal the relative importance and character of this hidden enterprise culture. Chapter 4 commences this process by reviewing the various methodologies and findings of those who have sought to chart the size and growth of underground enterprise and this is followed in Chapter 5 by a detailed portrait of the heterogeneous varieties of underground enterprise. Here, for the first time, new extensive empirical evidence is reported of the proportion of underground work that is conducted by off-the-books employees, fledgling entrepreneurs, more established self-employed people and not-for-profit 'social' entrepreneurs, along with numerous first-hand case study accounts of underground workers so as to highlight the diversity within each of these segments of the underground economy. The outcome is both a quantitative and qualitative portrait of the underground economy, which displays how most underground work is conducted by self-employed people and paints a fine-grained picture of the diverse types of worker in this hidden enterprise culture.

Chapter 6 then seeks to explain this hidden enterprise culture in western societies. Moving away from the conventional use of single and universal causes to explain its existence, this chapter promulgates that a multitude of individual factors can influence the decision to work on an underground basis and whether they apply in any time or place depends on whether a host of other factors are present and how they combine together. For example, high tax levels might lead to a relatively extensive underground economy. However, where trust in government is higher and there is awareness of the benefits of taxation for social cohesion, then a hidden enterprise culture will not necessarily be the inevitable outcome of higher tax levels. Here, therefore, it will be revealed that the reasons for the existence of a hidden enterprise culture are complex, multi-layered and subtle and that they can be captured only through dynamic explanatory models that include a whole range of factors and how they interrelate. This appreciation, as will become apparent, is important when considering the initiatives required for dealing with underground work.

In Part III, the various policy options are evaluated. Chapter 7 explores the implications of persisting with the deterrence option that until now has been the dominant public policy approach towards underground enterprise in most advanced economies. This will reveal that continuing with this approach will result in western governments deterring precisely the entrepreneurship and enterprise culture that it otherwise wishes to nurture. Chapter 8 therefore considers whether the policy option of laissez-faire might be a way forward. Indeed, until now, for those who have brought to the fore the presence of entrepreneurship in this realm (for example, De Soto, 1989, 2001), this has been the approach advocated. Their argument has been that the widespread prevalence of entrepreneurship in the underground economy is a rationale for freeing other business from the shackles of state intervention and deregulating the formal economy. In this chapter, however, strong justifications are set out for not pursuing this policy path, not least that it would result in a 'race to the bottom' in western economies.

Chapter 9 then sets out the arguments for a third policy option that is beginning to receive much greater attention, namely facilitating the transfer of this work into the legitimate realm. While a largely deterrence approach might remain appropriate for eradicating off-the-books employees working in sweatshops, it is here contended that for fledgling micro-entrepreneurs and the more established self-employed that constitute the vast bulk of the underground economy, conventional deterrents (push measures) need to be combined with more enabling (pull) initiatives that encourage such work to transfer into the legitimate sphere.

Part IV then focuses upon identifying in some detail the variety of pull measures that might be used in conjunction with the existing push measures to harness this hidden enterprise culture. First of all, and in order to help enterprise in future start up in a legitimate manner, Chapter 10 pinpoints a range of preventive measures to encourage enterprise and entrepreneurs to no longer start up their business ventures conducting a portion or all of their transactions in the underground economy. Measures evaluated here will include those that seek to: simplify the process of compliance; create new categories of work that legitimize underground entrepreneurship and enterprise; use direct and indirect tax incentives to encourage more firms to start off on a legitimate footing; provide support to micro-enterprise start-ups, and help smooth the transition from unemployment to self-employment.

Chapters 11 and 12 then turn towards more 'curative' remedies to pull into the legitimate realm those fledgling entrepreneurs and more established enterprises that are currently conducting a portion or all of their trade on an off-the-books basis. Chapter 11 evaluates a range of supply-side incentives to encourage underground enterprise and entrepreneurs to make the transition to the legitimate sphere, including the use of: societal-wide amnesties; individual-level voluntary disclosure; advisory and support services for those seeking to legitimize their operations; and formalization mentors or tutors. Chapter 12, meanwhile, evaluates the other side of the coin, namely demand-side measures to persuade customers to acquire goods and services from legitimate rather than underground sources. Here, three types of demand-side incentive will be evaluated: targeted indirect tax measures; targeted direct tax measures and a range of service voucher schemes that have been recently experimented with in some European nations.

Besides helping businesses start off in a legitimate manner and providing incentives (alongside deterrents) to encourage those already working underground to legitimize their activities, Chapter 13 explores the importance of first, raising awareness of the costs of underground work and benefits of working formally, and second, fostering societal commitment to legitimate work practices. This will contend that although it is important to use direct controls to ensure compliance, these need to be supplemented with indirect control methods so as to forge a 'high-commitment society' that relies more on internal control to elicit participation in the legitimate rather than underground economy.

Finally, Chapter 14 evaluates whether the issue of co-ordinating government thought and action when tackling the underground economy is as important as is sometimes asserted in public policy circles. Taking two polar opposite cases of a relatively fragmented style of governance in relation to the underground economy (that is, the UK) and a state with a highly co-ordinated institutional infrastructure (that is, France), this chapter reveals the paucity of current evidence to support the view that greater co-ordination of strategy and operations necessarily leads to greater effectiveness. Rather than write off joined-up approaches towards the underground economy, however, this chapter argues that there is thus a dire need for much more evaluation of the effectiveness of joined-up initiatives than has so far been the case.

In the concluding chapter, Chapter 15, the overall argument of the book will be then synthesized. Commencing by reviewing the case for the underground economy being represented as a hidden enterprise culture and thus an asset that needs to be harnessed rather than an obstacle to development, it then summarizes the arguments about how this might be achieved by combining deterrence (push) measures with enabling (pull) measures, concluding that unless concerted action is now taken in this policy direction, then western governments will with each new measure deter such work, ending up destroying precisely the enterprise culture that they are so desperate to nurture.

NOTES

1. Having reviewed the moral economy of paid favours in a previous book (Williams, 2004a) and the self-employed working on an off-the-books basis in this volume, the future intention in the final book in the trilogy will be to return to the segment of the underground economy conventionally focused upon, namely the so-called 'sweatshop' sphere where people work as off-the-books employees for legitimate or underground businesses. The objective will be to unpack the oversimplistic understandings of the nature of this sweatshop realm sometimes purveyed and reconsider conventional wisdom regarding public policy approaches towards this sphere.

PART I

Entrepreneurship and the underground economy: the missing link

2. Studies of entrepreneurship: the omission of the underground economy

INTRODUCTION

In this chapter and the next, the scene will be set for the rest of the book by highlighting how both those studying entrepreneurship and those studying the underground economy have widely omitted to explore how they are interrelated. While the next chapter deals with how, besides a few neo-liberals seeking to extol the virtues of deregulation, those researching the underground economy in the western world have until recently largely neglected its entrepreneurial features, the focus of this chapter is on the voluminous literature on entrepreneurship and enterprise culture, and how despite the depiction of entrepreneurs as risk-taking heroes and enterprise cultures as risk societies, this literature seldom if ever questions whether this means that the game is played always by the rulebook. Notable by its absence from nearly all literature on entrepreneurship and enterprise cultures, that is, is the notion that these risk-takers and risk societies might weigh up the costs of being caught and the level of punishments and then decide to do some or all of their business on an off-the-books basis. As will be displayed, however, such a clean and legitimate representation of entrepreneurs and enterprise culture does not seem to dovetail with the lived experience in the contemporary world.

Here, therefore, first the ways in which entrepreneurship and enterprise culture are depicted in the literature will be reviewed and following on from this, questions will be raised about this largely wholesome representation of entrepreneurship and enterprise culture. In doing so, the intention is to explain how the pure, clean and sanitized narratives of entrepreneurship and enterprise culture that dominate the literature have written out the underground economy from their portrayals, thus causing a rift between textbook representations and the everyday realities of entrepreneurship and enterprise culture.

DEPICTING ENTREPRENEURSHIP AND ENTERPRISE CULTURE

It takes only a cursory glance at the literature on entrepreneurship and enterprise culture to realize that these have long proven elusive concepts to define and that today, there still remains no widely accepted consensus on how to define them. As Cole (1969: 17) put it well over three decades ago, 'for ten years we ran a research centre in entrepreneurial history and for 10 years we tried to define the entrepreneur. We never succeeded'. Some two decades later, the literature remained still no closer to any widely agreed definition. As Brockhaus and Horowitz (1986: 42) conclude, 'there is no generic definition of the entrepreneur' while Shaver and Scott (1991: 24) argued that 'entrepreneurship is like obscenity: nobody agrees what it is, but we all know it when we see it'. It is similarly the case with 'enterprise culture'. If defining the 'entrepreneur' remains littered with confusion, so too does this closely linked concept. Indeed, most definitions lie somewhere on a spectrum of meaning that ranges from at the narrow end a view of enterprise culture as a society characterized by 'entrepreneurship' to at the broader end a view of enterprise culture as a society in which there is a positive, flexible and adaptable attitude to change (see OECD, 1989: 6–7).

In a now notorious phrase, Hull *et al.* (1980) have thus likened the search for a definition of the entrepreneur (and enterprise culture) as akin to 'hunting the heffalump'. For all of the effort put into defining these phenomena, the study of entrepreneurship and enterprise culture seems never to get any nearer to reaching an agreed definition. Why is this the case? In one recent very insightful analysis that attempts to explain this impasse, Jones and Spicer (2005: 235) contend:

> But what if research into the entrepreneur has, in its very failure, identified something critically important about the operation of the category of the entrepreneur, that is, that it is essentially indefinable, vacuous, empty? What if entrepreneurship has not failed at all, but has uncovered something significant about the underlying structure of entrepreneurial discourse, that is, that 'the entrepreneur' is an empty signifier, an open space or 'lack' whose operative function is not to 'exist' in the usual sense but to structure phantasmal attachment?

This is an important argument. Even though the literature on entrepreneurship and enterprise culture has been unable to reach any consensus on how to define these phenomena, there does seem to be strong and broad agreement on two issues.

Nearly all representations in the voluminous literature, first, depict entrepreneurship and enterprise culture in a positive and virtuous manner and second, portray them in a relatively clean and sanitized way. Indeed, for the purposes of this book, where the intention is to explain the failure to identify a relationship between these phenomena and the underground economy, it is this overarching desire to provide a positive, virtuous and clean portrait of entrepreneurs and enterprise culture, as will be shown, that is of crucial importance. As Jones and Spicer (2005: 237) explain, such a portrayal:

> offers a narrative structure to the fantasy that coordinates desire. It points to an unattainable and only vaguely specified object, and directs desire towards that object ... One secures identity not in 'being' an enterprising subject but in the gap between the subject and the object of desire. This lack is central to maintaining desiring ... it is precisely the ... mysterious nature of entrepreneurship discourse that allows it to be so effective in enlisting budding entrepreneurs and reproducing the current relations of economic domination.

In order to depict how nearly all definitions and depictions of entrepreneurship and enterprise culture represent them in positive, virtuous and clean terms as desirous objects, this section thus reviews first, how entrepreneurship and second, how enterprise culture is predominantly portrayed. By revealing how these objects of entrepreneur and enterprise culture are being endowed with positive attributes, and at the same time implicitly contrasted with subordinate 'others' that have no name but constitute the 'non-entrepreneur' and 'non-enterprise culture', it becomes apparent why the underground economy has been written out of representations of entrepreneurship in particular, and enterprise culture more generally. To detail how underground work is an inherent part of contemporary entrepreneurship and enterprise culture, to put it plainly, would tarnish this object of desire and curtail people's emotive attachment to achieving this fantasy state of being.

Depictions of Entrepreneurship

Throughout the advanced economies and well beyond, the endless search to define and depict the entrepreneur has resulted in a multiplicity of traits, qualities and characteristics being attached to this subject. Even if there remains no agreement on what these are, and heated debates over whether specific ones should be included or not, the widespread agreement, to repeat, is that what is being defined and delineated is essentially a wholesome and virtuous subject. Entrepreneurs are in the eyes of Cannon (1991) 'economic heroes'. They are, as Burns (2001: 1) proclaims, 'the stuff of "legends" ... held in high esteem and held up as role models to be emulated'. As he continues, they are 'super heroes' (Burns, 2001: 24).

This super-heroic and virtuous status is the case, as Table 2.1 displays, whichever theoretical approach to entrepreneurship is adopted. Whether one adopts the 'great person' perspective that views them as born (rather than made) and reads them as possessing a 'sixth sense' along with intuition, vigour, energy, persistence and self-esteem and contrasts them with 'mortals' who 'lack what it takes', or one adopts the more socially constructed theoretical approaches of the classical, management, leadership or intrapreneurship schools of thought, the assumption is that the entrepreneur is a superheroic figure possessing virtuous attributes that 'lesser mortals' do not. In none of these schools are negative attributes ever attached to the entrepreneur.

What, therefore, are these positive qualities possessed by the entrepreneur? This is the subject of much debate. Different commentators and schools of thought put forward contrasting attributes, champion certain qualities over others, argue over whether particular traits are applicable or not, and debate what emphasis should be given to which qualities, or sets of qualities. The outcome has been a very large and continuously expanding field of enquiry. Indeed, Armstrong (2005) identifies the emergence of over 20 academic journals dedicated to the study of entrepreneurship. Yet despite such a huge mountain of research and human effort, this large and rapidly expanding field of enquiry is still no closer to reaching agreement on the qualities of the entrepreneur.

Indeed, it feels somewhat like walking into a minefield to even attempt here to provide a list of the possible characteristics, traits and/or qualities possessed by entrepreneurs. Yet this needs to be done if one is to more fully understand how the entrepreneur is variously being defined and depicted in this voluminous literature as well as how this is always done by attributing virtuous characteristics to this heroic figure. Here, therefore, and following Burns (2001: 27), the various characteristics, traits and/or qualities possessed by entrepreneurs that are being debated in the literature are listed as:

- the need for independence;
- the need for achievement;
- internal locus of control;
- ability to live with uncertainty and take measured risks;
- opportunistic;
- innovative;
- self-confident;
- proactive and decisive with higher energy;
- self-motivated; and
- vision and flair.

Many other commentators have produced similar lists, albeit with slightly different emphases in each case (for example, Baty, 1990; Blanchflower and

Table 2.1 Summary of approaches to describing entrepreneurship

Entrepreneurial model	Central focus or purpose	Assumption	Behaviour and skills	Situation
'Great person' school	The entrepreneur has an intuitive ability – a sixth sense – and traits and instincts with which she or he is born	Without this 'inborn' intuition, the individual would be like the rest of us mortals, who 'lack what it takes'	Intuition, vigour, energy, persistence and self-esteem	Start-up
Psychological characteristics school	Entrepreneurs have unique values, attitudes and needs that drive them	People behave in accordance with their values; behaviour results from attempts to satisfy needs	Personal values, risk-taking, need for achievement and others	Start-up
Classical School	The central characteristic of entrepreneurial behaviour is innovation	The critical aspect of entrepreneurship is in the process of doing rather than owning	Innovation, creativity and discovery	Start-up and early growth
Management school	Entrepreneurs are organizers of an economic venture; they are people who organize, own, manage and assume the risk	Entrepreneurs can be developed or trained in the technical functions of management	Production planning, people organizing, capitalization and budgeting	Early growth and maturity
Leadership school	Entrepreneurs are leaders of people; they have the ability to adapt their style to the needs of people	An entrepreneur cannot accomplish his or her goals alone, but depends on others	Motivating, directing and leading	Early growth and maturity
Intrapreneurship school	Entrepreneurial skills can be useful in complex organizations; intrapreneurship is the development of independent units to create, market and expand services	Organizations need to adapt to survive; entrepreneurial activity leads to organization building and entrepreneurs becoming managers	Alertness to opportunities, maximizing decisions	Maturity and change

Source: Cunningham and Lischeron (1991: 47)

Meyer, 1991; Bolton and Thompson, 2000; Brockhaus and Horowitz, 1986; Carr, 2002; Chell *et al.*, 1991; Kanter, 1983; McClelland, 1961; Schumpeter, 1996; Storey and Sykes, 1996).

Given that the purpose here is simply to highlight the absence of underground endeavour from the entrepreneurship literature, there is no need to go too deeply into the heated debates that are complex and ongoing about the validity and/or importance of each attribute. All that is required here is a brief description of what is meant when commentators refer to each. Much more important is to recognize that all of these qualities possessed by the entrepreneur are being used as building blocks to construct a wholesome representation of the entrepreneur as a heroic figure.

First, that is, it is commonly assumed that the entrepreneur has a 'need for independence', often interpreted as meaning that they need to be their own boss. However, voluminous debates exist, not least because independence is seen to mean different things to different people, such as controlling your own destiny, controlling your working time, or the desire to do things differently. Similarly, the assertion that entrepreneurs have a 'need for achievement' is a very open-ended attribute since achievement might mean making money, for others money as an end in itself might be less important. Entrepreneurs are also often said to possess an 'internal locus of control'. If one believes that you can control your environment and destiny, you are said to have an internal locus of control and this is seen as a virtuous trait. If, however, you believe in destiny, then you have an external locus of control and you take what life throws at you (see Begley and Boyd, 1987; McClelland, 1961; Rotter, 1966).

A further set of positive attributes often accorded to entrepreneurs is that they are asserted to have the 'ability to live with uncertainty and take measured risks' (for example, Brockhaus, 1980). Human beings, it is often asserted, do not like uncertainty and one of the biggest uncertainties of all is whether one will have a regular income. Most people, therefore, are seen to be risk averse. They try to avoid risks and insure against them. Setting up your own business is risky and owner-managers are willing to take more risks than most people, a trait that is widely believed entrepreneurs possess, although again this is hotly debated. Entrepreneurs are also seen to be 'opportunistic'. By definition, entrepreneurs are said to seek out opportunities to make money. Often entrepreneurs see opportunities where others see problems associated with change and do not mind the uncertainty. They are also seen to be 'innovative' (for example, Mueller and Thomas, 2001). Indeed, possessing the ability to spot opportunities and to innovate is sometimes seen as the two most important distinguishing features of entrepreneurs. These characteristics set entrepreneurs apart from owner-managers and other mortals.

As such, entrepreneurs are sometimes viewed as 'self-confident', both in their own judgement and ability to start up businesses. Entrepreneurs are also asserted to be more 'proactive and decisive with higher energy' in the sense that they tend to be proactive rather than reactive and more decisive than others in the sense that they seek out opportunities and act quickly and decisively to make the most of an opportunity before somebody else does. They are also seen to be highly 'self-motivated', amounting almost to a driving urge to succeed in their goals; this is driven by their inner need for achievement, far stronger than in the average owner-manager (Chell *et al.*, 1991). They also possess 'vision and flair' in that entrepreneurs are seen to have a clear vision of what they want to achieve. That is part of the fabric of their motivation. It is also said to help them bring others with them, both employees and customers.

Whatever the validity of attaching any or all of these attributes to entrepreneurs, the important point here, to repeat, is that this heroic figure is always endowed with positive qualities. To witness this, one needs only consider that if the above are the qualities of entrepreneurs, then the dualistic opposite, the 'non-entrepreneur', is somebody who is dependent, lacks the will to achieve, believes in destiny, cannot live with uncertainty and avoids risks, fails to take opportunities, lacks the ability to innovate, lacks confidence, is reactive, indecisive and lacks energy, lacks the ability to motivate themselves and has no vision or flair.

In other words, one useful way of interpreting the category entrepreneur is through the lens of hierarchical binary thought. For Derrida (1967), western thought is characterized by a mode of thinking that first, conceptualizes objects/identities as stable, bounded and constituted via negation and second, reads the resultant binary structures in a hierarchical manner in that the first term in any dualistic opposite (the superordinate) is endowed with positivity and the second term, the subordinate (or subservient) 'other', is endowed with negativity.

This theorization of western ideas as premised on a hierarchical binary mode of thinking is here deemed a useful heuristic device for understanding entrepreneurship discourse. Viewing the above literature through this lens allows one to see how the majority of debates taking place surrounding the qualities of the entrepreneur represent an attempt to portray entrepreneurship/non-entrepreneurship as a binary hierarchy. Entrepreneurship is the superordinate term endowed with positivity while the unnamed non-entrepreneurship category is the subordinate 'other' endowed with negativity and whose meaning is established solely in relation to its superordinate opposite.

To contest such binary hierarchical thought, first, attempts can be made to revalue the subordinate term, namely the non-entrepreneur. The problem, however, and as Derrida (1967) points out, is that revaluing the subordinate in a binary hierarchy is difficult since it also tends to be closely associated with the subordinate terms in other binary hierarchies (for example, non-entrepreneur is associated as shown above with dependency, an external locus of control, risk avoidance, an inability to innovate, indecision, no vision, a lack of flair, motivation and energy). A second strategy is thus to highlight the interdependencies between the two sides of the dualism and a third strategy is to blur the boundaries between the terms so as to undermine the solidity and fixity of identity/presence.

It is this latter strategy that is adopted in this book and is a major driving force underpinning it. The intention throughout is to tarnish the largely positive representation of the entrepreneur (and enterprise culture) by showing the disparity between the ideal-type textbook representation and the everyday realities of entrepreneurship (and enterprise culture) where participants do not always play by the rulebook. The objective, in other words, is to sully the clean, sanitized and virtuous image of the entrepreneur by highlighting the lived practices of entrepreneurship so as to begin to deconstruct the binary hierarchical thought that endows the entrepreneur with wholly positive attributes. The principal way in which this is achieved in this book is by bringing to the fore the ways in which many entrepreneurs engage in underground transactions in their daily practices so as to challenge the notion that these are super-heroic figures that possess traits that are always virtues, which others should adopt.

Depictions of Enterprise Culture

It is not only the sanitized representation of the entrepreneur that needs to be contested if the relationship between the underground economy and entrepreneurship is to be more fully understood. So too must the depiction of enterprise culture. In much of the literature, that is, enterprise culture is very much treated in the same positive and virtuous way as entrepreneurship.

For Burns (2001: 40), for example, 'An entrepreneurial culture is one that fosters positive social attitudes towards entrepreneurship'. As such, an enterprise culture possesses the same traits as identified above for entrepreneurship, albeit writ large for the society rather than applied to the individual (see also Carr, 2002; Gibb, 1987; Hofstede, 1981; Timmons, 1994). Therefore, just as the 'entrepreneur' has been predominantly endowed with positive attributes and seldom discussed in a more negative fashion, the same applies so far as enterprise culture is concerned. On the whole, with some notable exceptions (for example, Armstrong, 2005; Deutschmann, 2001; Fournier, 1998; Jones and Spicer, 2005, 2006), few studies have sought to challenge the largely wholesome representation of enterprise culture.

Consider for example, the following celebratory ode to the entrepreneurial culture of the USA by Burns (2001: 40):

> many would consider the culture in the USA to be the most entrepreneurial in the world. It is an achievement-orientated society that values individualism and material wealth ... Americans are said to have a 'frontier culture', always seeking something new. They are restless, constantly on the move. They have a strong preference for freedom of choice for the individual; the individual is always free to compete against established institutions. Rebellious, non-conformist youth is the accepted norm. If there is an 'American dream' it is that the humblest of individuals can become the greatest of people, usually measured in monetary terms. Achievement is prized and lauded throughout society. Individuals believe they control their destiny. Americans think big. Nothing is impossible. They prefer the new or at least the improved. They worship innovation. Time is their most precious commodity. They are tolerant of those who make mistakes as long as they learn from them. Things need to get done quickly rather than always get done perfectly.

To explain why such odes are to the fore and more negative discourses on enterprise culture have not to any major degree prevailed, it is necessary to understand that enterprise culture (akin to entrepreneurship) is a prescriptive ideology. Written into all binary hierarchies, that is, is a narrative of 'progress' whereby the superordinate 'us' is privileged over the subordinate 'others' in the trajectory of historical development and this in turn locks mind-sets into particular ways of thinking about the past, present and future. As such, the rise to dominance of the superordinate over the subordinate is often somehow conjectured as some natural and inevitable (evolutionist) historical tendency. Enterprise culture, therefore, is conjectured as emerging to replace non-enterprise culture. Given that this prescription is often very closely associated with two other dominant prescriptions, namely the shift from a Fordist to a post-Fordist mode of production and from bureaucratic to post-bureaucratic organizations, such a binary hierarchy has proven difficult to contest in the contemporary period (see Du Gay and Salaman, 1998).

Indeed, rather than recede, enterprise culture as a prescriptive ideology has displayed colonizing tendencies. As Du Gay and Salaman (1998: 63–4) put it:

> In Britain attempts to construct a culture of enterprise have proceeded through the progressive enlargement of the territory of the market – of the realm of private enterprise and economic rationality – by a series of redefinitions of its object. Thus the task of creating an 'enterprise culture' has involved the reconstruction of a wide range of institutions and activities along the lines of the commercial business organization, with attention focused, in particular, on their orientation towards the customer. At the same time, however, the market has also come to define the sort of relation that an individual should have with him/herself and the 'habits of action' he or she should acquire and exhibit. Enterprise refers here to the

'kind of action, or project' that exhibits 'enterprising' qualities or characteristics on the part of individuals or groups. In this latter sense, an 'enterprise culture' is one in which certain enterprising qualities – such as self-reliance, personal responsibility, boldness and a willingness to take risks in the pursuit of goals – are regarded as human virtues and promoted as such.

Given the way in which this prescriptive ideology has apparently begun to pervade every nook and cranny of daily life, it is perhaps crucial that the so far wholesome reading of enterprise culture is subjected to greater critical evaluation.

Here, in consequence, the depiction of enterprise culture as composed of super-hero entrepreneurs playing by the rulebook in their business lives is transcended. Although there may be a gleaming 'whiter-than-white' version of enterprise culture, this is here asserted to represent but the tip of the iceberg and beneath the surface, so far largely ignored, exists a large hidden enterprise culture composed of entrepreneurs who do not always play within the bounds of the law. By shining a light on this hidden enterprise culture beneath the waterline, the aim is to begin to tarnish the sanitized and clean representation of enterprise culture by revealing the everyday lived realities.

THE OMISSION OF THE UNDERGROUND ECONOMY

To see how the underground economy is related to entrepreneurship and enterprise culture, it is necessary to question whether entrepreneurship and enterprise culture should always be depicted in first, such a positive and virtuous manner and second, a clean and sanitized way. To begin to understand that this is necessary, consider just one characteristic often associated with these objects, namely the desire to take risks. In many variants of entrepreneurship and enterprise culture, especially the UK case (Chell *et al.*, 1991), a great deal of emotional weight is given to the concept of risk. There is seen to be an inextricable bond between risk and entrepreneurship. As Lord Young in a 1987 speech to the Centre for Policy Studies stated, 'Risk-taking is at the heart of enterprise' (cited in Seldon 1991: 67). Meanwhile, David Potter, the founder of Psion, believes that the 'key equation is risk = opportunity' (Potter, 1998), while the DTI (1998: 6) asserts that 'Entrepreneurs sense opportunities and take risks in the face of uncertainty ... The UK needs more risk-takers ...'.

Until now, however, and despite the common representation of entrepreneurs as risk-taking heroes and enterprise cultures as risk societies, it has been seldom if ever questioned whether this means that they always keep to the rules. Notable by its absence from most literature on entrepreneurship and enterprise cultures, that is, is the notion that risk-takers and risk societies might weigh up the probability of being caught and the level of punishments and decide to do some or all of their business on an off-the-books basis.

Until now, perhaps the best known attempt to impute any negative attributes to entrepreneurship is the study by Kets de Vries (1977) that adopts a psychodynamic approach and suggests that many entrepreneurs are the product of unhappy family backgrounds, particularly situations in which the father is a controller and manipulator who is remote and often seen as a deserter. As a result of these experiences, these individuals develop an intense dislike of authority figures and develop suppressed aggressive tendencies towards persons in control, leading them to set up on their own. Although such an approach has been criticized due to the lack of empirical evidence, Delmar (2000) notes that it is one of the few theories contesting the view of the entrepreneur as an exceptional person with superhuman capabilities. Entrepreneurs here are portrayed as having problems, like everyone else, and are not immune to failure.

To move towards further tarnishing the overwhelmingly sanitized representation of the entrepreneur and enterprise culture, let me here take as my starting point the 'old adage that if you scratch an entrepreneur you will find a "spiv"' (Burns, 2001: 4). One does not need to look far beyond the celebratory textbook odes to find a wealth of support for such a view. As Armstrong (2005: 211) asserts, 'The few academic attempts to draw an ethical boundary around the concept of entrepreneurship so as to exclude the unethical and/or illegal, are unconvincing to say the least'. The classic study of the entrepreneur as somebody who does not always play by the rulebook is that of Collins *et al.* (1964). A one-off in the literature for many years, their mordant view of entrepreneurial opportunism has been partially corroborated by Bhide and Stevenson (1990). Expecting to find that reputation effects would keep entrepreneurs honest where morality failed, these authors find the opposite. They also conclude that most dishonesty by entrepreneurs is not found out.

Two contemporary volumes that further deconstruct the dominant super-heroic representation of entrepreneurs are *How Mumbo-Jumbo Conquered the World* (Wheen, 2004) and *Critique of Entrepreneurship* (Armstrong, 2005). Both provide detailed accounts of how well-known individuals often used in textbooks to exemplify the superheroic entrepreneur have been later identified as not always abiding with the law. They show how the Maltese advocate of lateral thinking, Edward de Bono (1985), in his book, *Tactics: the Art and Science of Success*, showcased a number of people who 'would generally by regarded as "successful"'. One was the US hotelier Harry Helmsley, later convicted of massive tax evasion, and another was Robert

Maxwell, subsequently exposed as one of the major fraudsters in British history. Jonathan Aitken, in his book, *The Young Meteors* (1967), meanwhile, sought to overcome the prejudice that he perceived British society to then have against entrepreneurs by drawing attention to the cases of Gerald Ronson, aged 27, 'one of Britain's youngest self-made property millionaires', and Jim Slater, the 'brilliantly successful' founder of Slater-Walker. Slater-Walker eventually had to be bailed out by the Bank of England and Jim Slater was found guilty of 15 offences under the Companies Act. Gerald Ronson, meanwhile, served a term in Ford open prison for his participation in an illegal share-ramping operation. Jonathan Aitken himself in June 1999, having served as a Cabinet Minister until 1995, found himself jailed for perjury and attempting to pervert the course of justice.

Jeffrey Robinson in *The Risk Takers* (1985) again paraded Gerald Ronson as somebody to emulate along with Robert Maxwell. Yet another entrepreneurial pin-up in his gallery was Asil Nadir, owner of the fruit-packing company Polly Peck. In 1990, Robinson published *The Risk Takers Five Years On*, boasting that some of his original interviewees, including Robert Maxwell and Asil Nadir, had 'gone from strength to strength'. Indeed, he predicted somewhat ironically that Maxwell would eventually retire in glory, leaving his sons Kevin and Ian with the existing challenge of 'keeping dad's ship afloat'. Maxwell's corpse was found floating off the coast of Spain on 5 November 1991, after a fall from his yacht. In this revised edition, he also included several 'big players' that he had missed in his first book. These included Gerald Ratner, 'the world's largest jeweller', and Michael Smurfit, an 'indisputable success'. Once again, however, these pin-ups went belly-up. Ratner transformed his firm's annual profit of £112 million into a loss of £122 million after admitting that one of his products was 'crap' and was forced to quit. Smurfit, furthermore, resigned as chairperson of Irish Telecom only a few weeks after Robinson's book was published when it was revealed that he had bought a new corporate HQ without informing his fellow directors and that he was a shareholder in a company which had previously owned the property.

John Bloom, meanwhile, the 1960s' washing machine tycoon, according to Armstrong (2005), financed his early operation by tax evasion and spent some time in jail at the end of his public career accused of deception and false accounting. Sir Richard Branson, meanwhile, another entrepreneurial pin-up, according to Bower (2001: 9–10) allegedly avoided purchase tax at the beginning of his career and the supposed reason why he escaped prosecution being that his parents guaranteed to repay the tax, and because the tax authorities' priority was to recover the money, not to punish.

As Armstrong (2005: 215) thus concludes, 'the entrepreneur-hero may be a liar, a thief and driven by greed and worse'. Of course, not all entrepreneurs engage in illegitimate and/or off-the-books transactions and it is not the intention here to say that they do. The point is solely that at least some so-called 'super-heroes' are not perhaps as clean-cut and above board as is sometimes asserted in textbook depictions. Denoting entrepreneurs as virtuous and always following the law is as erroneous as asserting that they always break the rules.

By displaying how the underground economy is often closely related to entrepreneurship and enterprise culture, the aim here is simply to move closer to a portrayal of the lived realities of entrepreneurship and enterprise culture than has so far been the case in most textbook representations. Perhaps, if the prevalence of people working on an off-the-books basis were in decline, there would be little reason to bring this facet of entrepreneurship and enterprise culture out into the open. However, and as will be shown, the fact that it is growing in western economies means that it is essential to do so. Indeed, this is especially the case when it is realized that many simply assume that such cheats will disappear from view in the fullness of time. As Gerschlager (2005: 1) puts it:

> competitive markets have traditionally been assumed to detect, punish, and finally eliminate cheats. In a curious reversal of Gresham's law, honest traders are meant to drive out dishonest ones. In bimetallic times, Gresham observed that 'bad' money drove out the good, consequently inflating the economy. In markets, however, it is assumed that merits will be gained only by those deserving it. The false and 'bad' ones will be detected, their reputations spoiled, and nobody will want to trade with them any longer. In this way, cheats are assumed to disappear from the marketplace. The general idea is that the mechanisms inherent in markets will rid them of liars and cheats.

Yet the fact that the underground economy today constitutes a large and growing proportion of most advanced economies suggests that this is not the case. Until greater understanding is achieved of the close relationship between the underground economy and entrepreneurship, then western economies will fail to fully appreciate the real nature of entrepreneurship and enterprise culture, and policies to harness a culture of entrepreneurship are likely to fall short of what is required.

CONCLUSIONS

This chapter has revealed that much literature on entrepreneurship and enterprise culture errs towards representing these phenomena in first, a positive and virtuous manner, and second, a clean and sanitized way. The problem, however, is that there seems to be marked discrepancy between such textbook odes to these phenomena and the lived realities. To move forward so far as understanding entrepreneurship and enterprise culture is concerned, therefore, the assertion is that it will be first necessary to move beyond the cult super-hero representation of what it means to be an entrepreneur and partake in enterprise culture and instead, investigate some of the everyday realities. In this book, this will be done through highlighting how many entrepreneurs work on an underground basis. Indeed, only once this has been more fully understood will it be possible for policy towards the development of entrepreneurship and enterprise culture to respond in a manner that reflects the reality of the contemporary business environment.

3. Studies of the underground economy: the omission of entrepreneurship

INTRODUCTION

This chapter charts both the changes and continuities in thought on underground work in western economies over the past three decades. It displays how despite some changes at the margins, the vast majority of this literature has continued to propagate a vision of underground work that focuses largely upon its negative characteristics and as such, represented it as a form of work that needs to be eradicated using deterrence measures. Recently, however, it will be revealed that a body of thought has begun to emerge that depicts some more positive attributes of this sphere. This emerging representation of the underground economy as a source of enterprise and entrepreneurship and therefore an asset to be harnessed, moreover, is revealed to be very different to earlier neo-liberal thought, encapsulated in the writing of Hernando De Soto (1989). Rather than using the identification of entrepreneurship in the underground economy as a justification for deregulating the formal economy to free it from state intervention, this emerging perspective will be shown to be exploring how this hidden enterprise culture can be transferred into the legitimate realm.

In order to frame the continuities and changes in how the underground economy has been represented over the past three decades, this chapter will draw upon Derrida's (1967) notion that western thought is characterized by a hierarchical binary mode of thinking that to repeat, first, conceptualizes objects/identities as stable, bounded and constituted via negation and second, reads the resultant binary structures in a hierarchical manner in that the first term in any dualistic opposite (the superordinate) is endowed with positivity and the second term, the subordinate (or subservient) 'other', is endowed with negativity. In the last chapter, it was shown how entrepreneurship and enterprise culture have been largely represented as superordinate terms endowed with positivity in comparison with their subordinate others, non-entrepreneurship and non-enterprise culture. In this chapter, in stark contrast, it will be displayed how the underground economy has been predominantly represented as a subordinate other. In the legitimate/underground economy binary hierarchy, that is, the legitimate economy has been attributed with positivity while the underground economy has been wholly endowed with negative attributes.

Such a binary hierarchical framing, as will be seen, represents a useful starting point for understanding the continuities and shifts in thought on the underground sector. Indeed, to start to see how the underground economy has been configured as a subservient 'other' endowed with negativity, and whose meaning is established solely in relation to its superordinate opposite, there is no need to look any further than the multitude of different adjectives variously used to denote this sphere. As Latouche (1993: 129) recognizes, 'most of them simply qualify – either directly or indirectly – whatever is meant, in a *negative* way'. The underground economy, that is to say, and as indicated in Chapter 1, is variously denoted as 'non-structured', 'non-official', 'non-organized', 'a-normal', 'hidden', 'a-legal', 'black', 'submerged', 'non-visible', 'shadow', 'a-typical' or 'irregular'. In other words, it is denoted as 'bereft of its own logic or identity other than can be indicated by this displacement away from, or even effacement of, the "normal"' (Latouche, 1993: 129). It is described by what it is not – what is absent from, or insufficient about, such work – relative to the formal sphere and this absence or insufficiency is always defined as a negative feature of its configuration compared with formal employment.

It is not simply at the level of the adjectives used to denote this sphere, however, that it is useful to frame understandings of the underground economy in terms of hierarchical binary thought. It is also valuable when seeking to understand the continuities and trajectories of thought as well as the advances being made in this book. As will become clear below, over time, what can be witnessed in the literature is a steady deconstruction of the underground sector as a subservient other in a legitimate/underground binary hierarchy. To show this, first, this chapter highlights the ways in which the underground economy was conventionally depicted as a subservient other in a formal/underground hierarchical binary and following this, the ways in which this hierarchical binary has been so far deconstructed along with the further contributions being made in this book.

CONSTRUCTING UNDERGROUND WORK AS A SUBORDINATE OTHER

Modernity and the Underground Economy

To understand how underground work was conventionally constructed as a subordinate 'other' in a formal/underground employment binary hierarchy, one needs look no further than the 'modernization thesis'. Here, the view prevailed that underground work was in long-term decline, a pre-capitalist vestige of the past awaiting incorporation into capitalism. In this evolutionist or staged reading of economic development, the narrative of progress privileges the superordinate term in the binary hierarchy over the subordinate other. The underground sector is read as primitive or traditional, stagnant, marginal, residual, weak, and about to be extinguished; a leftover of pre-capitalist formations that the inexorable and inevitable march of modernization will eradicate. Indeed, a universal natural and inevitable shift towards the formalization of goods and services provision is envisaged as societies become more 'advanced'. The persistence of supposedly traditional underground activities, therefore, is taken as a manifestation of 'backwardness' (for example, Geertz, 1963) and it is assumed that such work will disappear with modernization or economic 'progress' (Lewis, 1954; Ranis, 1989). Underground work is thus read as existing in the interstices, or as scattered and fragmented across the economic landscape. Formal work, by contrast, is represented as systematic, naturally expansive, and coextensive with the national or world economy. Such 'modernist' interpretations, in consequence, focus upon either its imminent destruction, its proto-capitalist qualities, its weak or its determined position, viewing it either as 'the mere vestige of a disappearing past [or as] transitory or provisional' (Latouche, 1993: 49). Never is the underground sector represented as resilient, ubiquitous, capable of generative growth, or as driving economic change in this conventional modernist representation.

The Underground Sphere as a Separate Economy

A further common depiction that reflects how the formal/underground dualism has been conventionally constructed as a binary hierarchy is that the underground realm is often treated as entirely separate to the formal sphere. Those engaged in underground work have been on the one hand, viewed as wholly off-the-books businesses and on the other hand, there has been a strong and resilient view, characterized by the 'marginality thesis', that represents individuals engaged in underground work to be those marginalized from formal employment and reliant on this sphere as a survival strategy (for example, Castells and Portes, 1989; De Soto, 1989; ILO, 2002; Lagos, 1995; Maldonado, 1995; Rosanvallon, 1980). As such, the formal and underground realms are read as separate, a dual labour market, where one set of individuals and firms engage in formal employment and another ('othered') set of individuals and firms participate in underground employment (for example, Mezzera, 1992; Tokman, 1989a, b).

The Underground Sphere as a Negative Realm

Third, and reflecting how binarism represents the subordinate other in any binary hierarchy as possessing negative attributes, the underground sphere in conventional readings is persistently and recurrently depicted as exploitative, low-paid and sweatshop-like in character. Indeed, and reflecting the power of binarism, it is this representation of underground work as a negative phenomenon that has proven most markedly resistant to change. To see this negativity, one needs look no further than how the populist commentator, Jeremy Seabrook (2003: 9–10), views those working in the underground economy: 'The Western poor are dead souls ... hustlers and survivors, economic shadows in the shadow economy, the discouraged and despairing who have fallen through the bottom line of accounting systems'.

Such negative depictions are not confined to populist accounts, or solely to media portrayals. Political economists, recognizing that the underground sector is persistent and growing, have depicted it as a new form of work emerging in late capitalism as a direct result of economic globalization (a dangerous cocktail of deregulation and increasing global competition), that is encouraging a race to the bottom. In this reading, underground workers are portrayed as sharing the same characteristics subsumed under the heading of 'downgraded labour': they receive few benefits, low wages and have poor working conditions (for example, Castells and Portes, 1989; Gallin, 2001; Portes, 1994; Sassen, 1997).

Such accounts, therefore, solely highlight the negative attributes of this sphere. It is seen as: fraudulent activity that causes a loss of revenue for the state in terms of non-payment of income tax, national insurance and VAT (for example, Bajada, 2002; Grabiner, 2000; O'Higgins, 1981); weakening trade unions and collective bargaining (for example, Gallin, 2001; ILO, 2002); creating unfair competitive advantage for firms who use underground labour over those who do not (for example, Grabiner, 2000; Small Business Council, 2004); generating circumstances of 'hypercasualization' as more formal workers are forced underground to compete effectively (for example, Evans *et al.*, 2004; Jordan and Travers, 1998; Small Business Council, 2004); leading to a loss of regulatory control over the quality of jobs and services provided in the economy (for example, Evans *et al.*, 2004; Grabiner, 2000; Small Business Council, 2004); eroding compliance with health and safety standards (for example, Small Business Council, 2004); creating circumstances conducive to the exploitation of workers due to the reduction of wage rates (for example, Gallin, 2001; ILO, 2002); and causing the loss of various employment rights (for example, annual and other leave, sickness pay, redundancy, training). The notion that it might also have more positive outcomes, as will be discussed below, is not considered.

In sum, the conventional depiction of the underground sphere is that it is a pre-modern sector composed of wholly underground businesses and workers engaged in exploitative, low-paid and sweatshop-like work, and thus a hindrance to 'progress'. In other words, it is read as a subordinate other. Recent decades, however, have started to witness a deconstruction of this conventional reading. Below, the ways in which this has occurred are documented along with how this book is further advancing the deconstruction of this binary hierarchy.

DECONSTRUCTING THE UNDERGROUND ECONOMY AS A SUBORDINATE OTHER

One way of making sense of the multifarious shifts in recent decades in how the underground sphere is conceptualized is to view them as a bid to deconstruct the formal/underground binary hierarchy, and more precisely, the representation of the underground sphere as a subservient 'other' endowed with negativity. If viewed through this lens, then much of the apparently diverse and unconnected shifts in thought become more coherent.

To deconstruct binary hierarchies, several approaches can be hypothetically employed. First, attempts can be made to revalue the subordinate term. Second, the boundaries between the terms can be blurred highlighting similarities on both sides of the dualism so as to undermine the solidity and fixity of identity/presence, showing how the excluded other is so embedded within the primary identity that its distinctiveness is ultimately unsustainable. Third and finally, the interdependencies between the two sides of the dualism can be depicted. As will now be seen, the literature on the underground economy over the past few decades has adopted all of these approaches.

Beyond Modernity/Formalization

To understand how the view of underground work as a subordinate other is being deconstructed, let us start with the modernization thesis that views the underground sphere as a primitive or traditional, stagnant, marginal, residual, weak, and about to be extinguished realm, and the formal economy as a modern, growing, strong and extensive sphere. For adherents to this 'modernization thesis', as aforementioned, there is seen to be a natural and inevitable shift towards formalization as societies become more 'advanced'. In this narrative, therefore, all economies are considered to witness the same linear and uni-dimensional trajectory of economic development whereby

underground work steadily disappears and is replaced by formal goods
and services provision.

To witness the dominance of this linear and uni-dimensional reading
of the trajectory of economic development, one has only to consider
how different nations are often viewed as at varying stages of economic
development. The extent of formalization, in this view, is frequently taken
as the measuring rod used to define third world countries as 'developing'
and so-called advanced economies as 'developed' (Williams and Windebank,
1999a). From the standpoint of the modernization thesis, in consequence,
the existence of supposedly traditional underground activities is taken as a
manifestation of 'backwardness' and it is assumed that they will disappear
with economic progress (modernization). In this conceptualization, and to
repeat, underground work is primitive or traditional, stagnant, marginal,
residual, weak and about to be extinguished. It is a leftover of pre-capitalist
formations and the inexorable and inevitable march of modernization will
eradicate such work. Such a view of underground work as some kind of
traditional outdated type of work contract that is in long-term terminal
decline and will vanish with the pursuance of modernization, however,
has come under considerable criticism in recent years, not least due to the
recognition that in the contemporary era, it is growing rather than declining
(see Chapter 4).

Indeed, there has been a marked decentring of the formal economy
in many contemporary texts. For a long time, the formal economy was
represented as a near hegemonic sphere with the informal realm existing
purely in some minor peripheral sites on the edges where the formal economy
had not yet penetrated. The recurring discourse today, however, is that even
in modern economies, the underground sector is not only persistent but a
large and even growing facet (for example, ILO, 2002; Williams, 2002a, b,
2003, 2004g, 2005a, f; Williams and Windebank, 2003a, b). As the ILO
(2002: 53) put it, 'In the world today, a majority of people work in the
informal economy – because most of them are unable to find jobs or start
businesses in the formal economy'.

Rather than depicting underground work as some leftover or a 'a mere
"lag" from traditional relationships of production' (Castells and Portes,
1989: 13), the narrative that has emerged is one of a new and expanding form
of advanced capitalist exploitation that is a direct product of the neo-liberal
project of deregulation taking hold (for example, Amin, 1996; Castells and
Portes, 1989; ILO, 2002; Sassen, 1997; Ybarra, 1989). The argument is that
economic globalization is causing an expansion of underground work (for
example, Castells and Portes, 1989; ILO, 2002; Sassen, 1997) and that this
exploitative form of employment is a new facet of contemporary capitalism.
Particularly prevalent in the USA, this 'globalization thesis' views such

work to be especially prevalent in global cities and among immigrant/ethnic minority populations (for example, Cornelius, 1992; Marie, 1999, 2000; Ross, 2001; Sassen, 1991, 1994a, b, 1996, 1997; Snyder, 2003; Sole, 1998; Waldinger and Lapp, 1993).

As will be shown throughout this book, however, even if replacing the modernization thesis with the globalization thesis results in a more accurate portrayal of the current state of affairs because it recognizes the growth of this sphere, great care needs to be taken. This is because first, it simply replaces one universal generalization of the direction of change with another and second, it ascribes a universal logic to the processes that are supposedly under way. This is ultimately misleading. On the one hand, underground work is not always and everywhere growing. Locations can be identified where the size of the underground sphere is either static relative to the formal economy or even declining (for example, Kesteloot and Meert, 1999; Williams, 2004a; Williams and Windebank, 1998). On the other hand, there is growing evidence that the underground sphere is not everywhere solely a product of neo-liberal economic globalization. Besides such an economic narrative, others argue that a fuller understanding will only derive from a socially, culturally and geographically embedded consideration of this sphere (for example, Renooy *et al.*, 2004; Williams, 2004a; Williams and Windebank, 1998). Once one starts unpacking the range of different processes taking place in various locations, therefore, it becomes apparent that universal generalizations about the trajectory of development and its causes need to be replaced by more embedded understandings if a fuller comprehension is to be achieved.

Even if the underground sector is today seldom if ever read as stagnant or dwindling, a widespread, often implicit, belief is nevertheless that this is a scattered and fragmented sphere that is transitory or provisional, as shown in attempts to map its uneven distribution both temporally, spatially and socio-economically (see below). If no longer seen as in demise, few commentators thus ultimately read underground work as equivalent to formal work. It is still more often than not seen as a by-product of, or response to, changes in the formal economy (see Smith, 2006). This in major part is because the modernization thesis has mostly been contested by pointing to the size and growth of the underground sphere in order to revalue it. The strategy of showing how the underground and formal spheres are mutually entangled and embedded in each other has not so far been pursued in any concerted manner. For example, few so far have engaged explicitly with the idea that the formal economy might shape, and be shaped by, the underground sphere in a process of mutual iteration, or attempted to address the complex interdependence between these realms. Until this is pursued, then the underground sphere as a subordinate, negative and opposite realm will not be brought into independent or perhaps more precisely co-dependent, existence in its own right. It will remain simply a sphere characterized by some absence or insufficiency contained within, in opposition to, or dependent on formal work. In consequence, until such time as it is shown that the excluded other (that is, the underground sphere) is so embedded within the primary identity (that is, the formal sphere) that its distinctiveness is ultimately unsustainable, the formal realm will remain viewed as naturally expansive and the underground sphere as scattered and fragmented across the economic landscape, and even dependent on the formal realm.

Beyond Separate Economies

Turning to the second aspect of the formal/underground binary hierarchy, that is, the treatment of these spheres as entirely separate, some significant advances can be identified in the literature. At first, this negation of their separateness resulted from the realization that the formal and underground sector are linked through networks of subcontracting and supply chains (for example, Barrientos and Ware-Barrientos, 2003; Doane *et al.*, 2003; Lund, 2003; Portes and Walton, 1981), although this argument persisted in viewing underground work as conducted by wholly underground businesses and workers who engage solely in underground work.

This dualistic thinking that treats people and businesses as either underground or formal, however, finds its clearest expression in the 'marginality thesis', which holds that underground work is concentrated among marginalized populations, whether these be poor nations, deprived localities and regions, the unemployed or illegal immigrants (for example, Castells and Portes, 1989; De Soto, 1989; ILO, 2002; Lagos, 1995; Maldonado, 1995; Rosanvallon, 1980). For some two decades or so, a Popperian-like mode of enquiry ensued so far as studies of the distribution of underground work are concerned. Numerous studies, that is, principally subjected this thesis to critical evaluation in order to either corroborate or refute it. The intention was to find out whether it is indeed the case that underground work is entirely conducted by wholly underground businesses and that workers exist who engage solely in underground work. Here, the results are reviewed.

Over the past two decades, a multitude of studies have revealed that the majority of underground work in many populations is conducted by formal businesses undertaking a portion of their trade on an off-the-books basis (for example, Ghezzi, 2006; Ram et al, 2001; Small Business Council, 2004; Williams, 2004a). Similarly, those in formal employment have been found to engage in more underground work than those excluded from formal employment. The widespread finding of direct surveys conducted throughout the developed nations has been that underground work chiefly benefits those already in formal employment. This has been found to be the case in France (Barthe, 1988; Cornuel and Duriez, 1985; Foudi *et al.*, 1982; Tievant, 1982), Germany (Glatzer and Berger, 1988; Hellberger and Schwarze, 1987), Greece (Hadjimichalis and Vaiou, 1989), Italy (Cappechi, 1989; Mingione, 1991; Mingione and Morlicchio, 1993; Warren, 1994), the Netherlands (Koopmans, 1989; Van Eck and Kazemeier, 1990; Van Geuns *et al.*, 1987), Portugal (Lobo, 1990b), Spain (Ahn and Rica, 1997; Benton, 1990; Lobo, 1990a), the UK (Economist Intelligence Unit, 1982; Howe, 1990; Morris, 1994; Pahl, 1984; Warde, 1990; Williams, 2001a, b, 2004a, d; Williams and Windebank, 1999b, 2001a, b, c, d, e, 2002a, b, 2003a) and North America (Fortin *et al.*, 1996; Jensen *et al.*, 1995; Lemieux *et al.*, 1994; Lozano, 1989). On the whole, therefore, the marginality thesis has been largely refuted so far as who engages in such work is concerned.

It is similarly the case that although earlier studies often assumed underground work to be concentrated in deprived regions and localities, this has become much less common recently. Even if some studies have presumed that such work is concentrated in deprived inner city localities (for example, Blair and Endres, 1994; Elkin and McLaren, 1991; Haughton *et al.*, 1993; Robson, 1988) and poorer peripheral regions (for example, Button, 1984; Hadjimichalis and Vaiou, 1989), the overwhelming finding of the detailed surveys conducted over the past two decades has been that this is not the case. Instead, lower-income areas have been found to conduct less underground work than more affluent localities. This has been identified in the Netherlands (for example, Van Geuns *et al.*, 1987), the UK (for example, Bunker and Dewberry, 1984; Williams, 2004e, f, 2005c, d, e; Williams and Windebank, 1993, 1994, 1995a, 1999a, 2001a), France (for example, Barthe, 1985; Cornuel and Duriez, 1985; Foudi *et al.*, 1982) and Italy (for example, Mattera, 1980, 1985; Mingione, 1991; Mingione and Morlicchio, 1993).

Although this at first led to one universal generalization (that is, the marginality thesis) being replaced by another (what might be called the 'reinforcement thesis' in that underground work was asserted to reinforce the socio-spatial inequalities produced by the formal economy), recent years have witnessed the emergence of a more refined understanding. The recognition that in some specific populations evidence is found to support the view that the majority of underground work is conducted by people marginalized from formal employment and wholly undeclared businesses (for example, Kesteloot and Meert, 1999; Leonard, 1994, 1998a) has resulted in a more embedded understanding which recognizes that there are particular economic, political, cultural and/or geographical circumstances where the reinforcement thesis does not hold in the western world. This, in turn, has led to a recognition that it is how various factors combine together in particular circumstances, rather than individual causal factors *per se*, that influence the extent and nature of the underground sphere (for example, Mateman and Renooy, 2001; Renooy *et al.*, 2004; Williams, 2004a; Williams and Windebank, 1995a, 1998). Today, therefore, and so far as the dualistic treatment of people and businesses as either underground or formal is concerned, considerable progress has been made in transcending such binary thought.

Beyond Underground Work as a Negative Phenomenon

Is it also the case, therefore, that the attribution of negative characteristics to underground work and positive attributes to formal employment has been transcended? One might think the recognition that usually relatively affluent populations engage in underground work in western nations would have led commentators to radically rethink the caricature of this work as exploitative, low-paid and sweatshop-like. However, on the whole, those who have sought to rethink this largely negative portrayal of underground work have been so far in the minority.

Of all of the negative attributes attached to underground work, it is probably its low-paid character that has been most widely questioned (for example, Fortin and Lacroix, 2006; Thomas, 1992; Williams, 2004a; Williams and Windebank, 1998). Indeed, it is now widely recognized that the wages and incomes from underground work display just as wide a distribution as those in the formal economy and the view that all underground work is low-paid has been widely refuted. Less questioned, however, is the assumption that such work is predominantly exploitative work conducted under sweatshop-like conditions. Recent years, nevertheless, have seen some significant reinscribing of the character of underground work.

Indeed, since the mid-1990s, it has been broadly appreciated that besides exploitative low-paid sweatshop-like work, there exist autonomous forms of underground employment (for example, Fortin *et al.*, 1996; Leonard, 1994, 1998a; MacDonald, 1994; Renooy, 1990; Warren, 1994; Williams, 2004a, d, 2005b, 2006b, c; Williams and Windebank, 1998, 2001a, b). The outcome is that rather than view underground work as a sweatshop realm sitting at the bottom of a hierarchy of types of formal employment, underground work is now often depicted as a heterogeneous or segmented labour market with a hierarchy of its own (Williams and Windebank, 1998). Following on from this recognition that underground work is conducted on an autonomous as well as an organized basis, the new millennium has witnessed the emergence of a small but growing corpus of thought that has begun to ask first, whether such work should always be viewed as a hindrance to development and second, whether greater emphasis needs to be placed on some of its more positive features. In some ways, this builds upon an earlier tradition of neo-liberal thought but comes to very different conclusions as to the way forward.

Earlier neo-liberal studies, that is, argued that entrepreneurship was apparent in the underground economy and that this sphere should be seen as possessing positive features and representing an asset rather than obstacle to development (for example Contini, 1982; De Soto, 1989, 2001; Minc, 1982; Sauvy, 1984). For these commentators, however, such a finding was seen as a rationale for unshackling formal enterprise from state intervention and deregulating the formal economy so as to allow all economic activity to take place on what in effect is an underground basis. Engagement in such work was read as a form of popular resistance to an unfair and excessively intrusive state and underground workers a political force that can generate both true democracy and a rational competitive market economy (see Chapter 8).

In recent years, however, a much wider group of scholars have started to recognize the existence of entrepreneurship in the underground economy and the presence of this hidden enterprise culture, and brought fresh perspectives that do not always read it as a site of resistance to the encroachment of the state. Similar to the neo-liberals, such enterprise and entrepreneurship is seen as an asset, but only if harnessed and brought into the legitimate realm. This notion of recognizing the underground sector as an asset and seeking to harness underground 'micro-enterprise' has for some years prevailed in majority ('third') world nations (for example, Cornwall, 1998; Franks, 1994; Rakowksi, 1994). As the ILO (2002: 54) state, for example, underground entrepreneurs display 'real business acumen, creativity, dynamism and innovation' and in consequence, this sphere is viewed 'as an incubator for business potential and ... a transitional base for accessibility and graduation to the formal economy'.

It is only in the last few years, however, that this representation has started to be also applied to the underground economies of western nations (for example, Evans *et al.*, 2004; Global Employment Forum, 2001; ILO, 2002; Small Business Council, 2004; Tabak, 2000; Williams, 2004a, c, d, 2005a, b). Viewing this sphere as a potential breeding ground and platform for entrepreneurship and enterprise creation, this stream of thought, rather than advocating the stripping away of all regulations so as to make formal employment like underground work, instead and akin to much of the literature in the majority world, argues that such enterprise and entrepreneurship is an asset but only if harnessed and transferred into the legitimate realm. Indeed, it is the development of this emerging perspective towards the underground economies of western nations and its implications for public policy that is the focus of this book.

CONCLUSIONS

This chapter has charted the continuities and changes in thought on the underground economy over the past three decades or so. Until recently, the vast majority of the literature on the underground economy focused upon its negative attributes and, as such, viewed it as a form of work that needs to be eradicated using deterrence measures. Recently, however, it has been here displayed that a body of thought has begun to emerge that highlights some of the more positive features of this sphere and how this is now leading to a rethinking of whether deterrence is always the appropriate public policy response.

This emerging strand of thought that is rereading the underground economy as an asset that needs to be harnessed rather than a hindrance to development, not least due to the recognition that this sphere is a site for entrepreneurship, is very different to the much earlier neo-liberal strand which argued that the formal economy needs to be deregulated. For these commentators, enterprise and entrepreneurship in the underground sphere of western economies is an asset only if it can be harnessed and transferred into the formal economy. It is the further development of this perspective that is the subject matter of the rest of this book.

PART II

The extent and nature of underground enterprise

4. Estimating the size and growth of underground enterprise

INTRODUCTION

Next time you receive your payslip, look at how much tax you have paid. If you work solely as an employee and have your tax withheld on a 'pay as you earn' basis, you are probably picking up part of the tab that others should be paying. But how much more tax are you paying because others do not? And is the amount growing or reducing over time? This chapter attempts to answer these questions by reviewing what is known about the magnitude of the underground economy and whether or not it is growing.

Both for those exploring the underground sector for the first time, as well as for more seasoned investigators, there is often a deep scepticism about whether it is possible to measure what is by its very nature a hidden phenomenon. Indeed, and as Table 4.1 displays, this scepticism appears at first glance justified. In all nations, vast variations exist in the estimates of its magnitude. In the UK, for example, they range from 1 to 34 per cent of GDP and in the USA from 5 to 28 per cent.

To understand these startling variations, this chapter evaluates the array of measurement methods that have produced these estimates. These range from indirect to direct techniques. At one end of the spectrum, that is, and for those assuming that research participants will not be forthcoming about whether or not they engage in underground work, evidence is sought indirectly in macroeconomic data collected and/or constructed for other purposes. The belief is that even if underground workers wish to hide their income from underground work, these will be nonetheless revealed at the macroeconomic level and it is these statistical traces of their underground work that are analysed by indirect approaches. At the other end of the spectrum are those assuming that despite the illegitimate nature of underground work, reliable data can be directly collected on the nature and extent of underground work using survey methods such as questionnaires.

Table 4.1   Estimates of the magnitude of underground work in advanced economies, as percentage of GDP

Country	Smallest	Highest	Average Estimate
Ireland	0.5	7.2	3.9
Austria	2.1	6.2	4.2
Norway	1.3	9.0	5.5
UK	1.0	34.3	6.8
Australia	3.5	13.4	8.4
Germany	3.4	15.0	8.7
Netherlands	9.6	9.6	9.6
Denmark	6.0	12.4	10.1
Sweden	4.5	14.1	10.1
Canada	1.2	29.4	10.7
Belgium	2.1	20.8	10.9
Spain	1.0	22.9	11.1
USA	5.0	28.0	11.3
France	6.0	23.2	11.4
Portugal	11.2	20.0	15.6
Italy	7.5	30.1	17.4
Greece	28.6	30.2	29.4

Source: Williams (2004a: Table 6.1)

To show why it is important to understand the precise method underlying any headline statement of its size, Table 4.2 reveals how in the UK different techniques produce widely varying measures of its magnitude. For the period 2000 until the present, for example, estimates of its volume in the UK range from 2 per cent of GNP using direct survey methods (Pedersen, 2003) to 12.3 per cent using the cash demand approach of Schneider (2001). Great care needs to be taken, therefore, to understand the method used to measure its size and to ensure when comparing its changing magnitude either over time or across nations that estimates are compared that employ the same method.

In modernization theory, as the last chapter showed, the underground economy was viewed as some pre-capitalist leftover that over time would naturally and inevitably become incorporated into the formal economy. Over the past three or so decades, however, the vast majority of attempts to measure its changing magnitude have revealed that such work is growing rather than declining relative to the formal economy. As Table 4.2 displays, whatever technique is used, the UK underground economy has been growing faster than the legitimate economy in that its relative size as a share of GDP has increased. This is far from unique to the UK. Whatever technique is used, the widespread finding whatever corner of the globe is analysed is that the underground economy is expanding relative to the formal economy. This is the case not only in the western world but also in the old 'second world' of central and east Europe as well as the majority ('third') world (ILO, 2002).

Table 4.2   The size of the UK underground economy as percentage of GNP: by year and measurement method

Measurement method	1970–5	1976–80	1981–5	1986–90	1990–5	1996–2000	2000–
Direct surveys	1.5						2.0
Tax auditing		9.7–12.9					
Income/expenditure discrepancy	2.5	3.6	5.5		10.6		
Physical input method				13.2	13.1		
Currency demand (Tanzi)	4.3	7.9	8.5	9.7	14.3	12.7	12.5
Cash deposit ratio (Gutmann)	14.0	7.2	6.2				
Transactions approach (Feige)	17.2	12.6	15.9				
MIMIC method (Frey–Weck)		8.0					
Cash demand (Schneider)	2.0	8.4		9.6	12.5	13.0	12.3

Sources: derived from Schneider and Enste (2002: Table 4.8); Williams (2004a, chapter 3)

Even if the growth of underground work in advanced market economies is a common finding across all methods, there are stark variations in both estimates of its overall size and the pace of its growth depending on the methods used. It is important, therefore, to understand the different methodologies and the assumptions underpinning them if sense is to be made of the somewhat bewildering array of estimates of its size and growth. Indeed, this becomes even more crucial when it is recognized that in recent years, a consensus has emerged that some methods are more dependable, authoritative and trustworthy than others. As will be shown, most commentators and institutions evaluating the diverse techniques have concluded that indirect techniques are less accurate as a measure of the volume of underground work and, perhaps more importantly so far as this book is concerned, wholly inappropriate for understanding the nature of this work (for example, Mateman and Renooy, 2002; Office of National Statistics, 2005; OECD, 2002a,b; Renooy *et al.*, 2004; Thomas, 2000).

Here, therefore, and to evaluate critically the contrasting methods used when measuring the size and growth of underground work, first, this chapter reviews the relatively indirect methods that seek statistical traces of the underground economy in data collected for other purposes. Second, it evaluates the more direct survey methods, including the method used by the author to identify the degree to which the underground sphere constitutes a hidden enterprise culture.

INDIRECT METHODS

Three types of indirect method have been used to evaluate underground work. First, there are those seeking statistical traces of underground work in non-monetary indicators, second, those employing monetary indicators and third and finally, those that analyse discrepancies between income and expenditure levels. Evaluating each in turn, this section will reveal that the problem with all of these approaches is that they are not only unreliable and inaccurate as proxies of the size of this realm but also provide very little information on the characteristics of this endeavour. Instead, in most cases, they are driven by some very crude assumptions concerning its nature that are far from proven.

Indirect Non-monetary Methods

Three of the most common indirect approaches using non-monetary surrogate indicators are first, those that seek traces in formal labour force statistics, second, those that use very small enterprises as a proxy and third and finally, those that use electricity demand as a surrogate.

Labour force estimates

Methods that measure the magnitude of underground work from formal labour force statistics are of two varieties. The first uses unaccountable increases in the numbers in various types of employment (for example, self-employment, second-job holding) as proxy indicators (for example, Alden, 1982; Crnkovic-Pozaic, 1999; Del Boca and Forte, 1982; Hellberger and Schwarze, 1986). The problem, however, is that the idea that underground work prevails in these categories of employment is an assumption, rather than a finding, of the technique, and there is no way of knowing the degree to which it is underground work, rather than other factors, that has led to such an increase. Second-job holding, for example, is not always a direct result of underground work except if such job holding is illegal *per se*. It is also the result of broader economic and cultural restructuring processes such as the demise of the 'breadwinner wage' and the proliferation of part-time work. To identify the proportion of growth in multiple-job holding attributable to such processes and the share attributable to underground work is thus a difficult if not impossible task.

The second technique seeks discrepancies in the results of different official surveys, such as the population census and firm surveys (for example, Denison, 1982; Lobo, 1990b; Mattera, 1985; US Congress Joint Economic Committee, 1983). Four problems exist with this method. First, such a method often erroneously assumes that individuals are either legitimate or underground workers and, in so doing, misses a vast amount of underground work conducted by those who have a formal job (Bajada, 2002; Williams and Windebank, 1998). Second, by analysing only those employed in businesses, it assumes that all underground work is conducted on an 'organized' basis and misses both more autonomous forms of underground sector activity as well as underground work conducted for households. Third, there is no reason to assume that an underground worker will describe him/herself as employed in a household survey while the employer will not in a business survey. And fourth and finally, the fact that such analyses have resulted in contradictory results, with some studies showing no change in the size of underground work in the post-war years (for example, Denison, 1982) and others showing growth (US Congress Joint Economic Committee, 1983) intimates the need for caution. Due to the inaccuracy of this proxy, in sum, this method has waned in popularity since its heyday in the early 1980s. This approach, moreover, and importantly so far as this book is concerned, provides little, if any, information on the character of underground work.

Very small enterprise (VSE) approach
An alternative is to use very small enterprises (VSEs) as a non-monetary proxy (for example, Fernandez-Kelly and Garcia, 1989; ILO, 2002; Portes and Sassen-Koob, 1987; Sassen and Smith, 1992; US General Accounting Office, 1989). This assumes that in advanced economies, most underground work takes place in smaller enterprises because of their reduced visibility, greater flexibility and better opportunities to escape state controls. Larger firms are viewed as subject to more state regulation and risk-averse to the potential penalties so will be less likely to directly employ underground workers, although they are purported to subcontract to smaller firms who use such labour.

As an indicator of underground work, however, the VSE approach is subject to two contradictory assumptions. On the one hand, not all VSEs engage in underground practices, which could lead to an overestimate. On the other hand, fully underground VSEs will escape government record keeping that could lead to an underestimate (Portes, 1994). As such, estimates can only be very approximate. More importantly, it totally ignores more individualized forms of underground work conducted by people on a one-to-one basis to meet final demand. As Portes (1994: 440–1) thus concludes:

> By themselves, ... such series represent a very imperfect measure of the extent of informal activity. It is impossible to tell from them which firms actually engage in irregular practices and the character of these practices. All that can be said is that small firms, assumed to be the principal locus of informality, are not declining fast and actually appear to increase significantly during periods of economic recession.

Yet despite this, such a proxy indicator remains widely used. Of the 54 countries from which the International Labour Office collects data on 'informal sector enterprise', 21 use the criterion of non-registration of the enterprise, either alone or in combination with other criteria such as small size or type of workplace location, when defining the underground economy while 33 countries use small size as a criterion, either alone or in combination with non-registration or workplace location (ILO, 2002). Hence, the VSE approach remains common with firm size being used as the principal criterion in some two-thirds of countries. It should not therefore be thought that this indirect non-monetary approach is in abeyance. If anything, quite the opposite is the case, despite its inappropriateness for understanding the full range of underground work in contemporary societies.

Electricity demand
Recent years have seen electricity demand employed as a non-monetary indicator of underground work (for example, Friedman *et al.*, 2000; Kaufmann and Kaliberda, 1996; Lacko, 1999). Kaufmann and Kaliberda (1996) assert that electric power consumption is the single best physical indicator of (official plus unofficial) economic activity. Overall, that is, economic activity and electricity consumption have been claimed to move in step with each other with an electricity-to-GDP elasticity of close to one. This means that the growth of total electricity consumption is a fairly reliable indicator for the growth of overall (formal and underground) GDP. By using this proxy measurement of the whole economy and then subtracting from this measure the estimates of official GDP, these analysts derive an estimate of unofficial GDP. Table 4.3 reviews some of the results produced.

As shown in Table 4.2 earlier, compared with other methods, electricity demand produces relatively high estimates. There are, of course, many criticisms that can be raised about using this single variable to assess the underground economy. First, not all types of underground work require a considerable amount of electricity (for example, personal services) and other energy sources can be used (for example, gas, oil, coal). Second, and when seeking trends in underground work, it is necessary to recognize how both the production and consumption of electricity is more efficient than in the past. How to disaggregate this from the volume of underground work is a difficult task since it is not known whether these improvements in energy efficiency are the same in both the legitimate and underground economies. There may also be considerable differences or alterations in the elasticity of electricity-to-GDP across countries and over time. Perhaps more importantly so far as this book is concerned, however, is the fact that such a measurement method tells us nothing about the nature of the underground economy.

Table 4.3   Estimates of underground economy: based on electricity demand

Country	GDP (%)	Country	GDP (%)
Australia	15.3	Lithuania	21.6
Bulgaria	36.2	Latvia	35.3
Belarus	19.3	Poland	12.6
Czech Republic	11.3	Romania	19.1
Estonia	11.8	Russia	41.6
Finland	13.3	Slovakia	5.8
Georgia	62.6	Ukraine	48.9
Hong Kong	13.0	Cyprus	21.0
Hungary	29.0		

Source: Friedman *et al.* (2000: Table 1)

Ultimately, therefore, and like other non-monetary proxy measures, this indicator provides nothing more than a crude measure of the extent of underground work and little, if any, information about the nature of underground work. As such, other analysts have turned to monetary indicators in the belief that this will enable a much closer estimate of underground work.

Indirect Monetary Methods

Indirect monetary methods have concentrated largely on four proxies, namely large denomination notes, the cash–deposit ratio, money transactions and currency demand.

Large denomination notes approach

For those believing that underground workers use exclusively cash in their transactions and that large sums are involved with high denomination notes exchanged, the circulation of high denomination bank notes is a useful proxy indicator of the magnitude of underground work (Bartlett, 1998; Carter, 1984; Freud, 1979; Henry, 1976; Matthews, 1982). First, however, this approach cannot separate the proportion of large denomination notes used for crime from their use in underground work, thus making estimates of the latter difficult (Bartlett, 1998). Second, the evidence is that many underground transactions are for relatively small amounts of money (for example, Cornuel and Duriez, 1985; Evason and Woods, 1995; Tanzi, 1982) and do not necessarily even involve cash. Third and finally, a multitude of other factors besides crime influence the use of large denomination bank notes. Although alterations in modes of payment (for example, credit and debit cards, store cards) imply a decline in usage, the restructuring of formal financial services in advanced economies, reflected in the 'flight of financial institutions' from poorer populations (Collard *et al.*, 2001; Kempson and Whyley, 1999; Leyshon and Thrift, 1994), has necessitated increased cash usage among the financially excluded. These counter-tendencies thus make identifying whether alterations in cash usage are due to crime, the restructuring of formal financial services, shifts in attitudes and behaviour, or the growth/decline of underground work difficult to discern. Indeed, many studies display no increase in the use of large denomination notes once inflation is taken into account (for example, Mirus and Smith, 1989; Porter and Bayer, 1989; Trundle, 1982).

The large denomination notes method, in sum, represents a very unreliable indicator of underground work and makes erroneous assumptions about the character of this work. It is, in conclusion, of little use for understanding the extent and nature of underground work.

The cash–deposit ratio approach

A further monetary proxy is the ratio of currency in circulation to demand deposits. Starting with the former, and similar to the large denomination notes approach, this is grounded in the assumption that in order to conceal income, illegitimate transactions will occur in cash. It then proceeds to estimate the currency in circulation required by legitimate activities and subtracts this from the actual money in circulation. The difference, multiplied by the velocity of money, is taken as the currency in circulation due to underground work. The ratio of this figure to the observed GNP measures the proportion of the national economy represented by underground work. Pioneered by Gutmann (1977, 1978) in the USA who made the courageous assumption that there was no underground work in the USA prior to the Second World War since levels of taxation were so low as to make underground work unnecessary, he takes the ratio for this period as the baseline norm and then finds that money was in circulation beyond the figure required for legitimate transactions. Assuming that this illegitimate cash circulated at the same velocity as the legitimate transactions, underground work was argued to represent more than 10 per cent of the officially calculated national income.

Despite this approach being subsequently widely adopted (for example, Atkins, 1999; Caridi and Passerini, 2001; Cocco and Santos, 1984; Matthews, 1983; Matthews and Rastogi, 1985; Meadows and Pihera, 1981; Santos, 1983; Tanzi, 1980), it suffers from at least seven serious problems. First, cash is not always the medium of exchange for underground transactions (for example, Contini, 1982; Smith, 1985). As Smith (1985) identifies in the USA, whether an undeclared payment is made in cash or by cheque depends on the same factors as determine the mode of payment in formal employment (that is, the size of the transaction and the seller's confidence in the purchaser's cheque). Second, this approach cannot distinguish the share of illegitimate cash circulation due to underground work and the proportion due to crime, nor how it is changing over time. Third, the choice of the cash–deposit ratio as a proxy is arbitrary and not derived from economic theory (for example, Trundle, 1982).

Fourth, the cash–deposit ratio is influenced by a myriad of tendencies besides underground work (for example, changing methods of payment, financial exclusion), often working in opposite directions to one another, which are not taken into account as contributing to changes in the currency ratio (for example, Bajada, 2002; Mattera, 1985). Even where taken into account (for example, Matthews, 1983; Matthews and Rastogi, 1985; Tanzi, 1980), problems remain (Smith, 1986; Thomas, 1988).

Fifth, the choice of a base period when underground work supposedly did not exist is problematic, especially given the sensitivity of the results to which base year is chosen (O'Higgins, 1981; Thomas, 1988). Little evidence exists of some period in history where underground work was zero. Such work has been in existence as long as there have been employment regulations. Henry (1978), for example, cites examples of fiddling and tax evasion from the time of Aristotle, whilst Houghton (1979: 91) shows that in 1905, when tax was at a uniform rate of less than one shilling (5 pence) in the pound in the UK, a departmental committee reported that 'In the sphere in which self-assessment is still requisite, there is a substantial amount of fraud and evasion'. Smithies (1984), moreover, in a detailed case study of underground work in five towns (Barnsley, Birkenhead, Brighton and Hove, Walsall and part of North London) between 1914 to 1970, clearly demonstrates a continuity in the prevalence of such activity. Any method that assumes a time when underground work did not exist is thus founded on suspect grounds (see Henry, 1978).

Sixth, this method assumes the same velocity of cash circulation in the underground and formal spheres. However, there is no evidence that they are the same (Frey and Weck, 1983). Seventh, it is impossible to determine how much of the currency of a country is held domestically and how much abroad. Finally, and perhaps most importantly, this approach does not uncover the nature of underground work. The next approach seeks to overcome some of the above problems by relaxing one assumption in particular, namely that underground transactions take place in cash.

The money transactions approach
Recognizing that cheques as well as cash are used in underground transactions, this approach estimates the extent to which the total quantity of monetary transactions exceeds what would be predicted in the absence of underground work (Feige, 1979). As evidence that cheques as well as cash are used in undeclared transactions in the USA, Feige (1990) quotes a study by the Internal Revenue Service (IRS) showing that between a quarter and a third of unreported income was paid by cheque rather than currency. In Norway, similarly, Isachsen *et al.* (1982) find that in 1980, about 20 per cent of underground services were paid for by cheque, while in Detroit, Smith (1985) provides a higher estimate in the realm of informal home repair, displaying that bills were settled roughly equally in cheques and cash.

By relaxing this cash-only assumption, the unsurprising result is that relatively high estimates of its size are produced. Feige (1990) reports that the US underground economy as a proportion of total reported adjusted gross income (AGI) rose from 0 in 1940 (the base year) to 20 per cent in 1945, declined subsequently to about 6 per cent in 1960, increased rapidly to reach 24 per cent in 1983 and then declined again to about 18 per cent in 1986. This approach, however, suffers exactly the same problems as the cash–deposit approach. The only problem it overcomes is the acceptance that cheques can be used in underground transactions. Here, in consequence, the above criticisms are not repeated. Instead, attention turns towards another monetary proxy approach believed by its advocates to be far more sophisticated.

Currency demand approach
This approach seeks to overcome some of the problems of the above methods by considering multiple indicators and multiple causes (for example, Schneider 2003; Schneider and Enste, 2001). Schneider (2001), for example, views the causes (and indicators) of the underground economy as: the burden of direct and indirect taxation, both actual and perceived;

the burden of regulation; and tax morality (citizens' attitudes towards the state). As will be shown later (see Chapter 6), it is not only possible to challenge all of these supposed causes (and indicators) but there also seems little recognition that it is not these factors *per se* but, rather, how they combine with a multitude of other factors that produce high or low levels of underground work.

This currency demand approach, nevertheless, has grown in popularity, particularly the DYMIMIC (dynamic multiple indicators multiple-causes) model that treats underground output as a latent variable and uses the above causal variables to measure its size (for example, Bajada and Schneider, 2003; Chatterjee *et al.*, 2002; Giles, 1999a, b; Giles and Tedds, 2002). Table 4.4 displays some results. Similar to other indirect measurement methods, this approach produces relatively high estimates of its size.

Table 4.4   Currency demand estimates of the size of the underground economy, 2000

Country	GDP underground economy 2000 (%)	Country	GDP underground economy 2000 (%)
Australia	15.3	Italy	27.0
Austria	10.2	Japan	11.3
Belgium	23.2	Mexico	30.1
Bulgaria	36.9	Netherlands	13.0
Canada	16.4	New Zealand	12.7
Croatia	33.4	Norway	19.1
Czech Republic	19.1	Portugal	22.6
Denmark	18.2	Spain	22.6
Finland	18.3	Sweden	19.1
France	15.3	Switzerland	8.8
Georgia	67.3	Turkey	32.1
Germany	16.3	UK	12.6
Greece	28.6	USA	8.7
Hungary	25.3		
Ireland	15.8		

Source: Schneider and Klinglmair (2004: Table 7.1)

Although adherents promote this multi-variable approach as more sophisticated, the important point to consider is whether there is a 'gigo' effect (that is, garbage in–garbage out). As Chapter 6 will reveal, it is by no means proven that the causes and indicators used in this model always and everywhere lead to its existence and growth. For this reason, a cautious approach is urged.

In conclusion, all of these indirect monetary methods have inherent problems that raise grave doubts about the validity of their findings (see Tanzi, 1999; Thomas, 1999; Williams and Windebank, 1998). Yet despite this, such approaches continue to be used (for example, Bhattacharyya, 1999; Dixon, 1999; Gadea and Serrano-Sanz, 2002; Giles, 1999a; Hill, 2002; OECD, 1997, 2000b, 2002). Most importantly for this book, however, these methods appear incapable of exploring the relationship between entrepreneurship and the underground economy. Indeed, given that 'the methodology underlying the monetary approaches ... rests upon questionable and generally untestable assumptions and ... the estimates they have generated are of dubious validity' (Thomas, 1988: 180), one can only conclude that 'Estimates of the size of the black economy based on cash indicators are best ignored' (Smith, 1986: 106). Here, therefore, another method that again uses monetary methods but in a more direct manner is evaluated.

Income/expenditure Discrepancies

This approach evaluates differences in expenditure and income either at the aggregate national level or through detailed microeconomic studies of different types of individuals or households, premised on the assumption that even if underground workers can conceal their incomes, they cannot hide their expenditures. An assessment of income/expenditure discrepancies thus supposedly reveals the extent of underground work and who does it.

First, therefore, aggregate level studies analyse the discrepancy between national expenditure and income so as to estimate the size of underground work. Such studies have been conducted in Germany (for example, Langfelt, 1989), Sweden (for example, Apel, 1994; Hansson, 1994; Park, 1979; Tengblad, 1994), the UK (O'Higgins, 1981) and the USA (for example, Macafee, 1980; Paglin, 1994), In the USA, for example, Paglin (1994) examines the discrepancy between household expenditure and income surveys published annually in the Bureau of Labor Statistics Consumer Expenditure Survey (CES). He finds that between 1984 and 1992, underground work declined from 12.4 per cent to 9.2 per cent of personal income, or from 10.2 per cent to 8.1 per cent of GDP over this period. This, he asserts, is principally due to the growth of formal employment during the 1980s in the USA. Nevertheless, he finds that in 1992, 10.2 per cent of households were income-poor but consumption-rich and views this to be a product of the existence of underground work. As Paglin (1994) finds, the poorest 20 per cent of households had an average after-tax income of US$5648 in 1991 but an average expenditure level of US$13464. He then takes a major logical leap by proposing that a sizeable number of them must engage in underground work, failing to consider whether this could be due to other factors (for example, retirement household spending, households between jobs, major one-off expenditures on costly items).

Second, others study income/expenditure discrepancies at the household level. In the UK, the Family Expenditure Survey (FES) has been analysed (see Dilnot and Morris, 1981; Macafee, 1980; O'Higgins, 1981). Comparing households' income and expenditure in 1000 out of the 7200 households surveyed for the 1977 FES so as to examine whether some households appear to live beyond their means, Dilnot and Morris (1981) employ a variety of 'traps' to exclude discrepancies that might be explained by factors other than underground work (for example, high expenditure due to an unusual major purchase or to the running down of accumulated wealth). After all adjustments, Dilnot and Morris (1981), assuming that tax evasion existed in any household whose expenditure exceeded its reported income by more than 15 per cent, derived upper and lower estimates of its extent. They reveal that 9.6–14.8 per cent of households evaded taxes and that tax evasion was equivalent to 2.3–3.0 per cent of the GNP in 1977. Such evasion, moreover, was found to be more prevalent among the self-employed (who understate their income by between 10–15 per cent) and part-time employees than those in full-time employment. Smith (1986) further reinforces this in a study of the 1982 FES, concluding that the self-employed understate their income by between 10 and 20 per cent.

O'Higgins (1981), however, casts doubt over the accuracy of this method. He suggests that it could be an underestimate because 30 per cent of households refuse to participate in the FES, and it is plausible that a greater proportion of non-respondents participate in underground work than the 9.6 per cent of respondents suggested by the lower-bound estimate of Dilnot and Morris (1981) and probably to a greater extent than the identified average weekly figure of £31. As O'Higgins (1981) argues, even if as few as 25 per cent of non-respondents engage in underground work to the extent of £31 weekly, the lower-bound estimate would be raised by almost half, yielding an adjusted lower estimate of 3.5 per cent of GNP.

Although this method has advantages over other indirect monetary methods, not least its reliance on relatively direct and statistically representative survey data, its problems remain manifold (see Thomas, 1988, 1992; Smith, 1986). For the discrepancy to represent a reasonable measure of underground work, one has to make a number of assumptions about the accuracy of the income and expenditure data. On the expenditure side, estimates depend on the accurate declaration of expenditure. Mattera (1985) suggests that it is somewhat naive to assume that this is the case. Equally convincing is the criticism that, for most people, spending is either over- or underestimated during a survey because records are kept by few members of the population compared with income, which for employees comes in regular recorded uniform instalments. Household level expenditure studies also suffer from the fatal flaw of only examining final demand, not intermediate demand for underground goods and services (Portes, 1994). Moreover, and as the RVA (2001) asserts, often no allowance is made for the fact that the self-employed are allowed to reduce their tax liability by allocating some items of income to reserves, or that their patterns of consumption may differ to those of wage earners.

On the income side, meanwhile, these studies cannot decipher whether the income derives from criminal or underground activities, or even whether it derives from wealth accumulated earlier such as money savings. In addition, and so far as studies such as the FES are concerned, there are problems of non-response as well as under-reporting (Thomas, 1992). Consequently, the accuracy of this method is doubtful. Weck-Hanneman and Frey (1985) clearly display this when reporting that the national income in Switzerland is larger than expenditure. According to this, Swiss underground work is negative. This is nonsensical and reveals that the discrepancy does not display the level of underground work but is due to other factors. As Frey and Weck (1983: 24) thus conclude about these monetary methods, 'One of the main shortcomings of all these approaches is that they do not concentrate on the causes and circumstances in which a shadow economy arises and exists'. Nor, moreover, do they explore the character of underground work beyond crude estimates of its sectoral or occupational concentrations. To do this, it is the more direct approaches to investigating underground work that need to be examined.

DIRECT SURVEY METHODS

Direct survey methods have been used to evaluate the magnitude and/or character of underground work in Belgium (Kesteloot and Meert, 1999; Pestieau, 1983, 1985), Canada (Fortin *et al.*, 1996), Germany (Frey *et al.*, 1982), Italy (for example, Bàculo, 2001; CENSIS, 1976), Norway (Isachsen and Strom, 1985), the Netherlands (for example, Van Eck and Kazemeier, 1985; Renooy, 1990), the UK (for example, Leonard, 1994; Pahl, 1984; Williams, 2004a; Williams and Windebank, 2001a, b, 2002a, 2003a), Sweden (Jönsson, 2001) and the USA (Ross, 1978; Jensen *et al.*, 1996; Nelson and Smith, 1999; Tickamyer and Wood, 1998). Such surveys can ask suppliers and/or purchasers of underground work about whether or not they participate, the volume or the value of their exchanges, what they did/received, for/from whom and/or why.

Measuring participation rates in underground work is a common feature of many direct studies (for example, Jönsson, 2001; Pedersen, 2003). Table 4.5 presents the results of one of the few cross-national surveys. It reveals that participation rates vary from 20.3 per cent of the population in Denmark to 7.8 per cent in the UK. It also displays that men are twice as likely to participate in such work as women, that younger age groups more extensively participate and that there are significant cross-national variations in the occupational groups engaging in such work.

Analysing the volume of underground work, studies can directly or indirectly ask either households or businesses about their use of underground

Table 4.5   *Proportion of population aged 18–74 participating in underground work in Denmark, Norway, Sweden, Germany and the UK: by gender, age and occupation*

	Denmark		Norway		Sweden		Germany		UK	
	%	No.	%	No.	%	No.	%	No.	%	No.
All	20.3	1796	17.3	2522	11.1	2181	10.4	5538	7.8	1572
Men	29.4	882	23.8	1276	15.4	1074	14.5	2717	10.3	753
Women	11.5	914	10.7	1246	7.0	1107	6.5	2824	5.4	819
18–19	42.0	50	22.2	108	(24.6)	65	16.6	198	(3.9)	55
20–29	26.8	281	23.9	518	17.1	369	19.1	802	13.0	268
30–39	24.5	383	20.3	572	17.4	425	13.2	1243	13.2	340
40–49	22.1	358	16.9	508	12.1	462	10.0	1049	7.8	334
50–59	15.9	370	12.8	430	(4.5)	420	7.4	896	(3.9)	272
60–69	11.5	252	9.3	269	(3.7)	323	5.6	901	(1.5)	217
70–74	(6.1)	99	(6.0)	117	(2.6)	117	(1.0)	449	(0.6)	86
Self-employed	27.8	162	33.3	165	17.5	137	12.1	336	(13.5)	122
Salaried	18.2	582	13.8	1242	7.2	559	7.1	1184	9.5	536
Skilled	29.2	308	41.8	184	15.8	462	19.2	826	12.5	161
Unskilled	28.6	168	20.3	227	13.4	262	8.2	723	(5.6)	210
Unemployed	(9.9)	81	(21.7)	60	(10.6)	151	20.7	247	(9.2)	40
Pensioners	9.5	326	(5.9)	186	(3.3)	391	4.2	1281	(1.1)	233
Students	25.2	135	18.7	112	23.5	162	27.3	256	30.6	26
Other	–	31	12.5	346	(7.8)	51	8.7	685	(3.7)	244

Note: Figures in parentheses mean that there are less than 20 observations in the cell.

Source: Pedersen (2003: 66)

work to acquire specific goods and/or services. Alternatively, they can ask people about their supply of underground work. In practice, most direct surveys assess the volume of underground work at a household level and request information from respondents both as suppliers and purchasers of underground work (for example, Leonard, 1994; Pahl, 1984; Warde, 1990). Few have used the enterprise as a unit of analysis (for exceptions, see Fries *et al.*, 2003; Ram *et al.*, 2001, 2002a, b, 2003). To explore the value of off-the-books purchases and/or sales, meanwhile, the amount of money earned by sellers, or spent by consumers, with regard to underground work can be analysed. Again, most studies have investigated respondents as both purchasers and sellers (for example, Fortin *et al.*, 1996; Isachsen *et al.*, 1982; Lemieux *et al.*, 1994), although some examine only purchasers (for example, McCrohan *et al.*, 1991; Smith, 1985).

These data can be collected, moreover, through either mail-shot questionnaires (for example, Fortin *et al.*, 1996), telephone interviews (for example, Jönsson, 2001) or face-to-face interviews of the unstructured (for example, Bàculo, 2001; Howe, 1988) or structured variety (for example, Williams and Windebank, 2001a). Reflecting the lack of data generally available, most have used relatively quantitative approaches composed largely of closed-ended questions and then frequently employed a variety of more open-ended questions and/or qualitative methods for in-depth exploration of particular aspects (for example, Leonard, 1994; Pahl, 1984). Indeed, even studies relying primarily on ethnography, such as that by Howe (1988), conduct some interviews as a quantitative precursor for their ethnographic material. Pahl (1984) in the UK and Jönsson (2001) in Sweden, meanwhile, use follow-up in-depth interviews with a limited number of households to explore specific issues.

Although direct studies could sample cross-national, national, regional or local populations, they have mostly studied particular localities (for example, Barthe, 1985; Fortin *et al.*, 1996; Leonard, 1994; Pahl, 1984; Renooy, 1990; Warde, 1990; Williams and Windebank, 2003a), socio-economic groups such as home-workers (for example, Phizacklea and Wolkowitz, 1995) or industrial sectors such as garment manufacturing (for example, Lin, 1995). Indeed, unless governments decide to invest in direct studies, it seems unlikely that direct surveys will move beyond this case study approach in the near future.[1]

The major criticism of direct surveys, that exclusively comes from commentators using indirect approaches, is that researchers naively assume that people will reveal to them, or even know, the character and magnitude of underground work in their lives. It is intimated that purchasers may not even know if such work is being offered off-the-books or legitimately and that sellers will be reticent about disclosing the nature and extent of their underground work since it is an illegal activity.

The former point might be correct. For example, if a purchaser has his/her external windows cleaned or purchases goods from a market stall, s/he might assume that this is not declared when this is not necessarily the case, or *vice versa*. In other words, although consumers might assume that goods and services bought in certain contexts are purchased on an underground basis while in other contexts they are not, their assumptions might be incorrect. Goods acquired in formal retail outlets, for example, may not only have been produced on an underground basis but may even be sold in such a manner (for example, in illegally inhabited shop premises) without the knowledge of the consumer. Not all those dealing in cash meanwhile may necessarily be working on an underground basis (for example, they may not have confidence in the purchaser's cheque), just as some accepting cheques may be tax evaders. On the whole, therefore, although people purchasing goods and services may be more willing to reveal whether they think it has been bought on a underground basis, they cannot necessarily be sure whether this is indeed the case unless the supplier informs them that this is so.

Despite such critiques of direct surveys, however, it is not necessarily the case that those supplying underground work will be untruthful in their dealings with researchers. Indeed, this criticism has been refuted many times. As Bàculo (2001: 2) states regarding her face-to-face interviews, 'they were curious and flattered that university researchers were interested in their problems' and were more than willing to share their experiences. Pahl (1984), in his study of the Isle of Sheppey, questioned people both as suppliers and purchasers and when comparing the results, found the same level of underground work. The implication is that individuals are not so secretive as sometimes assumed. Just because underground work is hidden from or unregistered by the state for tax, social security and/or labour law purposes does not mean that people will hide it from each other or even from academic researchers. It also intimates that customers are not as wrong as sometimes considered about whether or not a supplier is working on an underground basis. Similar conclusions have been drawn concerning the openness of research participants in Canada (Fortin *et al.*, 1996) and the UK (Evason and Woods, 1995; Leonard, 1994; MacDonald, 1994). As MacDonald (1994) reveals in his study of underground work among the unemployed, 'fiddly work' was not a provocative subject from their perspective. They happily talked about it in the same breath as discussing, for instance, their experiences of starting up in self-employment or of voluntary work. This willingness of people to talk about their underground work was also identified by Leonard (1994) in Belfast.

Perhaps a more salient criticism is that the direct approaches have so far largely investigated underground work in relation to final demand (spending by consumers on goods and services), not intermediate demand (spending by businesses). Final demand, however, accounts for only some two-thirds of total spending in most advanced economies. Such direct methods are thus missing the underground work that takes place in the other third of the economy. This is a valid criticism of those studies that focus upon only households as customers of underground work. Where respondents as suppliers of underground work are considered, however, it is to be expected that this would gather data on work that not only met final but also intermediate demand.

One of the few direct surveys of businesses, however, the 2002 EBRD/ World Bank Business Environment and Enterprise Performance Survey implemented in 26 countries of central and eastern Europe and the Commonwealth of Independent States (CIS), finds that businesses in Poland and the Czech Republic hid an average of less than 10 per cent of their sales from tax authorities, while tax under-reporting was higher in Hungary and the Slovak Republic but often over 20 or 30 per cent in CIS and Balkan countries (Fries *et al.*, 2003). Such a survey thus reveals that it is wholly possible to use direct methods when surveying businesses. There have also been several qualitative surveys that again reveal the willingness of both employers and employees to openly talk about their participation in the underground economy (for example, Jones *et al.*, 2004; Ram *et al.*, 2001, 2002a, b, 2003).

To conclude, therefore, the strength of direct over indirect survey methods is that they are specifically designed to generate data on underground work rather than make sense of data collected for other purposes (Harding and Jenkins, 1989). The result is that they can be tailored to meet the needs of the particular research problem being investigated. This is particularly relevant when wishing to explore its character, such as its entrepreneurial qualities. In consequence, and given the focus of this book, it is the data collected using direct methods that are largely the focus herein. To enable the reader to understand the data in the next chapter, the final section here focuses upon the direct survey method used in the English Localities Survey of underground work, an extensive survey that provides the most comprehensive dataset so far gathered of the relationship between entrepreneurship and the underground economy.

Implementing Direct Methods: the English Localities Survey

Between 1998 and 2001, primary data were collected on underground work by taking the household as the unit of analysis and then examining the economic practices used to undertake domestic service tasks along with the work that they supply on a paid and unpaid basis to others. This is known as a 'household work practices' approach (see Nelson and Smith, 1999; Pahl, 1984; Sik, 1993; Smith, 2002; Wallace, 2002).

A relatively structured face-to-face interview schedule was designed centred on a list of 44 common services, partly derived from the tasks used by Pahl (1984) on the Isle of Sheppey (see Table 4.6). Unlike this earlier study, however, the relations within which the work was conducted and the motivations of suppliers and consumers were also investigated.

Table 4.6   List of tasks investigated in the English Localities Survey

House maintenance
- outdoor painting
- indoor painting
- wallpapering
- plastering
- mending a broken widow
- maintenance of appliances

Housework
- routine housework
- cleaning windows outdoors
- spring cleaning
- cleaning windows indoors
- doing the shopping
- washing clothes and sheets
- ironing
- cooking meals
- washing dishes
- hairdressing
- household administration

Car maintenance
- washing car
- repairing car
- car maintenance

Caring activities
- daytime baby-sitting
- night-time baby-sitting
- educational activities
- pet care

Home improvement
- putting in double-glazing
- plumbing
- electrical work
- house insulation
- putting in a bathroom suite
- building a garage
- building an extension
- putting in central heating
- carpentry

Making and repairing goods
- making clothes
- repairing clothes
- knitting
- making or repairing furniture
- making or repairing garden equipment
- making curtains

Gardening
- care of indoor plants
- outdoor borders
- outdoor vegetables
- lawn mowing

The core of the questionnaire investigated the sources of labour last used to complete each of the above 44 tasks. The interviewee was asked whether each task had been undertaken in the household during the previous five years/year/month/week (depending on the activity). If not, they were asked why not. If undertaken, they were asked: who had conducted the task (for example, a household member, kin living outside the household, a friend, neighbour, previously unknown person on a self-employed basis, firm, landlord, and so on); whether the person had been unpaid or paid; and if paid, whether it was 'cash-in-hand' or not as well as how much they had paid. Moreover, the respondent was asked in an open-ended manner why they had decided to undertake each task using that labour so as to enable their motives to be understood as well as how they would have got the task done if they had not employed this labour. In addition, they were asked in an open-ended manner what other underground work they had obtained during the past year, from whom and the price paid.

Following this, the supply of both underground work and unpaid community exchange by household members was examined. The interviewee was asked whether a household member had conducted each of the 44 tasks for another household and if so, who had done it, for whom, whether they had received money, how much they had received and why they had decided to do the task. To collect data on other types of underground work conducted and received, meanwhile, a series of open-ended questions were used. This focused particularly on the type of work conducted, the length of time they had been conducting such practices and why they did so. In addition, data were collected on the current employment status of all household members, their ages, employment histories, ethnicity, household income levels and so forth so as to enable this underground work to be placed in the context of their overall work practices.

Similar to the above studies, the finding was that the interviewees had little reticence in openly talking about their underground work. Indeed, the total customers reported spending on underground work in deprived urban neighbourhoods was near enough exactly the same as suppliers of underground work received. So too was the mean price customers paid (£90.24) broadly equivalent to the mean price suppliers received (£84.48). This was similarly the case in affluent suburbs and rural areas. There is thus little evidence either of suppliers under-reporting such work and their incomes, or of customers falsely allocating economic activity to underground work when this was not the case.

Table 4.7 highlights the deprived and affluent neighbourhoods in both urban and rural English localities surveyed. The rationale for using the urban/rural and level of affluence variables to select localities was quite simply that previous research has indicated both of these to have important influences on underground work (for example, Jensen *et al.*, 1995; Kesteloot and Meert, 1999; Pahl, 1984; Renooy, 1990).

To select the localities, maximum variation sampling was employed. First, two cities were chosen that starkly varied in terms of their level of affluence. Southampton is a successful service-oriented economy with low

Table 4.7   Overview of locations studied in the English Localities Survey

Area-type	Locality	Description of area	Number of interviews
Affluent rural	Fulbourn, Cambridgeshire	'Picture postcard' rural village in high-tech sub-region	70
Affluent rural	Chalford, Gloucestershire	Rural village in Cotswolds.	70
Deprived rural	Grimethorpe, South Yorkshire	Ex-pit village with very high unemployment.	70
Deprived rural	Wigston, Cumbria	Village with one factory dominating the local labour market	70
Deprived rural	St Blazey, Cornwall	Village in a tourist region	70
Affluent suburb	Fulwood, Sheffield	Suburb in south-west Sheffield	50
Affluent suburb	Basset/Chilworth, Southampton	Sole affluent suburb within the city of Southampton	61
Deprived urban	Manor, Sheffield	Social housing estate with high unemployment	100
Deprived urban	Pitsmoor, Sheffield	Inner city area in deindustrializing city with high levels of private sector rented accommodation and high unemployment	100
Deprived urban	St Mary's, Southampton	Inner city locality in affluent southern city with high levels of private sector rented accommodation and high unemployment	100
Deprived urban	Hightown, Southampton	Social housing estate with high unemployment	100

unemployment rates in the affluent South East of England while Sheffield is a poorer northern English city, once famous for steelmaking but now suffering relatively high rates of unemployment. Continuing the maximum variation sampling, three neighbourhood-types in each city were then chosen using the Index of Multiple Deprivation of the ODPM that ranks all wards in England and Wales according to the level of their deprivation (ODPM, 2000). In each city, two of the most deprived wards and the most affluent ward were selected. Following this, and continuing the maximum variation sampling, a range of rural localities was chosen with a broad regional spread. Again, some very affluent and deprived rural localities were selected for investigation.

In each locality, meanwhile, a spatially stratified sampling procedure was used (Kitchin and Tate, 2001). The researcher called at every *n*th dwelling in each street, depending on the size of the neighbourhood and the number of interviews sought. In consequence, if there were 1000 households in the ward and 100 interviews were sought, then every 10th household was visited. If there was no response, then the researcher called back once. If there was still no response and/or they were refused an interview, then the 11th house was surveyed (again with one call back), then the 9th dwelling, 12th and so on. This provided a representative sample of the neighbourhood in terms of tenure and type of housing and prevented any skewness in the sample towards certain tenures, types of dwelling and different parts of the neighbourhood being interviewed rather than a spatially representative sample of the whole neighbourhood.

All target households had a covering letter put through their door a day or so prior to the researcher calling in order to provide information about the nature of the interview and to hopefully increase the response rate (30 per cent overall for the first choice household). This letter described the researcher as being interested in finding out how households manage to get everyday tasks completed and what prevents them being able to do more for themselves and others. Interviews took place not only during daytime hours on weekdays but also in the early evening and at weekends in order to capture working households. These interviews resulted in a wide array of data on unpaid work as well as overall household coping capabilities and work practices that have been reported elsewhere (Williams and Windebank, 2003a). Here in this book however, the focus is upon solely the findings with regard to the nature of their underground work.

CONCLUSIONS

That there is a substantial amount of underground work taking place in the advanced economies is nowhere disputed. However, measuring the precise amount of this work is a matter of heated debate. In this chapter, the contrasting methods used to evaluate the size of underground work in the advanced economies and resultant indications of its magnitude have been evaluated.

This has revealed that although nearly all methods find the underground economy to be expanding relative to the formal economy in western societies, indirect methods produce higher estimates of its magnitude than direct survey methods. It has also displayed the emerging consensus that direct methods are considered more accurate and reliable, especially when researching the character of the underground economy. In this book, therefore, where the purpose is to understand the nature of such work, indirect techniques are of little use. Such indirect methods are more the product of various untested assumptions about the nature of underground work rather than a means of acquiring understanding about its character. If knowledge is to be acquired on the nature of such work, especially the relationship between entrepreneurship and the underground economy, then it is to the direct methods that those with a desire to understand these issues have to turn.

NOTES

1. At the time of writing, the European Commission has put out a tender to evaluate the feasibility of conducting a direct survey of the underground economy in the European Union. If eventually implemented, it will be the first large-scale cross-national direct survey to be undertaken.

5. Portraits of underground enterprise

INTRODUCTION

What different types of underground worker can be identified? And in what sectors do they work? To answer these questions, this chapter transcends the conventional focus on which population groups engage in such work and moves towards an appreciation of both the various types of underground worker and the work that they undertake. In so doing, a significant gap in the literature concerning the nature of the underground economy in western nations is filled.

Conventional representations usually depict underground workers as low-paid employees working under exploitative sweatshop-like conditions. The widespread recognition that relatively affluent populations do most of this work, however, begs the question of whether it is always low-paid, exploitative and sweatshop-like in character. Although recognition that underground work is frequently conducted on an autonomous basis has hinted that such a depiction is far from the lived reality, until now, few studies have identified either the proportion of underground work conducted on an organized and autonomous basis, or attempted to differentiate the various types of autonomous work. The first section of this chapter thus seeks to answer these issues. Analysing the results of the English Localities Survey – one of the first data sets to unpack the heterogeneous character of underground work in advanced economies – this chapter will reveal first, that employees working on an off-the-books basis for formal or underground enterprises conduct only a very small proportion of all underground work and second, autonomous underground workers need to be differentiated according to their relations with the customer, motives for conducting such work and the stage of development of their business.

Here, in consequence, a distinction is drawn between fledgling underground micro-entrepreneurs starting up business ventures, the more established self-employed using underground work in a serial manner, and underground social entrepreneurs doing paid favours for others in order to help them out rather than for financial gain. In each instance, further divisions will be then made and portraits provided of individuals engaged in each type of autonomous underground work so as to provide a richer more textured understanding of this sphere than has so far been the case. The outcome will be a detailed account of the relationship between enterprise, entrepreneurship and the underground economy.

Until now, furthermore, there has been little investigation of the sectors in which underground enterprise is found. Instead, rather crude assumptions often prevail based on little more than hearsay evidence. In the second and final section of this chapter, therefore, the sectors in which such entrepreneurial endeavour is concentrated will be analysed. The net outcome will be a state-of-the-art review of the prevalence and nature of entrepreneurship and self-employment in the underground economy and the sectors in which such endeavour is concentrated. This sets the scene for later chapters that consider what should be done about underground enterprise in Parts III and IV.

TYPES OF UNDERGROUND WORKER

As Chapter 3 highlighted, it is now widely recognized that underground work is not normally concentrated in marginalized populations. The outcome is that the depiction of such work as exploitative, low-paid and sweatshop-like work conducted by employees for businesses is no longer accurate and a more refined understanding is required. The only way that this has been achieved until now, however, is by arguing that besides 'organized' underground employment composed of employees working on an off-the-books basis for formal or underground businesses, there exists 'autonomous' underground work involving people working on a self-employed basis (for example, Fortin *et al.*, 1996; Lazaridis and Koumandraki, 2003; Leonard, 1994, 1998a; MacDonald, 1994; Pahl, 1984; Renooy, 1990; Warren, 1994; Williams, 2004a, b, c; Williams and Windebank, 1998, 2001a, b). Few attempts have been so far made to explore the heterogeneous types of autonomous underground worker.

Here, in consequence, the results of the English Localities Survey are drawn upon to distinguish three broad types of autonomous underground worker. Analysing the data on the types of underground work conducted, along with information on the employment and work strategies of households, there emerged from this data set four broad forms of underground worker. On the one hand, and as in previous studies, underground workers were identified who work on an 'organized' basis as off-the-books employees for formal and underground businesses. On the other hand, three distinct types of autonomous underground worker were distinguished according to the nature of their relationship with the customer/employer, their motives and the stage of development of their business venture. These three types are:

- *Underground micro-entrepreneurs*   Starting-up fledgling business ventures, underground work here is often a short-term risk-taking strategy to either test out the business venture or to establish themselves. They are usually either employees in employment or classified as 'economically inactive' and in the process of setting themselves up as self-employed. These are usually small-scale operations. When their ventures grow and establish themselves, they move into a second category if they continue to do some trade off-the-books.
- *Established off-the-books self-employed workers*   Although some of these self-employed people are wholly underground, most are either in formal employment and conducting self-employed off-the-books work on a relatively continuous basis, or registered self-employed conducting a portion of their trade off-the-books in a serial and on-going manner as a means of 'getting by'. Usually, underground trading is heavily embedded in their working practices.
- *Off-the-books social entrepreneurs*   As monetary exchange has penetrated deeper into everyday life, exchanges that previously took place on an unpaid basis between friends, family and acquaintances now often involve money. Giving 'cash for favours' mostly involves casual one-off tasks, especially in deprived populations where the provision of paid favours is a widespread practice, not least because it prevents relations from turning sour if a favour is not returned. These paid favours, however, are not conducted for profit. They are undertaken to help others out (see Williams, 2004a for an in-depth treatment of this form of autonomous underground worker).

Below, portraits of both off-the-books employees as well as each of these three broad types of autonomous underground worker will be provided in turn. Before doing so, however, the proportion of underground work conducted by each of these groups in England is estimated so that the reader can get some feel for their relative importance.

Estimating the Prevalence of Various Types of Underground Worker

In one recent study, one in 13 people were found to engage in underground work in the UK (Pedersen, 2003). Until now, however, few have investigated the types of underground work that they conduct. Analysing the findings of the English Localities Survey, Table 5.1 reveals that just 18 per cent of all underground work is conducted by employees working on an off-the-books basis, meaning that 82 per cent is conducted on an autonomous basis, with 11 per cent of all underground work being conducted by fledgling micro-entrepreneurs, 22 per cent by more established self-employed off-the-books workers and 49 per cent by underground social entrepreneurs.

Table 5.1   Distribution of underground work in affluent and deprived
English localities: by type of underground worker

	Higher-income areas	Lower-income areas	All areas
Off-the-books employees	1	19	18
Fledgling underground micro-entrepreneurs	27	9	11
Established off-the-books self-employed	60	8	22
Underground social entrepreneurs	12	64	49

Source: English Localities Survey

The sample of the English Localities Survey, however, was heavily skewed towards deprived urban neighbourhoods (46 per cent of the total sample). Given the significant variations between deprived and affluent areas in the portions of underground work conducted by each type of underground worker, the overall findings heavily reflect the configuration of underground work in deprived areas. These overall proportions, therefore, will not reflect the national situation.

To guesstimate the share of all underground work conducted by each of these groups nationally, it is first necessary to recognize that in affluent areas, the proportion of all underground work conducted by off-the-books employees and underground social entrepreneurs is significantly lower than in deprived populations (see Table 5.1). Any national estimate of the configuration of the underground economy will thus result in the share of underground work conducted by fledgling entrepreneurs and the more established self-employed being much higher than identified in the findings above.

In order to guesstimate the national situation, a very crude approach is here employed due to the limitations of the data set because of its maximum variation sampling method. Using the ODPM Index of Multiple Deprivation (IMD), a national estimate is here derived by assuming that some 75 per cent of wards nationally display the same overall magnitude and character of underground work as the affluent areas studied and 25 per cent have the same size and character of underground work as the deprived neighbourhoods. Given that this English Localities Survey only surveyed wards at the extremes of the IMD, the middle-ranking localities have been thus assumed to display similar characteristics to relatively affluent localities.

Based on this heroic assumption, the resultant estimate is that some 5 per cent of all underground work in England might be conducted by off-the-books employees, 23 per cent by micro-entrepreneurs, 47 per cent by the more established self-employed and 25 per cent by underground social entrepreneurs (see Figure 5.1). This, however, should be treated with caution. It is a very rough approximation based on limited evidence from 861 interviews and on the untested assumption that the configuration of the underground economy in the three quartiles of wards witnessing the least multiple deprivation replicate the configuration of the affluent wards studied in the English Localities Survey, which all fall into the top decile of most affluent wards. This national guesstimate is therefore a very rough thumbnail portrait. A nationally representative sample survey is required before such data can be confirmed.

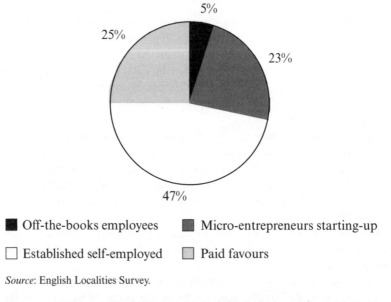

■ Off-the-books employees   ■ Micro-entrepreneurs starting-up

□ Established self-employed   ▨ Paid favours

Source: English Localities Survey.

Figure 5.1   Estimate of the structure of the underground economy in England: by type of labour

In sum, until further research is conducted in advanced economies to break down the underground economy, then public policy will not know for certain whether the emergent emphasis that seeks to harness this hidden enterprise culture, composed of fledgling micro-entrepreneurs and established self-employed, is dealing with a large or relatively small segment of the overall underground economy.

In order to understand the nature of underground enterprise, the rest of this chapter turns away from quantitative measures of the portion of all underground work conducted by each of type of underground worker and towards a more qualitative investigation using the data from the English Localities Survey of each of the four broad types of underground worker. The intention, in so doing, is to provide a richer and more textured portrait of the underground sphere and begin to highlight how some underground workers display entrepreneurial attributes and can be thus read as constituting a hidden enterprise culture.

UNDERGROUND EMPLOYEES

The conventional representation of underground workers is of employees working for wholly or partially underground businesses on low wages and engaged in exploitative sweatshop-like work. Here, it is not denied that such underground work exists. Indeed, a wealth of literature highlights in no uncertain terms the exploitation and low pay suffered by many working in 'sweatshop' conditions (for example, Barlett and Steele, 2000; Bender, 2004; Castree *et al.*, 2004; Espenshade, 2004; Hapke, 2004; A. Ross, 2004; R. Ross, 2004), especially in the garment manufacturing sector (for example, Bender, 2004; Espenshade, 2004; Hapke, 2004; Ram *et al.*, 2002a; R. Ross 2004) and as day labourers (for example, Valenzuela, 2003). There is also a large literature on how domestic servants and home-workers suffer from low pay and exploitative working conditions (for example, Anderson, 2001a, b; Baylina and Schier, 2002; Boris and Prugl, 1996; Dagg, 1996; Hondagneu-Sotelo, 2001; Pfau-Effinger, 2006; Salmi, 1996).

Until now, however, relatively few studies have sought to analyse the wide variety of forms of underground employment in western economies. Yet multiple types of underground employee exist. Besides working on a full-time basis, they can be employed part-time, intermittently or occasionally either for wholly underground or legitimate businesses. For some, moreover, such work will provide their primary wage and for others, additional income. For some, this work will be part of their formal job (for example, when the salaries of formal jobs are not fully declared), for others it will be a secondary job not related to their formal employment and for yet others, their formal employment will be underground work because the employer pays them less than the official minimum wage but the books show that they are paid at or above this minimum level (see, for example, Aniello and Coppola, 2003). Many different forms of underground employee thus exist whose underground work varies in its importance, permanence and centrality to their working lives. Each type, moreover, will prevail to different degrees in various socio-spatial contexts.

In the particular context of the English Localities Survey, with its sample bias towards deprived urban neighbourhoods, four principal varieties of underground employee were identified. First, there were temporary or occasional underground employees seeking additional income. Examples include an unemployed man who cleaned a truck for £10 which took him three hours, a woman doing bar work for two weeks for £50, a woman who worked for three weeks in a canteen on a building site for £50 and a man who refurbished a pub for one week for £100. This was the most prominent type of exploitative and low-paid off-the-books employment identified. Second, there were those doing it for additional income but in regular and sometimes permanent off-the-books employment. An example was a man working early mornings in a small bakery for £20 per month and then going to his formal job each day and a man who regularly staffed an ice-cream stall at weekends for £2.80 per hour. Third, and the smallest group, were those working on a more permanent and regular basis as underground employees who gained their primary income through their off-the-books work for what were otherwise legitimate businesses. Here, examples include a man working on a full-time permanent basis in a restaurant for £2.00 per hour (when the national minimum wage was £3.60 per hour) and a woman working five-hour evening shifts as a telephone receptionist in a taxi company for £2.80 per hour.

Not all off-the-books employees, however, are low-paid and engaged in exploitative work, and neither perhaps should such work always be seen as possessing wholly negative attributes. A fourth and final category of underground employee is relatively well paid and working under anything but sweatshop conditions. The examples from the English Localities Survey are mostly of skilled craftsmen (for example, plumbers, electricians, plasterers) who engage in off-the-books work for formal businesses for which they are relatively well paid and over which they have considerable autonomy concerning their working conditions.

A further example of how off-the-books employees are not always low-paid and exploited and such work far from negative is the growing industrial districts literature that pinpoints how local and regional growth clusters have resulted from co-operation between enterprises heavily relying on skilled off-the-books employees who are well-paid and witness relatively good working conditions (for example, Cappechi, 1989; Ghezzi, 2006; Holmstrom, 1993; Pérez Sáinz, 1989; Trinci, 2005). As Ghezzi (2006) reveals in her study of underground employment in several central Italian industrial districts, such employees can be well paid for their highly skilled work.[1] Benton (1990) reveals much the same in the electronics industry in Madrid where people working as off-the-books employees are on high wages and engaged in skilled work for advanced highly capitalized firms.

Besides low-paid exploited off-the-books employees, such as in labour-intensive small firms with low levels of capitalization, utilizing old technology and producing cheap products and services for local markets and export, which involve on the whole marginal populations (for example, Lin, 1995; Sassen, 1997), other underground employees are thus better paid, more skilled and have more autonomy and control over their work, often in highly capitalized firms which are modern and use high-technology equipment to produce higher-priced goods and services, with relations between employers and employees based more upon co-operation than domination (Benton, 1990; Cappechi, 1989; Warren, 1994). The outcome is that a segmented underground labour market can be identified ranging from low-paid, exploitative and sweatshop-like jobs to higher-paid, more skilled and rewarding jobs, and which is segmented along similar gender and ethnicity lines to the formal labour market (for example, Fortin *et al.*, 1996; Lobo, 1990a, b; Williams and Windebank, 1998).

It is not only this industrial districts literature, however, that displays the link between underground work and successful enterprise cultures. In recent years, the examination of autonomous underground has begun to forge in a more direct manner this close relationship between underground work and entrepreneurship.

Underground Micro-entrepreneurs

Previously, largely neo-liberals highlighted the existence of underground micro-entrepreneurs. More recently, however, a wider group of commentators have recognized such entrepreneurial endeavour (see Chapter 3). Who, therefore, are these micro-entrepreneurs that have become the focus of attention of both academic commentators and public policy-makers? Until now, despite the rapidly growing interest in this group, especially among governments and policy-oriented agencies (for example, European Commission, 2002, 2003a, b, c; Grabiner, 2000; ILO, 2002; OECD, 2002; Small Business Council, 2004), few studies in advanced economies have documented the characteristics of these 'low-flying heroes' operating below the radar screen of many government agencies. Here, therefore, the evidence currently available is reviewed.

Bàculo (2001: 2) in the Italian city of Naples found that among micro-entrepreneurs, 'informal employment is often a way of getting round difficulties and carrying out certain tasks in particular phases of a company, especially at the outset'. For her, therefore, such transactions are commonly used as a short-term strategy in the initial phase of business ventures such as to test out the market or establish the enterprise. A recurring question in many studies, nevertheless, is whether these micro-entrepreneurs engage in underground work out of necessity or choice. Although some studies in North America, especially among ethnic minority and immigrant communities, view engagement in underground work as a necessity (for example, Portes and Walton, 1981; Raijman, 2001), others do not. For Gerxhani (2004: 274), these micro-entrepreneurs:

> choose to participate in the informal economy because they find more autonomy, flexibility and freedom in this sector than in the formal one, In other words, participants have the freedom of operating their own business; they have flexibility in determining hours or days of operation; they can use and develop their creativity.

For yet others, however, both choice and necessity are variously identified among different groups of micro-entrepreneur.

In Lozano's (1989) detailed study of flea markets in Northern California, involving interviews with 50 dealers, a difference is drawn between voluntary and involuntary entrants to this market. Voluntary entry occurs when an individual decides to leave their job in order to earn income through self-employment, or when underground employment is conducted as a source of additional income beyond that necessary to cover normal living expenses and levels of indebtedness. One-fifth of respondents fell into this category. Involuntary entry, meanwhile, takes place when: a person loses a job; income from employment, pensions or welfare payments is insufficient to cover normal living expenses and levels of indebtedness; or a person leaves school to enter the formal labour market and is unable to find a job. The remaining 80 per cent of dealers experienced one of these situations prior to their involvement in the flea market. As Lozano (1989) asserts, there are also important differences in the motivations of those who enter the flea market voluntarily or involuntarily. The former explain their participation in terms of intense dissatisfaction with the routine and authority of the formal employment place and opt for self-employment for reasons of personal autonomy and flexibility and to 'be my own boss'. The involuntary joiners, however, are very different. Although a quarter claim to enjoy the autonomy of this work, none give this as a principal reason for their participation. They run such micro-enterprises because they need the money and, provided they have not been out of work for long, because their desire for a job is strong. In the work of Cross (1997, 2000) on street vendors in Mexico City and Cairo, one again sees this structure-agency dualism at work. He argues that while the self-employed have conventionally been seen as exploited workers stripped of the legal benefits of formal employment (for example, Alonso, 1980; Portes and Walton, 1981) and struggling to earn survival wages, his finding is that many conduct this work out of choice.

Similarly, a study by Snyder (2004) of New York City's East Village neighbourhood finds that although most literature focuses on external pressures (for example, discrimination, economic restructuring, unemployment) that force people into the underground economy, most of the 50 self-employed workers she studied were doing so out of choice in order to meet a personal goal, namely forging a new work identity. Most used the underground economy to set their careers on a new path in order to transform their work identity or to reveal their true selves. Even those originally joining due to constricted opportunities in the formal economy developed a commitment to their work in the underground economy as a long-term career plan.

For Snyder (2004), four types of underground worker were identified based on their degree of reliance on their underground jobs as first, an economic and second, an identity resource. High economic dependency refers to being reliant on underground work for their primary income. Low economic dependency refers to using the income as an extra source of money. High identity dependency indicates that the underground job is considered a main occupation or source of work identity while low identity dependency identifies with their current or anticipated formal sector job. Table 5.2 indicates the proportions of Snyder's 50 off-the-books self-employed workers in each group.

Table 5.2   Routes to the underground economy in New York's East Village

| | | Economic dependency | |
		High (76%)	Low (24%)
Identity dependency	High (54%)	42%	12%
	Low (46%)	34%	12%

Source: derived from Snyder (2004: Table 1).

Three-quarters of underground micro-entrepreneurs, therefore, rely on their underground work for their primary income and about half seek their work identity primarily through their underground work. For some 12 per cent of these underground micro-entrepreneurs, their underground job is not highly important. They do it simply to earn extra spending money. Most are financially secure and in full-time formal employment doing this as a sideline. For another 12 per cent, although not dependent on this work for their primary income, often because they are in full-time employment, such work is central to how they identify themselves outside of their formal careers. Often, these underground micro-entrepreneurs only charge minimal fees to cover their expenses. A further 34 per cent depend on their underground work financially but not for their work identity. However, they do enter the underground economy to fulfil an identity need, which is to achieve their work or career goals, such as becoming a professional artist or performer. They occupy the underground position until their career goals materialize. The remaining 42 per cent rely on their underground jobs for both their main income and work identity. Even if they have an additional formal job, they identify more with the underground one and see it as their long-term career plan.

Underground entrepreneurs, therefore, set up off-the-books business ventures for various reasons. Contrary to the arguments of neo-liberals, not all underground entrepreneurs are casting off the shackles of an over-intrusive state (for example, De Soto, 1989, 2001), but neither are they, as some political economists assert, simply reeling from the universal and homogeneous restructuring of capital (for example, Castells and Portes, 1989). Participants have multifarious motivations. While, for some their engagement is determined by structural factors, there is also often agency involved to varying degrees; they have options. Such underground entrepreneurship is not simply a voluntary choice but neither is it solely structurally determined.

This finding is strongly reinforced in the case studies of specific fledgling micro-entrepreneurs identified in the English Localities Survey. For the majority, such micro-entrepreneurship is a voluntary choice into which they are both pushed, often due to dissatisfaction with their formal employment and at the same time pulled due to their interest in the activity involved. Rarely is such endeavour viewed as wholly involuntary and due to a lack of choice rather than a matter of choice, and nor is it viewed as wholly voluntary. To show this, case studies of specific individuals collected during the English Localities Survey are here presented. Here, two groups of micro-entrepreneurs are distinguished: those whose micro-enterprise spun in various ways out of their formal employment and those whose entrepreneurial ventures derived from some hobby.

Spin-offs from formal employment
In many cases, attempts to set up a business venture arise directly out of the skills that underground micro-entrepreneurs used in their formal employment.

The painter and decorator   While working as an employee of a painting and decorating company, Geoff had begun to take on cash-in-hand jobs at weekends on a word-of-mouth basis through friends, neighbours and acquaintances in order to set up on his own. Two rationales had driven this decision. On the one hand, his work as an employee was not satisfying. He did the preparatory tasks with the more fulfilling final stages being undertaken by the owner of the business. Self-employment was a way for him to undertake the more interesting work in the final stages of each job. On the other hand, however, he also wanted to become self-employed because he had recently divorced and had custody of the child, and wanted more control over his working hours so as to spend more time with his child and fulfil his familial obligations. At the time of interview, Geoff had swiftly built up a client base large enough to resign from his job and to work full-time on a self-employed basis. He had also bought a van and all the necessary equipment and had started to do commercial contracts such as decorating the common areas of blocks of flats, often on a cash-in-hand basis. For him, conducting off-the-books work was an inherent part of his working practices to allow him to get established. Although a small part of his business was now declared, he continued to conduct a large proportion off-the-books and this was his primary income. He was adamant, nevertheless, that he wanted to create a 'legitimate' business. As he put it, he had 'too much to lose' if caught. But he had no knowledge on how to put everything 'right' (and even asked the interviewer if they could help).

The consultant   Another instance of how skills acquired in formal employment are used to establish a micro-enterprise 'on the side' is the case of Chris. Working in a large public sector organization, he sometimes undertook self-employed consultancy specializing in what he did for his formal employment for clients. Whenever possible, especially when working for foreign clients, he paid the money received directly into his personal bank account and never declared these payments for taxable purposes. He had every intention of eventually setting up in business on his own and was busy at the time of interview exploring whether there was a sufficient market for his services. For him, this work was conducted on an off-the-books basis because he had 'not yet established as being properly self-employed' and was 'testing the market' for his services. His income was presently additional income.

The landscape gardener   A final example of using skills acquired in a formal job to set up a micro-enterprise was Bob. Having worked on building sites for many years as a bricklayer, he had decided to set up his own landscape gardening business, specializing in small garden projects such as building patios and terraces. Underground transactions were being used to undercut others so as to establish a client base. At the time of interview, he had two employees both of whom were paid as casual cash-in-hand day-labourers. He had 'hated' working for others and saw this enterprise as a way of achieving an internal locus of control over his working life.

Spin-offs from a hobby or interest
Micro-enterprises arise not only from skills acquired in formal employment but also from some hobby or interest people have outside of their formal job, or what Stebbins (2004) calls 'serious leisure', by which he means the systematic pursuit of an amateur, hobbyist or volunteer activity that participants find so substantial and interesting that they launch themselves on a career centred on acquiring and expressing its special skills.

The canary breeder   Eric's life outside employment revolved around breeding canaries. He had begun with a canary given to him by a friend, and had slowly developed his hobby over the years so that he now kept and bred up to 150 at any time in a large shed in his garden. He sold 'good quality' canaries to fellow members of local and regional canary breeding clubs for anything up to £400 and the rest to pet shops for £5–£8 each. He had also set up a thriving business making canary cages, having first made them as a favour for close friends and later expanded further outwards as demand grew. Indeed, he was one of the only producers of such cages in the region and had a well-defined niche market with good access to his target market via bird shows and specialist weekly newspapers. All of the money he made from these activities was 'earmarked' for birdfeed, buying 'higher-quality' birds for breeding and showing at bird shows, and so on. In other words, he had reinvested all profits into his business venture. The outcome was that a thriving micro-business was emerging that produced a relatively significant additional income to complement his pension.

The sailing fanatic   Mick in his mid-40s had worked continuously since leaving college, and recounted how he had reached a stage in his life where he was searching for something more fulfilling and was tired of working long hours in a job that he did not enjoy (that is, as an executive in a large insurance company). His response had been to set up a web business selling antique yacht chandlery that he acquired at auctions on the south coast of England. This business not only reflected his hobby but also that living near one of the global centres of sailing, he could easily obtain chandlery that people elsewhere could not. For him, this was at first a voluntary initiative pursued in order to enable him to 'downshift' from a hectic and stressful working life, and to do something that he found more personally rewarding.

However, he had then been made redundant and had chosen to pursue this micro-entrepreneurial venture full-time rather than seek another permanent job. This work, for him, was appropriate to what he wanted to achieve. It was an attempt to downshift and to make use of his location in one of the world's yachting centres as a platform for a successful virtual business. Indeed, he had registered a business in order to do this but only put a small proportion of his trades through the formal company. The vast majority were off-the-books transactions. His justification was that he was not claiming 'dole' and was 'standing on his own two feet', so felt that the state should treat him with respect rather than disdain for his efforts to fend for himself. After some months, he had begun to find that acquiring such goods was rather more competitive than imagined and that he was generating insufficient income. He thus went part-time deciding to work in temporary formal jobs during the winter months each year through agencies and then spend his summers both yachting and developing his micro-enterprise. However, he found that his time spent out of the labour market was having a deleterious effect on his search for even temporary employment and at the time of interview was trying to decide whether to re-enter the formal labour market on a full-time basis or to pursue his entrepreneurial venture full-time. For him, therefore, underground work was being used as part of a downshifting strategy to enable him to establish his business and compete with others in the same market.

Stained glass window maker Having read a book on how to make stained glass windows because she wanted to apply the technique in her own home, Rita had found that friends and neighbours admired her work and asked if she could do the same for them. From this do-it-yourself (DIY) activity, she had developed a micro-business. Rita was registered unemployed and very fearful of what would happen to her if she were caught. She wanted to formalize this work by taking the 'self-employed' option on New Deal but was afraid of letting the authorities know of her micro-business for fear of the consequences. She had thus kept claiming social security payments. The problem, however, was that she remained at the time of the interview fearful of signing off in case the Department for Work and Pensions investigated her. She was thus continuing to work on a self-employed basis while claiming and could not envisage a situation when she could escape from this situation. Indeed, Rita raised the idea of an amnesty so that people like her could 'come clean'. If this occurred, Rita argued, she would be able to set up formally and claimed that she was now turning away business because she did not feel able to take on any employees, even on an underground basis, in case she was found out. For her, as for many others, there was a perceived level of work beyond which she was unwilling to venture for fear that she would be discovered.

The carpenter   Rick did carpentry as a hobby (arising out of the fact that his father had been a carpenter and had taught him) and a lot of DIY activity around the home. Employed as a furniture remover, he was finding the hard physical work increasingly difficult. When a job arose in the depot of the removal firm that involved making boxes and packing them for people moving abroad, he had successfully applied for the job. Here, therefore, a skill acquired through DIY activity had been used to acquire a different formal job. Once his carpentry skills had been discovered, many offers from those working in the company were received to do additional work on an underground basis. As he put it, 'The Director's daughter wanted some windows replacing so he asked me if I wanted to do it. Then one of the estimators asked me if I could do some things for him and it sort of snowballed from there'. There was an implicit agreement, moreover, that he could use materials from the workplace. For him, this was not 'pilfering' as it was wholly condoned by the owners as a perk of the job for this employee (and the employees having the work done). A DIY hobby thus not only resulted in a new higher-paid formal job but a range of underground work that was taking up nearly every weekend. This provided him with additional income but also a new work identity.

The painter and decorator   John had acquired skills decorating his own home and had so enjoyed it that he also then decorated his parents' house and later his brother's. His brother had paid him for the work and one of his brother's friends had then asked him to decorate some rooms in his house. His wife, who worked as a secretary in a large company in the city had then found colleagues at her workplace also interested in him doing work for them. From this, he had now set up as a self-employed painter and decorator and just about had sufficient customers on an ongoing basis for this to be his sole occupation and his primary income.

Most of these examples of entrepreneurship in the underground economy are small-scale. These micro-entrepreneurs were operating in the underground economy largely as a short-term risk-taking strategy to either test out the business venture or to establish themselves. They are usually either employees in employment or classified as 'economically inactive' and in the process of setting themselves up as self-employed. Of all fledgling micro-entrepreneurs identified in the English Localities Survey, about one-fifth display a high economic dependency on their underground work with the remaining 80 per cent earning additional income from such endeavour. For some three-quarters, this activity was more of a voluntary choice than a response to constraints, especially among those already in formal employment and developing some hobby or interest into a business venture. When they begin to establish themselves, they are here defined as moving into the category below if they continue to engage in underground transactions. Although the dynamics involved cannot be ascertained from this snapshot survey, the finding that fledgling ventures are operated mostly by the economically inactive and formal employees but more established off-the-books ventures by the formally self-employed intimates that if these ventures persist, many of their founders become formally self-employed rather than continue to work as an employee or claim benefits. Indeed, a number of the individual case studies below reinforce this proposal.

Underground Work and the Established Self-employed

For the more established self-employed conducting underground work, such work is generally used continuously and serially, and is heavily embedded in their working practices, often seen as a means of 'getting by'. Although a few of these more established self-employed operate wholly underground, the vast majority of these underground transactions are conducted by the formally self-employed (80 per cent of all off-the-books transactions conducted by established self-employed off-the-books workers in the English Localities Survey). Just 15 per cent of underground transactions by the established self-employed were by those who were also formal employees, and 5 per cent by people classified as economically inactive or unemployed. This finding that most established off-the-books self-employed workers are also formally self-employed is reinforced in other studies (see General Accounting Office, 1994; O'Higgins, 1981; Pahl, 1988; Small Business Council, 2004). For some three-quarters of such established self-employed, moreover, there was a high economic dependency on off-the-books work as a principal means of 'getting by'.

The formally self-employed with established off-the-books operations

The picture framers   Tony and Mo are self-employed people who are serial and continuous users of underground transactions in their formal business. This couple own a number of picture framing and mirror retail shops and the husband also manufactured picture frames and mirrors in the workshop at the rear of his main shop. Most trade was on an on-the-books basis. However, whenever close social contacts asked for pictures to be framed or mirrors, they nearly always did this on an off-the-books basis. As Mo put it, 'you would never make any profit if you put everything through the books'.

Although normally it was friends, neighbours and acquaintances offered an off-the-books rate this sometimes expanded a little further, especially when money was tight. Having recently bought a new house, their response had been to conduct more off-the-books transactions than normal for a wider range of customers. This couple, therefore, were serial and ongoing users of underground work as a coping strategy and it was very heavily embedded in their trading practices. They currently had a high economic dependency on such transactions.

A building firm   Dave and his father run a building firm doing mostly house extensions for domestic customers. They employ one other full-time formal employee. All other work is subcontracted. At the time of interview, they had gone through a number of very good years, when they had a pick of projects and had been able to charge 'extortionate' prices. Having been established for many years, a large proportion of their business went through the books. Indeed, they were resentful of the wider attitude that builders always did off-the-books work. For them, the only time underground transactions occurred was when doing a customer a favour and/or they saw it as an insignificant minor job. An example they gave was a home extension project they were doing at the time of interview. They had dug up the drive of the neighbouring house to lay pipes and then put scaffolding on their drive for 2–3 months. Dave and his father had already paid for them to have their drive resurfaced and also for a satellite television dish to be repositioned. When the neighbour had asked for them to carry out minor roof maintenance work, they had done so on an off-the-books basis. For them, the scaffolding was already in place and they felt that the neighbour deserved a favour for the disruption caused. However, because of the work already paid for, they felt it necessary to charge but only a minimum rate. For this more established business, therefore, off-the-books work was a relatively minor component of their income but still often used by them on an ongoing basis in their daily practices albeit for minor rather than major jobs.

The kitchen design business   David for many years worked as an employee of a retail chain that offered a kitchen design and installation service. After learning the trade, he decided to set up his own kitchen design business first alongside his full-time employment but by the time of the interview, on a full-time self-employed basis. The way in which he had moved towards this was first by conducting some off-the-books jobs at weekends and in the evenings and having built up sufficient trade, he then went 'solo'. Indeed, he still took his customers back to his old store to choose their goods. When installing, however, his strategy was very much grounded in the underground economy.

He lived in a relatively affluent suburb and worked from home offering a kitchen design service. Once people had chosen the goods they wanted, he then employed kitchen fitters, plumbers, electricians and plasterers all on an off-the-books basis. He made his profit on the units, not their labour. By employing the labour on an off-the-books basis, however, he could give the customer a more competitive rate than they would otherwise receive formally. For the underground craftsmen, the rates paid on a cash-in-hand basis for jobs in this affluent suburb were higher than they could earn formally elsewhere since the charging of premium rates by tradesmen was the custom and practice in this area. David thus had a thriving small business and a long waiting list of clients. Although he expressed a desire to formalize his operations, he felt that this would be a slow process. If he could employ the tradesmen on a more formal basis, without incurring significant extra costs, he said he would 'go legit tomorrow'.

The domestic cleaner   Diane is a long-standing user of underground work as a coping strategy. Living in a deprived neighbourhood, she was for a long time employed on a cash-in-hand basis by a taxi company but due to a dislike of the owner had decided to start working on a self-employed basis as a household cleaner mostly for clients in a neighbouring affluent suburb. At first, this work as an off-the-books employee for the taxi firm had been combined with her work on a self-employed basis for a formal company that supplied household cleaning services. Using the latter to establish contacts with customers, however, she had then asked customers given to her by the company about others she could clean for on an underground basis. In this way, she had broken into the local market where there is a shortage of cleaners and in a manner that enabled her to overcome the principal barrier to employment, which is a distrust of strangers being left in their homes and given door keys. She used the formal cleaning company to establish both relations of trust and 'word-of-mouth' recommendations. For her, nevertheless, this endeavour was purely a means of earning extra cash to get by. She received £5 per hour when working on a self-employed basis for the formal cleaning company with the customer paying some £7 per hour in total. By conducting the work on a cash-in-hand basis for £6 per hour, both she and the customer financially benefited. She had no desires, however, to expand beyond finding sufficient work for herself and no intention of formalizing this work. Indeed, attempts were continuously made to move into the underground economy any formal work received from the cleaning company if the clients were willing, not least because she had also grown to dislike the franchise owner of the domestic cleaning company whom she saw as exploiting her. The job history of Diane, therefore, was heavily embedded in the underground economy and her move towards off-the-books self-employment was a voluntary response to her considerable disdain for both her formal and underground employers and desire for autonomy in her work.

Another painter and decorator Ken is a painter and decorator who had been in self-employment for some 30 years at the time of the interview. Many of his jobs were through word-of-mouth, not least through his wife who worked for a large organization. A large proportion of his business was formal and he only conducted jobs on an off-the-books basis for what he termed 'deserving' customers (for example, long-standing customers who might now be retired), and the proportion conducted on such a basis had significantly declined over the years.

Formal employees with established self-employed business ventures
A 'parasitic' enterprise An example of where skills acquired in a formal job were used to establish an off-the-books micro-enterprise was Martin who worked for a large garage door installation company. Alongside his employment, he had his own 'parasitic' wholly underground business venture. When he visited clients for his company, he would whenever appropriate give them a quote for the company doing the job and then another quote if he did the job at the weekend or in the evening. In his case, there was never any intention of leaving his formal job since this gave him the necessary contacts for his own micro-enterprise. In one sense, this can be seen as an example of 'intrapreneurship' (see Chapter 2), albeit not of a sort that has been so far quoted in any textbooks on entrepreneurship.

The solicitor Ben worked as a solicitor for a fairly large solicitor's firm but regularly informed clients and other acquaintances that if they phoned him at home, he could provide his services for less than if it was put through the firm. This was a long-standing practice and he saw these off-the-books jobs as both a useful 'top-up' to his salary and a way of helping out people he knew who might return him a favour in the future.

The economically inactive/unemployed with established self-employed business ventures
The upholsterer As a school leaver, Mary had worked in her Uncle's furniture shop and learned upholstery, how to make loose covers for chairs and sofas, and curtain making. After marrying and her children reaching school age, during which time she had been a 'wife at home', Mary decided to set up in business on her own and had slowly built up a customer base.

This network had expanded through word-of-mouth. She always worked on a cash-in-hand basis and her annual earnings were usually over the personal income tax threshold. For her, this was additional income for the household since her husband had a full-time job and a way of making money for herself and her family and at the same time having the autonomy in terms of working time to be with her children.

Off-the-books Social Entrepreneurs

Although it has been increasingly recognized that underground work is conducted on both an organized and autonomous basis, few until recently queried whether all autonomous underground work was conducted under market-like economic relations for the purpose of monetary gain. Two stimuli, however, have led to this being questioned.

First, in the broader field of monetary exchange, there has been a growing opposition to the 'thin' representation of monetary exchange as always market-like and motivated by monetary gain. Arguing that 'the major defect of such market-based models of exchange is simply that they do not convey the richness and messiness of the exchange experience' (Crewe and Gregson, 1998: 41), 'thicker' descriptions have been increasingly promulgated that recognize the diverse economic relations and motives underpinning monetary transactions (for example, Bourdieu, 2001; Carrier, 1997; Community Economies Collective, 2001; Gibson-Graham, 1996; Slater and Tonkiss, 2001).

Second, empirical data on underground work have resulted in a questioning of whether underground work is always market-like and profit-motivated (for example, Cornuel and Duriez, 1985; Jensen *et al.*, 1995; Nelson and Smith, 1999; Pfau-Effinger, 2003; Williams, 2004a, c, e, g, 2005c, d, 2006c; Williams and Windebank, 2001a, b, 2002b, 2003a). As Travers (2002: 2) points out, 'most research on [underground work] gives short shrift to the motivations of people to do this work. It is usually said that people do the work to earn extra money and left at that'.

However, as early as the 1980s, Cornuel and Duriez (1985) in their study of relatively affluent households in French new towns highlighted how favours were exchanged on a paid basis between neighbours primarily in order to forge fledgling networks of support rather than to make extra money. At the time, such a finding resulted in few analysts pursuing a wholesale rethinking of the character of underground work. Recently, nevertheless, the number of studies identifying the presence of non-market relations and rationales other than financial gain has started to reach the critical mass necessary to raise doubts about the validity of the dominant market-centred reading of underground work.

Studying underground work in non-metropolitan Pennsylvania, for example, Jensen *et al.* (1995) have clearly shown that underground work is by no means always motivated by financial gain. They find in some 61 per cent of all reported cases of underground work in this rural area that the chief rationale was to help out neighbours. Nelson and Smith (1999), again studying small town America, highlight how 'ersatz entrepreneurial activity' (for example, vehicle repairs) by men displaced from traditional male occupations, although superficially appearing to be undertaken for money-making purposes, is uncovered on closer analysis to be motivated by the need to maintain masculine identities and often to cost rather than generate money.

As reported in Williams (2004a), moreover, the English Localities Survey found that for-profit underground work, although predominant in affluent localities (constituting 84 per cent of all reported instances of underground work), constitutes only a relatively small share of all underground work in deprived areas (32 per cent). In these latter areas, 68 per cent of underground work is by friends, neighbours and kin primarily for redistributive and community-building purposes. Here, employers often paid people for 'helping them out' so as to give money to those in need in a way that avoided all connotations of charity. Similarly, underground workers often did jobs for those they knew for a token fee well under the market price again so as to help out those who would otherwise be unable to get necessary work conducted. Indeed, they find that some 84 per cent of all material support provided by friends and neighbours in deprived neighbourhoods involved cash payments, signifying the existence of a culture of cash for favours (Williams, 2004a).

In sum, besides autonomous underground workers working for-profit, others undertake such activity on a not-for-profit basis for family, friends and acquaintances. As monetary exchange has penetrated ever deeper into areas of everyday life in western economies where unpaid exchange previously prevailed, it appears that exchanges that used to take place on an unpaid basis now often involve money. Giving cash for favours occurs mostly when casual one-off tasks are undertaken for friends, family and acquaintances, especially in deprived populations where paying cash for favours is a widespread practice, not least because it prevents relations from turning sour if the favour is not returned (for a detailed evaluation, see Williams, 2004a).

IN WHICH SECTORS ARE UNDERGROUND ENTERPRISES CONCENTRATED?

Although numerous studies pinpoint the prevalence of underground work in particular sectors and occupations, such as the hospitality industry (Williams and Thomas, 1996), restaurants (for example, Ram *et al.*, 2002a, b), domestic service (for example, Anderson, 2001a, b; Boris and Prugl, 1996; Dagg, 1996; Hondagneu-Sotelo, 2001; Pfau-Effinger, 2006; Salmi, 1996), garment manufacturing (for example, Bender, 2004; Espenshade, 2004; Hapke, 2004; Ram *et al.*, 2002b; A. Ross 2004) and taxi drivers (Jordan and Travers, 1998), there has been little overarching evaluation of the sectors in which such work is concentrated.

Recently, however, this gap has started to be bridged. Pedersen (2003) reveals in his cross-national survey that although the underground economy is apparent in all sectors, albeit to varying degrees, in the UK for instance, just under half of all underground work (46.7 per cent) takes place in the 'construction sector' and another quarter (23.8 per cent) in a range of consumer services (see Table 5.3).

This finding about the sectors in which underground work is rife is supported by other studies. Construction services, particularly in the domestic sector, are commonly acknowledged as a sphere in which underground work is rife. Indeed, Capital Economics (2003) cite how RMI (repair, maintenance and improvement) in the UK private housing sector was worth £12.8 billion in 2002 in current prices, of which £7 billion was conducted in the underground economy.

Domestic services, similarly, have been widely imputed to heavily rely on underground labour. As Cancedda (2001) reports, somewhere between 50 per cent and 80 per cent of all domestic workers are employed on an underground basis in western economies. In Austria, for example, where 70 per cent of jobs in household services are conducted on an underground basis, it has been estimated that while 5000 formal employees are registered with the authorities, underground employees number somewhere between 60000 and 300000. In France, meanwhile, it was estimated that there were five underground workers for every declared worker in the household services sector in 1997 and in Germany, over half of household service workers (more than 2 million people) are asserted to work on an underground basis. In Italy, the ratio of legitimate to underground workers in this sector is estimated to be one to three.

The English Localities Survey, moreover, identified remarkably similar results concerning its overall distribution to the Pedersen (2003) study. As Table 5.4 displays, some 43 per cent of all underground work is concentrated in the home repair and maintenance sector (46.7 per cent in the Pedersen

Table 5.3 Distribution of the underground economy in five countries: by sector, 2000

Sector	All underground work (%)				
	Denmark 2001	Norway 1998/2000	Sweden 1997–8	Germany 2001	UK 2000
Agriculture, forestry and fishing	(5.2)	(0.8)	9.1	(4.3)	(1.1)
Manufacturing	(1.0)	(3.0)	4.9	(1.3)	14.0
Trade	(0.3)	(0.6)	(1.6)	–	(0.7)
Construction	53.3	43.5	27.2	29.0	46.7
• painting and decorating	11.1	5.3	5.5	17.0	17.2
• carpentry and joinery	12.5	14.9	7.2	(0.9)	11.1
• bricklaying	13.0	(10.6)	–	(1.1)	1.3
• other (for example, electrical and plumbing)	16.7	12.8	14.6	10.0	17.2
Service functions	34.1	39.5	48.4	42.5	23.8
• repair work	9.8	5.9	5.8	3.7	11.6
• auditing and legal advice	(2.3)	(0.7)	2.0	(0.2)	
• cleaning	(1.2)	(2.1)	2.5	4.3	
• childcare	1.8	16.6	–	3.9	
• garden work	10.6	2.6	1.8	10.6	
• other services (for example, hairdressing)	8.4	11.6	36.4	19.8	12.2
Other (for example, transport)	(2.2)	(1.9)	6.4	5.0	(4.8)
Activity not stated	(3.9)	10.7	(2.3)	17.9	8.9
Total	100.0	100.0	100.0	100.0	100.0

Note: In parentheses when respondents in a cell are less than 20

Source: Rockwool Foundation Research Unit, 2003 (cited in Renooy *et al.*, 2004: Table 4.4).

study) and just over a quarter in domestic service activities. Indeed, the tasks most frequently using underground labour are: making/repairing garden equipment such as repairing lawnmowers or sharpening tools (one in three of such tasks are conducted on an underground basis); attic conversions (one in four are primarily done off-the-books); installing a bathroom (24 per cent); car repairs (19 per cent); plumbing (13 per cent); electrical work (12 per cent); plastering (12 per cent); baby-sitting (12 per cent); maintaining appliances (11 per cent); outdoor painting (10 per cent) and window cleaning (10 per cent).

Table 5.4   Tasks conducted in the underground economy in England

	Conducted in underground economy (%)	Share of underground economy (%)
House maintenance	8	24
Home improvement	10	19
Routine housework	3	28
Making and repairing goods	2	3
Car maintenance	9	12
Gardening	2	3
Caring	8	11

Source: English Localities Survey (*n* = 861 households) (see Williams, 2004a: Table 5.2)

This finding that the vast majority of underground work takes place in the domestic service and construction sectors has been also identified in Sweden (Jönsson, 2001). In Denmark, moreover, it has been estimated that some 50 per cent of such work involves home repairs, 30 per cent domestic services such as cleaning and 20 per cent car repairs (RSV, 2000). In Germany, meanwhile, building, renovating and repair work have been found to constitute 44 per cent of all underground work while in Austria, renovating and building work is estimated as constituting some 35 per cent of this sphere with the vast majority of the rest in consumer services such as hairdressing, baby-sitting, appliance repair and so forth (Schneider and Enste, 2002: 13–14).

This common finding that underground work in western economies is concentrated in the construction sector and a range of consumer services has important consequences for designing policy initiatives to tackle this sphere. For example, if UK policy measures were to deal with the realms of home maintenance and repair (43 per cent of all underground work), routine housework (28 per cent), gardening services (3 per cent) and caring

(11 per cent), they would deal with some 85 per cent of all underground work. In other countries, similarly, policies focused upon home construction and maintenance along with domestic services would deal with the vast majority of the underground sector.

CONCLUSIONS

In sum, this chapter has unpacked how the conventional depiction of underground work as exploitative organized employment conducted by marginalized populations in sweatshop-like conditions is descriptive of only a small segment of the underground economy. Here, three broad types of autonomous underground worker have been identified, namely fledgling micro-entrepreneurs, the established self-employed off-the-books workers and underground social entrepreneurs. These autonomous underground workers, moreover, have been tentatively argued to conduct the vast majority of underground work. In each case, the heterogeneity within each category has been here portrayed along with numerous case studies so as to provide a richer and more textured portrait of this hidden enterprise culture.

The outcome has been to map the relationships between entrepreneurship, enterprise culture and the underground economy. It has revealed that most fledgling micro-entrepreneurs working on an off-the-books basis are either employees in employment or economically inactive, and their micro-enterprise is either a spin-off from their formal employment or an outcome of some hobby or interest, while the more established off-the-books self-employed are usually also formally self-employed and their underground work is closely associated with their formal business venture. This snapshot portrait of the character of the hidden enterprise culture, however, cannot be used to imply that fledgling micro-entrepreneurs necessarily become formally self-employed. Not only do many of the case studies suggest that this is not the case but one cannot assume from a snapshot picture a trajectory in work histories. Further research is thus required on the dynamics involved in this hidden enterprise culture.

Nevertheless, this chapter has begun to display the close relationship between entrepreneurship, enterprise culture and the underground economy, and to portray the wide variety of forms that this can take. It has also shown that even if autonomous underground workers are to be found in all economic sectors, they are concentrated in the home improvement and maintenance sector along with the consumer services sphere. This has important consequences for policy formulation. It clearly reveals not only that a deterrence approach towards underground work will destroy precisely the entrepreneurship and enterprise culture that other spheres of public policy are seeking to nurture but also the economic sectors that need to be targeted. How public policy can deal with this hidden enterprise culture is the subject of the rest of this book.

NOTES

1. In her study of Brianza in Lombardy, Ghezzi (2006) identifies among the dense network of small industrial and artisan firms, most of which are family-run businesses, the pervasive practice of 'co-operatives of porterage' (*cooperative di facchinaggio*). Here, legally registered co-operatives who should only provide labour for specific tasks not central to the production process (for example, cleaning or repairing, packaging, loading, and moving the commodity outside the workshop) in practice hire skilled workers able to perform highly qualified tasks on an off-the-books basis to businesses that temporarily need it.

6. Explaining the hidden enterprise culture

INTRODUCTION

Conventionally, the existence of the underground economy was often attributed to single causes, such as the level of taxation or the prevalence of very small enterprises. Increasingly, however, it is recognized to be the product of not only a multiplicity of factors but also how these factors variously combine in different populations to produce high or low levels of underground work. A plethora of very small enterprises in an area, for example, is no longer seen as a proxy indicator of a sizeable underground economy. Rather, it is whether a host of other factors also exist and how these factors interrelate, that matter (Mateman and Renooy, 2001; Renooy et al., 2004; Williams, 2004a; Williams and Windebank, 1995a, 1998).

In this chapter, this mode of explaining the general underground economy is applied to understanding the existence of a hidden enterprise culture in western economies, by which is meant the prevalence of fledgling underground micro-entrepreneurs and more established self-employed off-the-books workers. To do this, the multiplicity of structural, institutional and individual-level conditions that influence whether a hidden enterprise culture prevails will be reviewed. Emphasis throughout, moreover, will be on understanding how these structural, institutional and individual-level factors combine together in different populations to produce particular outcomes. As Renooy et al. (2004: 9) put it:

> There are no general, universal causes for the existence and development of an underground economy. It is brought about by a complex interplay between various variables that varies between countries.

Given this recognition that the hidden enterprise culture cannot be explained using mono-causal explanations (for example, higher tax levels, illiteracy, local cultural traditions) and that individual factors will have varying impacts depending on how they blend with the overall constellation of conditions in existence at any time in a particular population, this chapter highlights the need for a more embedded understanding of the hidden enterprise culture that moves away from simple mono-causal narratives and towards understanding how factors combine in any time and/or place to produce a large/small and growing/declining hidden enterprise culture.

The outcome will be to show that concentrating on one condition (for example, reducing taxes, simplifying formalization procedures) to reduce the hidden enterprise culture is insufficient. As will become apparent, a multi-pronged attack on the host of conditions likely to stimulate its existence is required. In other words, by displaying that the reasons for the hidden enterprise culture are complex, multi-layered and often quite subtle, this chapter will reveal how the hidden enterprise culture needs to be tackled in a way that moves beyond simplistic uni-dimensional solutions such as a reduction in the general rate of income tax. To here review the factors that produce a hidden enterprise culture, first, the structural-level conditions that result in its existence are reviewed, second, the institutional-level conditions and third and finally, the individual-level characteristics.

STRUCTURAL-LEVEL CHARACTERISTICS

Economic Regulators

Whether or not a hidden enterprise culture emerges is in part influenced by a host of structural economic conditions (Benton, 1990; Portes and Sassen-Koob, 1987). Here, some of the more important are identified.

Level of affluence and employment

During the past decade or so, it has been found in many western nations that underground work in general, and autonomous underground work more particularly, is concentrated in affluent populations and among those in formal employment (see Chapter 3). The problem, however, is that a few studies have found the opposite (for example, Kesteloot and Meert, 1999; Leonard, 1994). This is not because some studies are correct and others false. It is because affluence or the level of employment alone does not lead to the development of a hidden enterprise culture. It is just one of a number of factors that when combined together, result in its development (Mateman and Renooy, 2001; Renooy *et al.*, 2004; Williams, 2004a; Williams and Windebank, 1995a, 1998).

As Barlett and Steele (2002) assert with reference to the USA, although growing economic pressures on households struggling to make ends meet can lead to a hidden enterprise culture, this is only the case where other conditions also exist such as a growing contempt for government, a turn towards self rather than society, declining moral and ethical standards and distrust. As will be seen below, there are many more additional factors. The important point is that although affluence and high employment rates are commonly prevalent in populations where hidden enterprise cultures thrive, they do not necessarily always and inevitably result in a large hidden enterprise.

Industrial structure

The size and diversity of enterprises in an area is an important determinant of whether a hidden enterprise culture prevails. Many find that relatively little autonomous underground work takes place in areas dominated by a few large companies because the skills acquired in larger companies are less transferable and large companies less often use underground work than smaller firms (Barthelemy, 1991; Howe, 1988; Van Geuns *et al.*, 1987). Underground entrepreneurship and self-employment usually flourishes, meanwhile, in local economies with a plethora of small firms (Barthelemy, 1991; Blair and Endres, 1994; Cappecchi, 1989; Pahl, 1988; Sassen, 1996; Van Geuns *et al.*, 1987) since there is greater scope for subcontracting and the skills acquired in formal jobs are more likely to be useful. Similarly, many have drawn a strong positive correlation between the level of self-employment and the prevalence of autonomous underground work (O'Higgins, 1981; Pahl, 1988; Small Business Council, 2004; Williams, 2005a).

However, one cannot automatically read-off a hidden enterprise culture from the level of formal self-employment or very small firms. The magnitude of underground work among very small firms and the self-employed will vary considerably between nations, regions and localities due to a host of other factors, such as the structure of taxation and the level of affluence and employment. Indeed, although the English Localities Survey in Chapter 5 found a strong correlation between formal self-employment and those engaging in serial off-the-books work, this does not mean that such a correlation always holds. Indeed, in other circumstances where there are self-employed people working wholly underground, there might be a substitutive relationship rather than one of reinforcement.

Level of subcontracting

It might be assumed that a hidden enterprise culture flourishes in areas where the flexible production process of subcontracting prevails. Indeed, many studies hint at this when discussing industrial districts (for example, Benton, 1990; Ghezzi, 2006; Williams and Thomas, 1996). However, although a growth of subcontracting leads to a proliferation of underground employees (for example, Barlett and Steele, 2000; Bender, 2004; Castree *et al.*, 2004; Espenshade, 2004; Hapke, 2004; A. Ross, 2004; J. Ross, 2004), as displayed in Italian industrial districts (for example, Cappecchi, 1989; Ghezzi, 2006), it is not established that subcontracting leads to greater levels of underground self-employment. Although Benton (1990) identifies this in the electronics industry around Madrid, others note thriving hidden enterprise cultures in areas where subcontracting is largely absent, such as Grand Failly in France (Legrain 1982), not least due to the dense social networks and relative geographical isolation of the population. Subcontracting, therefore, although sometimes leading to the existence of a hidden enterprise culture, is not a precondition for its emergence.

Social Regulators

Besides various structural economic conditions, a host of social structures also influence the development of a hidden enterprise culture.

Cultural traditions, norms and moralities

Underground work is more acceptable in some populations than others, for example because feelings of resentment and of being let down by the state lead to less acquiescence to its laws (for example, Howe 1988; Legrain 1982; Leonard 1994; Torgler, 2003; Van Geuns *et al.* 1987; Wintrobe, 2001). Frey and Weck (1983) for example, find significant cross-national differences in tax morality (that is the willingness to cheat on taxes) and Chavdarova (2002) in Bulgaria also identifies clear differences between localities, with low tax morality being highest in big cities.[1] On the whole, where there is contempt for government, the conditions are ripe for the emergence of a hidden enterprise culture. Where there is an ever-growing obsession with self rather than neighbourhood, community and society, it develops. Where there is a decline in moral and ethical standards, it develops. Where there is widespread disagreement with government spending priorities, it develops (Wintrobe, 2001).

There are also variations in the degree to which different types of underground work are deemed acceptable. In Sweden, Jönsson (2001) shows that there is a relatively high acceptance of small-scale and occasional underground work by people working on an autonomous basis. When it is conducted by businesses paying employees on an off-the-books basis, however, this is less acceptable, especially when it is continuous and large scale. Moreover, working while claiming is deemed unacceptable by a large share of the Swedish population. This is similarly the case in the UK. As Cook (1989, 1997) argues, working while claiming is seen as stealing 'our' money while tax evasion by the self-employed is seen as people keeping 'their' money for themselves. MacDonald (1994) finds much the same in North East England. Such a finding is replicated in many other western nations.

Underground entrepreneurship tends to be more acceptable when there is widespread resentment of the state and less acquiescence to its laws. As Bàculo (2001) displays in the Italian city of Naples, poor relations between citizens and the state is a primary reason for the existence of a thriving hidden enterprise culture in the city. As she states, first, many small entrepreneurs take pride in being 'self-made', without the help of the authorities. Second, the inefficiency and corruption of the state contribute to a general sense of mistrust, leading underground entrepreneurs to escape not just the state but also organized criminal gangs. In other nations where there is more acquiescence to the state and appreciation of its redistributive role, such as in Scandinavia, hidden enterprise cultures may be less acceptable.

The nature of social networks

Dense social networks are often a major contributory factor in explaining high levels of autonomous underground work (Legrain, 1982; Mingione, 1991; Morris, 1994; Van Geuns *et al.*, 1987; Warde, 1990). Leonard (1994: 3) concludes that 'stability of residence, duration of unemployment, social homogeneity, extensive kinship and friendship networks and low levels of access to external resources are all conducive to the development of informal economic practices'. It is here considered that such a factor is important to the development of a hidden enterprise culture that, at least to an extent, depends on social networks (see the case studies in Chapter 5).

Dense social networks alone, however, are insufficient to lead to the growth of a hidden enterprise culture. Although dense social networks in conjunction with other factors (for example, in areas with a wide socio-economic mix or rural areas) can lead to the prevalence of autonomous underground work (Jessen *et al.*, 1987), if members are unable to pay for such goods and services, as Turner *et al.* (1985) find in a study of a former coal-mining village in Scotland, then little autonomous underground work will take place. Lysestol (1995) finds the same in Norway.

Socio-economic mix/disparities

Populations combining people with high incomes but little free time and those with low incomes but much free time witness higher levels of autonomous underground work (Barthelemy, 1991; Pestieau, 1985; Portes, 1994; Renooy, 1990). This, nevertheless, is not always the case (see Kesteloot and Meert, 1999). Where social apartheid prevails, resulting in little overlap between their networks, this will not occur. So too may strict enforcement of social security regulations coupled with a low tax regime restrict its development since this would reduce supply and provide little incentive to customers.

Size and type of settlement

Rural areas undertake more autonomous underground work than urban areas (Hadjimichalis and Vaiou, 1989; Jessen *et al.*, 1987) and their underground economies are more skewed towards autonomous work than urban areas (Duncan, 1992; Levitan and Feldman, 1991; Kesteloot and Meert, 1999). There are, however, many exceptions. Van Ours (1991), examining how households get small home repairs, car repairs and maintenance and ladies' hairdressing done, finds that rural households use less underground work than households in small and large cities. Mogensen (1985), in Denmark, meanwhile, shows that the frequency of participation slowly decreases as one moves from large urban areas such as Copenhagen (17 per cent participation in underground work) to the rural areas of Western Jutland (10 per cent participation). In Canada, furthermore, Fortin *et al.* (1996) find that the participation rate in underground work is much lower in the rural area of Bas-du-Fleuve than in Quebec and Montreal. The implication, therefore, is that the urban–rural continuum alone is an insufficient determinant of the level of autonomous underground work. Whether it prevails depends on the presence or absence of a range of additional factors and how they combine together. One cannot universally state that rural areas have larger hidden enterprise cultures than urban areas or that more affluent urban areas have larger ones than poorer urban areas.

INSTITUTIONAL-LEVEL CONDITIONS

Tax Contributions

A vast literature examines the relationship between underground work and tax levels (for example Gutmann, 1977; O'Higgins, 1981; Tanzi, 1980). Although some argue that this condition alone is sufficient to explain the growth of a hidden enterprise culture (Geeroms and Mont, 1987; Klovland, 1980; Matthews, 1982), it is but one, albeit important, part of the 'cocktail' of explanatory factors. Generally, as taxes rise, the differential cost increases of using formal rather than underground work for both consumers and suppliers (Frey and Weck, 1983; Gutmann, 1977; Renooy, 1990). However, not all individuals will employ or offer themselves as underground workers. Instead, some consumers will engage in self-provisioning. Neither do all self-employed people and companies automatically switch some or all production to underground modes. It depends on the other options open to them.

Indeed, it is not just the level but also the structure of tax that influences the prevalence of a hidden enterprise culture. In general, places where taxes are raised more from companies than individuals, fledgling and established self-employed workers might be more prone to work off-the-books, while if these contributions are raised to a greater extent from individual workers, then employees working off-the-books might be more likely (see Barthelemy, 1991). The way in which the level and structure of taxation influences the configuration of underground work, moreover, depends on a range of other factors. A lack of trust in government and little 'buying into' the necessity of taxation for social cohesion and inclusion might lead higher taxes to cause a growth of a hidden enterprise culture. However, where trust in government is higher and there is awareness of the benefits of taxation for social cohesion, a hidden enterprise culture will not necessarily result from higher tax levels (see, for example, Wintrobe, 2001). On its own, therefore, higher taxation is a necessary but insufficient condition (of an unnecessary but sufficient causal field) for the emergence of a hidden enterprise culture.

Welfare Benefit Regulations

In many north European countries, those claiming benefit constitute a small proportion of those starting up fledgling micro-enterprises or the more established underground self-employed (see Chapter 3). However, this is not everywhere the case. The unemployed in countries with poor access to permanent state benefits will engage in such autonomous underground work as a survival strategy (Del Boca and Forte, 1982; Williams and Windebank, 1998) because they have little to lose if caught, thus helping to explain the higher levels of autonomous underground work in southern EU nations and the USA. In contrast, those eligible to claim more generous benefits will have the major disincentive of losing them, as Wenig (1990) has highlighted in Germany. Again, however, this general tendency will be mediated by other factors. Leonard (1994) in West Belfast, for example, displays that local cultural traditions, social networks and the lack of buoyancy in the local labour market as well as poor enforcement of regulations can lead to high levels of autonomous underground work among the unemployed.

Labour Law

By definition, government regulations create a hidden enterprise culture. As labour law differs between nations, so too does the level and nature of the hidden enterprise culture. For example, in Spain before 1980, and in contrast to nations such as the Netherlands and the UK, industrial home-working was illegal and thus by definition underground work. Although home-working again became legal after 1980, the tradition of home-working being conducted underground had become established and continued (Van Geuns *et al.*, 1987). Labour law, in sum, structures the character of the hidden enterprise culture.

State Interpretation and Enforcement of Regulations

Hidden enterprise cultures are shaped not only by regulations but also how they are interpreted and enforced. Some authorities, both national and local, deliberately overlook such entrepreneurship and self-employment so as to help individuals and families raise adequate incomes, which would be difficult if regulations were strictly enforced (Cappechi, 1989; Freeman and Ogelman, 2000; Jones *et al.*, 2004; Lobo 1990a, b; Mingione, 1990; Portes and Sassen-Koob, 1987; Van Geuns *et al.*, 1987; Warren, 1994). Freeman and Ogelman (2000: 118–19) for example, discuss 'purposeful failure' on the part of the state, which adopts 'a casual attitude towards the violation of formal rules if the ends of economic efficiency are being served'. Hidden enterprise cultures emerge, moreover, not only through passive tolerance but also through active practices. For example, there is well-documented evidence of a deliberately laissez-faire approach being adopted towards underground entrepreneurs by local governments or even active support (Bàculo, 2001; Ghezzi, 2006; Portes and Sassen-Koob, 1987; Vinay, 1987; Warren, 1994). However, on its own, this is again insufficient to result in the emergence and growth of a hidden enterprise culture.

INDIVIDUAL-LEVEL CHARACTERISTICS

Besides structural determinants and institutional conditions leading to the emergence of a hidden enterprise culture, a host of individual-level characteristics shape who is involved in such work.

Employment Status

As shown throughout this book, a close correlation exists between employment status and autonomous forms of underground work. Many running established off-the-books operations in England for example, are formally self-employed, while many fledgling underground entrepreneurs are currently employees and appear to be in transition to formal self-employment via off-the-books work (see Chapter 5). Whether this applies elsewhere, however, depends on a host of variables including the configuration of labour law, welfare benefit provision and regulations, the industrial structure, the levels and nature of taxation, and so forth.

Education and Skill levels

The more educated the person, the more likely s/he is to perform autonomous well-paid underground work whilst those with fewer qualifications engage in lower-paid underground work of both an autonomous and organized variety (Fortin *et al.*, 1996; Lemieux *et al.*, 1994; Pestieau, 1985; Renooy, 1990). Relatively deprived areas, which have lower qualification levels, will thus generally perform less autonomous underground work and that which takes place will be of lower-paid varieties. In Italy, however, Bàculo (2001) argues that one of the reasons for the prevalence of a large hidden enterprise culture has to do with the incapacity and difficulty of many entrepreneurs managing their own company in compliance with the rules. Many she interviewed were former employees or shopkeepers capable of producing or selling but not able to keep accounts or relations with the public authorities. Qualitative interviews with underground micro-entrepreneurs in the London borough of Newham come to the same conclusion (Copisarow, 2004; Copisarow and Barbour, 2004).

Again, therefore, there is a need to break down this factor, this time by the type of education and training necessary, and to recognize that there will be various configurations depending on the way in which human capital is mediated by other structural- and institutional-level factors in any population (for example, the structure of tax and welfare benefits and the degree to which they are enforced). It is increasingly apparent, nevertheless, that if one lacks the skills to participate in the legitimate economy, then opportunities to work in the hidden enterprise culture are likely to be similarly limited. Indeed, this is perhaps why many underground fledgling entrepreneurs are currently working as employees in employment and using the skills gained to set up independently. Similarly, it perhaps explains why so many who have more established off-the-books ventures are also formally self-employed.

Stage in Lifecycle

There is some evidence that underground workers are concentrated in younger age groups (Fortin *et al.*, 1996; Pedersen, 2003; Renooy, 1990). Until now, however, little research has been conducted on the age profile of underground entrepreneurs. Are those starting up for example, mostly younger age groups, those with young families seeking to transfer from employment to self-employment in order to achieve what they perceive as greater autonomy over their working time and/or a more family-friendly style of working? Or are they in older age groups being made redundant as employees and seeking to start up on their own? Or some mix of these groups? To some extent, this will depend on the structural economic conditions and how this combines with a variety of other factors. Populations subjected to recent bouts of de-layering in larger companies for example, might find a concentration in the latter group. Those with poor welfare entitlements and underdeveloped family-friendly working policies, however, might find the former group predominating. This requires further research. Until now, there is little understanding.

CONCLUSIONS

Anybody taking a cursory glance at the literature will quickly identify the all too common tendency to posit mono-causal explanations for the existence of underground endeavour. In recent years, however, there has been increasing recognition that it is how the host of conditions that might lead to underground work combine together, in particular circumstances, rather than individual causal factors *per se*, that result in businesses operating in the underground sector (for example, Mateman and Renooy, 2001; Renooy *et al.*, 2004; Williams, 2004a; Williams and Windebank, 1998). As Williams and Windebank (1998: 46) assert, what is important is 'the ways in which economic, social, institutional and environmental conditions combine in multifarious "cocktails" in different places to produce specific local outcomes'.

In this chapter, the same argument has been made when explaining the reasons for the prevalence of hidden enterprise cultures. By displaying that the reasons for entrepreneurship and self-employment in the underground economy are complex, multi-layered and often subtle, and that the causes can include a whole range of structural, institutional and individual-level conditions, this chapter has set the parameters for an evaluation of how the hidden enterprise culture might be tackled, displaying the need to move beyond simplistic solutions calling for reductions in the general rate of income tax and so forth. Before seeking specific policy initiatives to deal with the multiplicity of factors that lead people to join the hidden enterprise culture, however, a decision needs to be made on the overarching goal of such policy interventions. Is the primary goal to eradicate underground entrepreneurs? Is it to adopt a laissez-faire approach so that they might flourish? Or is it to actively intervene so as to enable them to start up on a legitimate basis and help those already working in this sphere to make the transition to the formal realm? Depending on the answer given, the policy initiatives required will significantly differ.

NOTE

1. This does not mean, however, that off-the-books workers possess a different set of cultural values to those who do not engage in such work. This has been widely refuted (for example, Engbersen *et al.*, 1993; Lysestol, 1995; Renooy, 1990).

PART III

What should be done about the hidden
enterprise culture? Policy options and their
implications

7. The deterrence option

INTRODUCTION

Here, the policy approach towards underground work that has been dominant across the western world is evaluated. This seeks to eradicate the underground economy using deterrence ('push') measures, notably the probability of detection and the level of punishments, in order to change the cost–benefit ratio confronting potential participants. To identify why its dominance has begun to recede, first, the practicality and second, the desirability of deterring such work is evaluated. In so doing, this chapter will reveal that although eradication is a wholly appropriate goal due to the negative impacts of this sector on consumers, suppliers, formal businesses and society, deterrence is not the appropriate means of achieving this objective.

THE DETERRENCE APPROACH TOWARDS UNDERGROUND WORK

Like other approaches towards underground work, the objective of the deterrence approach is to eradicate such work. The difference between this approach and others, however, rotates largely around how it seeks to achieve this. In this approach which has dominated public policy in most western countries, driven by a view that underground work is largely exploitative work conducted by off-the-books employees and has purely negative consequences, the belief is that eradication can be achieved by using tougher regulations and more punitive measures so as to deter people from participating in such work. First, therefore, it is necessary to outline how it views underground work along with what it considers to be the major consequences arising from its existence and following this, its approach to dealing with such work.

Representing the Underground Economy

In this approach, underground work is predominantly represented as an exploitative and low-paid form of work situated at the very bottom of a hierarchy of types of employment and a form of work that weakens formal workers' bargaining position (Castells and Portes, 1989; Gallin, 2001; Pfau-Effinger, 2003; Portes, 1994). Read in this manner, underground work is criticized alongside all other forms of exploitative work which unscrupulous employers oblige a vulnerable and unprotected workforce to undertake.

To more fully comprehend this reading of underground work, it is necessary to understand how such work is being situated in modern economies. Whereas in the past, and as discussed in Chapter 3, underground work was sometimes seen as a leftover from the past that would gradually disappear with modernization, the majority of commentators viewing it as a form of exploitative labour do not now see it in such marginal and peripheral terms. For them, underground work in the contemporary period is an inherent part of capitalism and a direct result of economic globalization that under neo-liberalism is encouraging a race to the bottom (Amin, 1996; Castells and Portes, 1989; Frank, 1996; Gallin, 2001; Ybarra, 1989). A strong correlation is thus drawn between the advent of underground work under neo-liberal globalization and the impoverishment of workers since firms are believed to turn to the underground economy so as to avoid the costs associated with protective labour legislation. Underground work, in consequence, is part of the current process of reversing unionization that is resulting in the disenfranchisement of a large section of the working class (often with the acquiescence of the state) in the name of economic growth and remaining competitive in an era of economic globalization (for example, Castells and Portes, 1989; Gallin, 2001; Roberts, 1991). As such, underground labourers are seen to share characteristics subsumed under the heading of 'downgraded labour': they receive few benefits, receive low wages and have poor working conditions.

Representing the Consequences of the Underground Economy

Based on this representation of the underground economy, advocates of the deterrence approach largely view this realm in wholly negative terms. In order to review its negative consequences, the impacts on underground employees, underground enterprises, legitimate businesses, customers and society at large will be here appraised in turn.

The negative consequences for underground workers, to commence, are seen to be that they: lack access to health and safety standards in the workplace (Evans *et al.*, 2004; Gallin, 2001; ILO, 2002); do not have various employment rights such as annual and other leave, sickness pay, redundancy and training (Evans *et al.*, 2004); have low job security (Jordan and Travers, 1998; Ross, 2001; Williams, 2001a); are unable to get an employer's reference (ILO, 2002); lack access to a range of other legal rights such as the minimum wage, tax credits and the working hours directive (Jordan and Travers, 1998; Leonard, 1998; Renooy *et al.*, 2004; Sassen, 1997; Williams and Windebank, 1998); are unable to gain access to credit (Kempson, 1996; Leonard, 1998); cannot build up rights to the state pension and other contributory benefits, and lack access to occupational pension schemes (Gallin, 2001; ILO, 2002; Sassen, 1997); lack bargaining rights (Dagg, 1996; ILO, 2002; Ross, 2001); lose employability due to their lack of evidence of engagement in employment; and suffer a constant fear of detection and risk of prosecution due to their activities being illegitimate (Cook, 1989, 1997; Grabiner, 2000).

Businesses working off-the-books, meanwhile, find themselves in a disadvantaged position operating outside, or at the margins, of the formal sector, resulting in their: pressurization into exploitative relationships with the formal sphere (Benton, 1990; Gallin, 2001; Lobo, 1990a, b; Williams and Windebank, 1998); lack of legal protection relative to formal businesses (Castells and Portes, 1989; ILO, 2002; Williams and Windebank, 1998); and an inability to develop and grow due to structural constraints with regard to gaining access to capital and securing the support available to formal businesses (Copisarow, 2004; ILO, 2002; Jurik, 2005).

For formal businesses, underground work results in: an unfair competitive advantage for off-the-books businesses over legitimate business transactions (Evans *et al.*, 2004; Grabiner, 2000; Renooy *et al.*, 2004; Small Business Council, 2004; Williams, 2005a); the emergence of micro-level deregulatory cultures enticing law-abiding firms into a local 'race to the bottom' and away from regulatory compliance (Grabiner, 2000; Renooy *et al.*, 2004; Williams, 2005a; Williams and Windebank, 1998); and situations of 'hyper-casualization' as more legitimate businesses are forced to turn to cash-in-hand work to compete effectively (Evans *et al.*, 2004; Gallin, 2001; Mateman and Renooy, 2001; Small Business Council, 2004; Williams, 2005a).

Customers employing underground labour, meanwhile, find themselves without: legal recourse if a poor job is done; insurance cover; guarantees in relation to the work conducted; and certainty that health and safety regulations have been followed (Williams, 2006a).

There are also broader societal costs in that: it is fraudulent activity that causes a loss of revenue for the state in terms of non-payment of income tax, national insurance and VAT (Evans *et al.*, 2004; Grabiner, 2000; Williams, 2005a; Williams and Windebank, 1998); it has knock-on effects on attempts to create social cohesion at a societal level by reducing the money available to governments to pursue social integration (Williams and Windebank, 1998); it results in weakened trade union and collective bargaining (Gallin, 2001); it leads to a loss of regulatory control over the quality of jobs and services provided in the economy (Gallin, 2001); and if a significant segment of the population is routinely engaged in such activity, it may well encourage a more casual attitude towards the law generally (Renooy *et al.*, 2004).

For all of these reasons, in consequence, underground work needs to be eliminated. This is irrefutable. However, is the deterrence approach the most appropriate means of achieving such a goal? Before answering this, one important point needs to be made. For adherents to this deterrence approach, the notion that underground work might have some positive as well as negative consequences is not entertained. The inevitable outcome of this blinkered view is that the aim is simply to stop people from engaging in such activity.

The Deterrence Policy Approach

Grounded in this negative representation of underground work, the way to eradicate it is to deter participation by ensuring that the expected cost of being caught and punished is greater than the economic benefit of engagement. This is achieved through improving detection rates and increasing the punishments in order to change the cost benefit calculation (for example, Allingham and Sandmo, 1972; Falkinger, 1988; Hasseldine and Zhuhong, 1999; Milliron and Toy, 1988; Sandford, 1999). For many years, this approach was adopted by most western governments (for example, Grabiner, 2000; Hasseldine and Zhuhong, 1999) and supported by supra-national agencies (for example, European Commission, 1998; ILO, 1996, OECD 1994; 2002) and many academic commentators (for example, Castells and Portes, 1989; Mingione, 1991; Sassen, 1989). To see how such an approach has operated in practice, a case study of UK public policy towards the underground economy is here provided.

The deterrence approach in practice: the case of the UK
In order to understand the UK approach towards the underground economy, two groups of underground worker need to be distinguished. First, there are 'ghosts' who earn over the personal tax allowance but do not declare their tax liability. Second, there are those 'working while claiming benefits' whose weekly income is over the 'earnings disregard' levels set by the Department of Work and Pensions (DWP) and/or they do not declare these earnings.

Starting with 'ghosts' (that is, those not claiming benefits but earning undeclared income over their personal tax allowance), under section 7 of the Taxes Management Act 1970, they are meant to notify Her Majesty's Revenue and Customs (HMRC) if there is a tax liability via a self-assessment tax return. There is also an additional requirement if turnover exceeds a certain amount to register for VAT. If they do not, then the situation has been that wherever possible, HMRC makes settlements or uses civil proceedings against offenders. It only rarely initiates criminal prosecution. This is simply because HMRC has the power to recover the tax owed, together with interest under section 86 of the 1970 Taxes Management Act. Under section 93, moreover, it also has the power to impose a civil penalty up to the value of the evaded tax but has discretion to mitigate or remit any penalty applied or, in cases where penalty proceedings would be appropriate, to make a 'contract settlement' with the tax payer. This settlement is an agreement not to take formal proceedings in exchange for an appropriate payment, to reflect the lost tax, interest and abated penalties.

If a 'ghost' comes forward, makes a spontaneous and full disclosure of past profits and co-operates with further enquiries, HMRC in practice has reduced the maximum penalty (100 per cent of the tax evaded) to 10 per cent or even less (Grabiner, 2000). This is because HMRC has a general responsibility for 'care and management' of taxes which enables it in appropriate circumstances to waive tax which is in law due and payable. Furthermore, where a person has been unable to realistically fund all or part of a settlement, the practice has been to treat the tax in question as irrecoverable. Although HMRC has been entitled to take proceedings under the criminal law, under section 17 on false accounting of the Theft Act 1968 or for the common law offence of 'cheat', this rarely happens. The relative inefficiency of criminal investigation and prosecution as a method for recovering sums owed means that there are just 50–100 prosecutions per annum and only in the most serious cases.

Such an approach to recovering money owed and criminal prosecution stands in stark contrast to how those 'working while claiming' are dealt with by the Department for Work and Pensions (DWP). Entitlement to some social security benefits depends on the means of the claimant. Claimants thus have a responsibility to declare any earnings. If they work for 16 hours or more per week, they are generally not entitled to benefit. If they declare earnings, their benefit is reduced pound for pound above the 'earnings disregard' thresholds of £5 for any weekly part-time earnings for single people, £10 for a couple or £15 a week for certain other groups such as lone parents and disabled people. These levels have been largely unchanged since their introduction in 1988. Estimating the level of 'working while claiming', the DWP assert that it constitutes some 40 per cent of all benefit fraud and effects the means-tested benefits of Income Support, Jobseekers Allowance as well as Housing Benefit. Indeed, the DSS has calculated that at any one time, 120 000 people are fraudulently working and claiming. Table 7.1 indicates the nature and level of the resulting fraud.

Unlike the low prosecution rates among 'ghosts', the DWP recovers all benefit overpaid and initiates criminal proceedings against those caught working while claiming. Indeed, in 1998/9, the DWP prosecuted some 6000 people for failing to declare earnings. Some such as Cook (1989, 1997) have compared these figures with the 50–100 cases prosecuted by HMRC in order to highlight the inequities in the system. Such comparisons, nevertheless, ignore that HMRC is entitled to recover money owed while the DWP is not. Indeed, it was in part due to these differential powers of HMRC compared with the DWP, that in late 1999, the Chancellor of the Exchequer asked Lord Grabiner to conduct a review of policy towards underground work.

Table 7.1   *Benefit overpayments due to fraudulent failure to declare earnings (£ million)*

Claimant failed to declare	Income Support	Jobseeker's Allowance[a]	Housing benefit[b]	Total
Full-time earnings	125	178	n/a	
Part-time earnings	16	5	n/a	
Partner's earnings	10	11	n/a	
Total	151	194	120	465

Notes:
[a] This only covers the means-tested part of Jobseeker's Allowance, not the part that is based on NICs.
[b] The figure for Housing Benefit is based on different methodology. And a full breakdown is not available.

Source: DSS Area Benefit Reviews April 1998/9; National Housing Benefit Accuracy Review, 1997/8 (cited in Grabiner, 2000: Table 1).

In his report, Grabiner (2000) recommended: the launch of a confidential phone line to give advice to people on how to put their affairs in order; measures to prevent identity fraud; a barrage of measures to improve the rate of detection (for example, information sharing, greater co-operation between central government departments); increasing the level of punishments; and greater use of publicity as a deterrent. For Grabiner (2000: 19), therefore:

> As long as people can profit by not declaring their work, it will be impossible entirely to eradicate the hidden economy. Therefore, the most effective way of tackling the problem is significantly to improve the likelihood of detecting and penalizing offenders. What is needed is a strong environment of deterrence.

In the March 2000 Budget Statement by the Chancellor of the Exchequer, his recommendations were fully accepted and responsibility for their implementation given to the cross-government Grabiner Steering Group, later renamed the Informal Economy Steering Group (IESG). Starting in

May 2000, a confidential phone line was launched to advise people on how to legitimize their activity followed from January 2001 onwards by various tougher rules and penalties to those who failed to respond (for example, HM Customs and Excise, 2003; Home Office, 2003a, b; Small Business Service, 2003).

As such, both the narrative of underground work adopted by the UK government as well as its resulting policy approach has been firmly grounded in this deterrence discourse that views underground work in mainly negative terms. Given the dominance of this discourse not just in the UK until very recently but also elsewhere, the rest of this chapter thus evaluates critically the practicality and desirability of this perspective.

A CRITICAL EVALUATION OF THE DETERRENCE OPTION

This deterrence approach that focuses upon its negative impacts fails to consider aspects of the underground economy that could be construed as potentially positive if brought into the formal sector. In this section, therefore, first, the practicality of deterring underground work will be evaluated critically and second, the desirability of attempting to do so.

Is it Practical to Try to Deter Underground Work?

A major problem with this deterrence approach is whether sufficiently stringent regulations and punitive measures can be implemented to eliminate underground work. On the one hand, this is because of 'resistance cultures' in that many local and regional state authorities do not wish to abolish underground work and it will be difficult to persuade them to do otherwise in the context of an increasingly competitive international economic system (see Chapter 6). On the other hand, even for those wishing to deter such work, inherent problems exist. First, there are 'practical barriers' to achieving such an end since this is a form of work deeply entrenched in everyday life. Second, there are 'unintended impacts' of implementing tougher rules and regulations that may not be those intended.

The first barrier, therefore, is that of 'resistance cultures'. It will be difficult to persuade many local, regional and state authorities to deter underground work since it is currently used as a strategy for promoting economic competitiveness. This is especially the case in southern European nations (Benton, 1990; Cappechi, 1989; Mingione, 1991) and state authorities in numerous localities, regions and nations have become heavily implicated (Cappechi, 1989; Van Geuns *et al.*, 1987; Husband and Jerrard, 2001;

Marchese, 2002; Portes and Sassen-Koob, 1987; Warren, 1994). Indeed, this has sometimes been an active economic development strategy. As Vinay (1987) reports, in Italy both the Communist Party in the regional government of the central regions and the Christian Democrats in the North-East collaborated in the underground practices of small- and medium-sized enterprises in their regions through their influence on industrial relations. Such situations have also been reported in Spain (Benton, 1990; Lobo, 1990a; Recio, 1988).

More usually, however, it has simply been a case of lax enforcement rather than active promotion (for example, Lobo, 1990a, b; Marchese, 2002; Mingione, 1990). In Greece, for example, Mingione (1990) reports how industrial home-working legislation is not enforced. In 1957, a bill was approved for the Greek clothing industry, compelling employers to pay social insurance contributions for home-workers. This was never implemented. According to another bill, approved in 1986, all home-workers must be considered as waged workers. This also was not enforced due to employer opposition as well as opposition from the self-employed. Lobo (1990a, b) reveals a parallel lax attitude in Spain and Portugal. In Portugal, for example, Lobo (1990b) argues that interviews with unionists and public administrators reveal that the dominant government attitude is one of 'tolerance'. This is first, because it is seen to help the Portuguese economy compete in a world market where regular conditions would make them uncompetitive, second, because the welfare state is weak and this sector gives many households a level of income not possible if they relied on solely formal employment, and third and finally because inspection of employment places is inefficient and cannot control such work.

Overcoming such active rejection and/or lax enforcement of employment regulations is difficult. Most northern European nations desire stronger regulation, especially since such businesses are in direct competition with them. Ultimately, this is a delicate matter of national sovereignty because in the majority of cases, what is being discussed is enforcement of national legislation and the protagonists in the 'fraud' all want to or must continue with for their survival. The EU, moreover, cannot police laws when no cases come before the European Court and if it introduces tougher penalties or tries to toughen up on the policing of underground work in order to reduce unfair competition, it may find that there is not the 'political will' in the southern European nations to comply with and implement such policies. The issue, therefore, is essentially one of whether the political will, especially in these southern European nations and the new accession states, exists to deter underground work.

It is also the case that there is a lack of opposition to underground work in many populations. In Quebec, for example, Fortin *et al.* (1996) find that

14.7 per cent of the population believe that underground work is morally acceptable and 42.7 per cent perceive it as neither moral nor immoral, while just 31.0 per cent see it as immoral. With less than a third of the population being opposed, it is thus questionable whether deterrence could ever be successful. This is similarly found to be the case in the UK. A study by Travers (2002) in the London borough of Newham finds that 64 per cent of respondents would not report someone who works for cash while claiming benefit since they are not seen as motivated by greed.

Deterrence approaches deal with this by increasing either the probability of detection or the penalty. Given the high cost of increasing the probability of detection, the tendency is to increase the cost of the penalty. However, this may not be politically viable given public attitudes. Punishments cannot be set in isolation from other crimes and there will be strong public reaction if the penalty for underground work is thought to be unfair in relation to broader criminal acts. Consequently, there may be limits to the range and degree of the penalties that can be implemented.

The only option, therefore, may be to increase the rate of detection but this involves high administration costs that again may be politically unacceptable both to governments and populations. Even if money is forthcoming, however, significant problems may be still encountered. Take, for example, Northern Ireland. Here, attempts to increase the rate of detection must confront significant barriers due to the lack of co-operation of the population, particularly, according to Howe (1990) and Leonard (1994), in the Catholic areas of Belfast. Indeed, Maguire (1993: 278) argues that 'the use of intimidation by terrorist groups on social security inspectors means that their work cannot be of the same level of efficiency and effectiveness as that of their colleagues on the mainland'. Although such oppositional tendencies to state regulations may not be the same elsewhere, the important point is that regulations cannot be implemented without compliance from the population. As shown above in the context of Quebec and the London borough of Newham, the proportion of the population desiring deterrence is not perhaps sufficient to allow this to happen.

A further problem concerns the unintended impacts of deterrence policy. A principal reason for deterring underground work is so that taxes can be raised. In practice, however, this may not occur. The implicit belief in the deterrence approach is that underground work reduces the amount of revenue raised through taxation and that by eliminating it one can raise more revenue and reduce the burden on the honest taxpayer. To display that one cannot simply assume that all underground work would become formal employment if such work was eradicated, Mogensen (1985) evaluates the notion that if the 200 million hours of underground work provided in 1984 in Denmark was converted into jobs for the unemployed, some 110 000 new full-time jobs could be created, thus lowering the unemployment rate of 10.8 per cent in 1984 to 7.8 per cent. He states that this could only be achieved if the price differentials between the formal and off-the-books labour supply could be abolished. Purchasers of underground work in his survey, however, stated that they would rather resort to do-it-yourself activities (34 per cent) or simply not consume the services (30 per cent) than pay the official formal price. Hence, nearly two-thirds of the work currently undertaken through underground work would not be converted into formal jobs if it were successfully eradicated. One cannot expect, therefore, underground work to be fully replaced by formal jobs.

There is also evidence that using tougher rules and regulations will have the opposite effect to that intended: it will increase, not decrease, the level of underground work. As Portes (1994: 433) argues, 'state efforts to obliterate it through the expansion of rules and controls can exacerbate the very conditions that give rise to these activities'. Put another way, 'order creates disorder. The formal economy creates it own informality' (Lomnitz, 1988: 54), as displayed in the former Central and East European socialist states where state policies gave birth to a vast range of underground work (Bernabe, 2002; Boren, 2003; Burawoy and Lukacs, 1985; Chavdarova, 2002; Illie, 2002; Neef, 2002; Portes, 1994; Salmi, 2003; Sik, 1994; Smith, 2002; Wallace and Haerpfer, 2002). This is because, as Peck (1996a: 41) has stated, '*Pressures* for regulation do not necessarily result in effective regulation'. As Portes (1994: 444) thus contends:

> The more state policies prevent the satisfaction of individual needs and access to inputs by firms, the wider the scope of informalization that they encourage. The response will vary, of course, with the specific characteristics of each society. Yet recent evidence on the extent of irregular activities suggests that state officials have more often than not underestimated the capacity of people to circumvent unwanted rules.

The universal persistence of such work thus reflects in part the considerable capacity for resistance in most societies to the exercise of state power. The consequent paradox confronting western governments is that extensive regulation, despite being needed, is problematic because it encourages more underground work rather than less. Implementing policy towards underground work and understanding their consequences thus 'requires a keen sense of the limits of state enforcement and of the ingenuity and reactive capacity of civil society' (Portes, 1994: 444).

Indeed, underground work will grow if civil society rejects the principles of the tax and welfare system. An analysis of the 1987 American Taxpayer Opinion Survey by Smith (1992) for instance, reveals that perceived procedural fairness and responsiveness in providing a service were positive incentives that increased taxpayers' commitment to paying taxes. Kinsey (1992), meanwhile, discovers that while detection and punishment attempt to force people to comply with the law, these processes also alienate taxpayers and reduce willingness to comply voluntarily. An increase in the perceived severity of punishment may therefore amplify fraud and reduce respect for the fairness of the system. Consequently, it is no surprise that in some nations, the deterrence model is starting to be superseded.

Is it Desirable to Eradicate Underground Enterprise? The Implications for Entrepreneurship

The perception until recently of nearly all governments (see Hasseldine and Zhuhong, 1999) and many academics (for example, Castells and Portes, 1989; Sassen, 1989) was that deterring underground work is a positive move that will have beneficial impacts for all concerned. This is wholly correct with regard to the small proportion of underground work undertaken by employees on an off-the-books basis for unscrupulous employers. Such work is fraudulent activity that represents unfair competition for formal activity has a deleterious effect on formal employment and undermines the welfare state by depriving it of income that could be used for social cohesion purposes. It is also work that unscrupulous businesses oblige a weak and unprotected workforce to undertake and a form of work that needs to be brought back within the bounds of the law so as to help eliminate exploitative labour market conditions (see, for example, Ram *et al.*, 2003).

However, is it beneficial to deter the underground entrepreneurs and self-employed described in Chapter 5? Indeed, given the current desire of western governments to nurture an enterprise culture, pursuing deterrence towards such entrepreneurs and enterprise appears paradoxical. To deter such underground work is to stifle precisely the enterprise culture that governments wish to foster. As will be seen later, therefore, it is perhaps not the deterrence of such workers that is required through tougher regulations and punitive measures but, rather, their transfer into the legitimate realm through more enabling initiatives.

Indeed, this has started to be recognized in the last few years by both western governments as well as some academics, reflecting how the west is now taking on board an approach adopted much earlier in a third world context. The growing belief is that tackling the underground economy in a more positive manner might not only help the emergence of an enterprise culture across the western world and the establishment of full(er) employment, but also be a more effective way of dealing with this sphere.

CONCLUSIONS

This chapter has evaluated critically the dominant approach towards underground work, namely the deterrence approach that sought to eradicate such work by using stringent regulations and punitive measures. Here, it has been shown that such a policy option is grounded in a reading of underground work that highlights only its negative features. It does not recognize any of the more positive aspects of underground work (for example, as a seedbed for entrepreneurship).

As such, this chapter has argued that this deterrence approach might be wholly appropriate with regard to the small proportion of the underground work undertaken by employees on an off-the-books basis. However, such a deterrence approach is not appropriate in relation to the vast bulk of underground work conducted on an autonomous basis. Given the current desire of western governments to develop an enterprise culture and achieve fuller employment, the pursuit of a policy that seeks to deter enterprise and entrepreneurship seems, to say the least, problematic. In consequence, some other policy approach must be sought. In the next chapter, one possibility is explored. This is the laissez-faire approach, an option that has been until now the principal approach advocated by those who have long recognized the existence of entrepreneurship in the underground economy.

8. The laissez-faire option

INTRODUCTION

If deterrents are relatively ineffective at preventing engagement in the underground sector and have the unintended consequence of hindering the development of enterprise culture and fuller employment, then the question that begs an answer is the following. What alternative approach could be adopted towards underground work? In this chapter, one possible answer is explored.

Here, the intention is to evaluate critically the policy prescriptions of neo-liberal economists, such as De Soto (1989), who until now have been the principal propagators of the view that underground workers are entrepreneurs and that the underground sphere represents a hidden enterprise culture. For them, a laissez-faire approach should be adopted towards underground enterprise and entrepreneurship and a deregulatory approach towards the formal economy. The argument of this chapter will be that although such an approach would enable people to freely engage in entrepreneurship and thus help cement and forge an enterprise culture, the net result would be a levelling down rather than up of material and social circumstances for the majority of the population in the advanced economies. First, therefore, this laissez-faire approach will be outlined and then the implications of pursuing such a policy approach will be analysed.

THE LAISSEZ-FAIRE APPROACH TOWARDS UNDERGROUND WORK

To understand this policy option, it is necessary to distinguish between its approach towards first, the formal economy and second, underground work. As will now be shown, neo-liberals contend that the way forward is to pursue the deregulation of the formal economy and a laissez-faire approach towards underground enterprise and entrepreneurship.

Deregulating the Formal Sphere

In the sense that neo-liberals desire a return to full 'formal' employment, they are no different to the interventionists discussed in the last chapter. However, their explanations of and solutions to the problem of unemployment, the lack of enterprise culture and so forth in western economies could not be more different. For neo-liberals, over-regulation of the market is to blame for the economic ills befalling society (Amado and Stoffaes, 1980; De Soto, 1989; Minc, 1980, 1982; Sauvy, 1984; Stoleru, 1982). As Peck (1996a: 1) so incisively summarizes, 'From this viewpoint, failure is seen to have occurred *in* the market, not *because* of the market'. The solution is thus to give the market free reign by liberating it from external interference.

In consequence, the growth of unemployment and the lack of enterprise culture are viewed to be a result of state regulation (Sauvy, 1984; Minc 1980, 1982; Stoleru, 1982). Sauvy (1984), for example, blames mass unemployment on the rigidity of the economy, expressed in terms of legal controls on employment (for example, redundancy laws, health and safety legislation, minimum wages), on the social security system and on the general way in which the state imposes itself on the lives of the population. For him, however, legislation in itself is not the cause of rigidity. In the individualistic fashion characteristic of this approach, he asserts that this legislation is a product of the general desire of individuals for stability and security, resulting in inflexibility. He contends that workers do not seek work as such but a stable job and job seekers are encouraged to seek such jobs by the welfare system. Sauvy (1984) maintains that it is these attitudes that have led to protective legislation and produced a society in which needs go unmet while workers claim benefit. The way to tackle unemployment and the lack of enterprise culture is thus first, to allow wages to fall so that employers will be induced to create jobs and absorb surplus labour and second, to cut back on welfare payments so as to give workers an incentive to be less fastidious about the work they accept. Consequently, the future of work is one in which market forces hold sway, enabling supply and demand to return to equilibrium. If implemented, the goal of full employment and the advent of an enterprise culture will be achieved.

The various policies and initiatives that comprise this neo-liberal ideology add up to an economic strategy that places low-waged labour and deregulated labour markets at the forefront of the solution to resolve the 'jobs deficit' and lack of entrepreneurship. The implicit and sometimes explicit consequence of such a strategy is to make underground work less necessary. By stripping away regulations, the need for people to operate in the underground sector is reduced. To some extent, therefore, this approach is precisely what the commentators in the last chapter were referring to when they discuss how underground work is becoming embedded in the mainstream in late capitalism as the neo-liberal project takes hold. As regulations are stripped away in neo-liberal regimes, formal employment starts to become akin to underground work since employees are left without protection and with minimal safeguards *vis-à-vis* working conditions.

If the neo-liberal project with regard to employment is to deregulate and give the market free reign, what is its approach towards welfare provision? Similar to interventionist approaches, neo-liberals view the welfare state and the economy as adversaries in that one is usually seen as the root cause of problems in the other. The difference is that while interventionists largely favour the welfare state and view free market capitalism as hindering social equality, laissez-faire theorists support the free market and dislike any structure that constrains it. The former, in consequence, read the welfare state as a necessary institution for the functioning of modern capitalism and indeed, a prerequisite for efficiency and growth as well as individual self-realization. Neo-liberals, in marked contrast, read the welfare state as interfering with individual freedoms and the ability of the market to optimize the efficient allocation of scarce resources.

Although debates exist within neo-liberalism over the degree to which a welfare state should be provided (see Williams, 2004a), this should not mask that laissez-faire commentators are largely negative about the welfare state due to its deleterious influence on economic performance. For them, competitive self-regulatory markets are superior allocation mechanisms from the viewpoint of both efficiency and justice. It follows, therefore, that government interference in allocation processes (aside from marginal cases of imperfections, externalities or market failure) risks generating crowding-out effects, maldistribution and inefficiency with the inevitable end result that the economy will produce less aggregate wealth than if a laissez-faire approach were adopted (Lindbeck, 1981; Okun, 1975). Some even insist that current inequalities must be accepted, and perhaps even encouraged, because their combined disciplinary and motivational effects are the backbone of effort, efficiency and productivity (Gilder, 1981).

If this laissez-faire option were merely 'academic' theory in the most derogatory sense of the word (that is, of little or no importance), then perhaps it would not even matter. But this narrative of economic progress and development is so much more than simply an academic theory. This is not just an abstraction that is seeking to reflect reality but an ideology that has been, and continues to be, used to shape the material world. As Carrier (1998: 8) puts it, there is a 'conscious attempt to make the real world conform to the virtual image, justified by the claim that the failure of the real to conform to the idea is a consequence not merely of imperfections, but is a failure that itself has undesirable consequences'. In this virtualism, economic theory and practice thus act to shape each other in an ongoing recursive and reflexive loop 'driven by ideas and idealism [and] the desire to make the world conform to the image' (Carrier, 1998: 5).

Anybody in doubt has only to consider how this theory has been a mirror against which the reality of the economy and welfare has been held up and found wanting. Indeed, it is somewhat ironic that despite this theory being heavily opposed to state-led change, it is precisely the states of Anglo-Saxon nations such as the UK and the USA that have been the primary vehicle for implementing this vision. Indeed, this recognition is not new. Well over half a century ago, Polanyi (1944: 140) realized that 'the road to the free market was opened and kept open by an enormous increase in continuous, centrally organised, and controlled interventionism'. The laissez-faire approach, therefore, is not just an attempt to reflect reality but also a narrative used to shape the material world.

From the late 1970s until the change of government in 1997 in the UK, for example, the state pursued its implementation by increasing labour market flexibility, eroding employment rights and removing or privatizing welfare protection and regulatory institutions (see Beatson, 1995; Crompton *et al.*, 1996; Deakin and Wilkinson, 1991/2; Peck, 1996a, b; Rubery, 1996). The significance of this experiment was that it was an attempt to dissolve any visible social and labour market institutions that might provide a check on the supposed operation of market forces (Rubery, 1996) or what Hutton (1995) terms all 'intermediary institutions between state and individual' so as to construct a reality more reflective of the theory.

In the USA, similarly, the reconstruction of reality by deregulating formal employment and welfare provision to conform to the theory is perhaps even more acutely witnessed (see Esping-Anderson, 1996; Myles, 1996). In the realm of employment legislation, there has been a slow and continual whittling away of labour laws while in the welfare sphere, there has been a rolling back of welfare provision as displayed in the 1996 Welfare Act (see Peck, 1996b). As Barlett and Steele (2000) highlight, moreover, a series of Congresses and Presidents, both Democratic and Republican, have emasculated the Internal Revenue Service (IRS) preventing it from pursuing effective detection. This laissez-faire approach, therefore, is much more than an academic exercise. It has been implemented, sometimes with ardent fervour, across many western economies and well beyond.

The Laissez-faire Approach Towards Underground Work

For neo-liberals, the growth of a hidden enterprise culture is interpreted to be a direct consequence of state over-regulation. Contini (1982) calls its expansion the 'revenge of the market'. Underground workers are viewed as heroes who are casting off the shackles of an over-burdensome state (for example, Biggs *et al.*, 1988; Matthews, 1982; Sauvy, 1984; De Soto, 1989). In this narrative, underground work is not read as undermining the creation of formal jobs and short-circuiting the macro-economy but instead, as responding to 'needs expressed by people' (Sauvy, 1984: 274). They are meeting material needs that would otherwise go unmet due to state interference in the formal sphere that has had the inevitable consequence of market distortion. Underground enterprise and entrepreneurship is thus the people's 'spontaneous and creative response to the state's incapacity to satisfy the basic needs of the impoverished masses' (De Soto, 1989: xiv–xv). As Sauvy (1984: 274) explains, such work represents 'the oil in the wheels, the infinite adjustment mechanism' in the economy. It represents the elasticity that facilitates a snug fit of supply to demand that is the aim of every economy. It is the mechanism through which enterprise culture can express itself.

Underground workers are thus only breaking rules and regulations that are inherently unfair. Such work is a form of popular resistance to an unfair and excessively intrusive state and underground workers are a political force that can generate both true democracy and a rational competitive market economy. Given this view of underground work as one of the last bastions of untrammelled enterprise culture in an over-rigid economic system, these neo-liberals view in its supposedly recent growth a resurgence of the free market against state regulation and union control. According to them, underground work is the 'essence of liberalism' (Sauvy, 1984). The Italian economist, Martino (1981: 89) for example, considers underground work 'a masterpiece of my countrymen's [*sic*] ingenuity, a second Italian economic miracle which has saved the country from bankruptcy, and an example for the other "free" countries to follow'. Milton Friedman, moreover, asserts that 'the clandestine economy is a real life belt: it effectively limits collective coercion … allowing individuals to get round the restrictions imposed by government on personal enterprise' (cited in De Grazia, 1982: 480).

Here, therefore, underground work is the locus for the development of pure and perfect competition which is prevented from spreading into the 'modern sector' by the many barriers imposed by the state such as protectionism, legal measures, excessive bureaucracy, wage rigidity and so on (De Soto, 1989). These measures maintain barriers to entry that prevent the 'modern sector' from working competitively. In order to cast off these shackles, the (universal) entrepreneurial spirit currently has to operate on the fringes of laws and regulations. An example is the set of underground activities known as the 'second economy' in the now defunct state socialist regimes of Central and Eastern Europe (Grossman, 1989; Lomnitz, 1988). Indeed, some Hungarian sociologists assert that the free-market forces unleashed by the second economy were the key solvent that undermined the political legitimacy of state socialist regimes and led to their demise (Borocz, 1989; Gabor, 1988).

Such a neo-liberal reading of the underground economy as the true expression of the entrepreneurial spirit is not confined to these countries. Today, such a view is most widely articulated in the majority ('third') world. The study by Keith Hart of urban labour markets in Africa was the first work in the modern era to use the term 'informal economy' and is the origin of a now vast literature (Hart, 1973). In his report to the ILO, Hart postulated a dualistic model of income opportunities of the urban labour force, or what Hart (1990: 158) later referred to as 'people taking back in their own hands some of the economic power that centralized agents sought to deny them'. Neo-liberal theorists such as the Peruvian economist, Hernando De Soto can be seen as giving this original theme, lost in subsequent ILO documents, renewed impulse. In *The Other Path* (1989), De Soto recaptures this by representing underground work as the popular response to the rigid 'mercantilist' states in Peru and other Latin American nations that survive by granting privileges of legal participation in the economy to a small elite. Hence, unlike its portrayal in the ILO (2002) as a survival mechanism in response to insufficient formal employment, the view that such enterprise represents the irruption of real market forces in an economy straitjacketed by state regulation draws upon a relatively long tradition.

Indeed, the influence of *The Other Path* (De Soto, 1989) cannot be underestimated. Offering a vision of underground workers as budding entrepreneurs whose greatest desire was not to bring down the market economy but to join it, he provided an alternative pro-market way forward for Peru to that of the Shining Path of proletarian revolution. Indeed, De Soto and his *Instituto Libertad y Democracia* (ILD) implemented many of their ideas from the mid-1980s onwards, working first with the government of Alan Garcia (1985–90) although most of their reforms were implemented under the government of Alberto Fujimori (1990–5). According to De Soto (1989), by 1994, over 270 000 formerly underground entrepreneurs had entered the legal economy, creating over half a million new jobs and increasing tax revenues by US$1.2 billion.

How, therefore, was this achieved? For De Soto (1989) and other neo-liberals, although heaping praise on underground entrepreneurs, their intention was not to promote such work. That is a popular misconception. Instead, their desire was and is to eradicate underground work as much as the interventionists outlined in the last chapter. For them, however, the way to achieve this is by reducing state regulations in the realms of formal sphere so as to both unshackle formal employment from the constraints that force up labour costs and prevent flexibility and remove the welfare constraints that act as a disincentive to those seeking formal jobs. With fewer regulations, the notion is that the distinction between formal and underground work will wither away so that the legitimate and underground spheres become inseparable since all activities would be performed in the manner now called the 'underground economy', although such activity would be 'formal' since it would not be breaking any rules.

Indeed, this was the approach adopted in Peru. Through a process of what De Soto (1989) calls 'administrative simplification', the underground economy was legalized. As De Soto (2001: 162) puts it, 'all we had to do was make sure the costs of operating legally were below those of surviving in the extralegal sector'. The solution was to bring the legal sector into line with the extralegal sector. For him, this was not seen as problematic because in Peru, legally employed proletarians make up less than 4.8 per cent of the Peruvian population and 'extralegal entrepreneurs' together with their families, he argues, constitute around 60–80 per cent of the nation's population. They construct seven out of every ten buildings, they operate 56 per cent of all businesses; they retail over 60 per cent of all foodstuffs; and they operate 86 per cent of all buses (De Soto 1989). For De Soto (2001: 27): 'Extralegality is often perceived as a "marginal" issue ... In fact it is legality that is marginal; extralegality has become the norm in developing nations.' He was simply bringing the legal sector into line with the vast bulk of economic endeavour. As De Soto (1989: 255) thus concludes in his final remarks in *The Other Path*, 'the real problem is not so much informality as formality'.

This project to deregulate the economy so that those currently in the formal economy become more like those currently working in the underground or extralegal economy has since been widely viewed as a solution in many other majority world nations. It is also a discourse prescribed as the medicine to cure the minority world (that is, the western economies) of its ills (for example, Matthews, 1982; Minc, 1982; Sauvy, 1984; De Soto, 1989).

A CRITICAL EVALUATION OF THE LAISSEZ-FAIRE APPROACH

To evaluate critically this policy solution, first, its approach towards deregulating formal employment is addressed and second, its laissez-faire approach towards underground work.

Evaluating Critically the Deregulation of Formal Employment

The core narrative of this approach is that full employment and an enterprise culture will emerge only if market forces are allowed to operate unhindered.

Measured purely in terms of whether this deregulatory approach is more effective in achieving the goal of full employment than more interventionist approaches, there is little doubt that this is the case. It does indeed appear that unemployment is lower in advanced economies such as the UK and the USA that have pursued such a deregulatory strategy with greater fervour than in the more social democratic nations of mainland Western Europe. However, this sound performance in terms of job creation must be seen both in terms of the quality of the jobs created and the degree of social polarization that this 'success' has entailed (see Conroy, 1996; Esping-Anderson, 1996; European Commission 1996b, 2000a; Fainstein, 1996; OECD, 1993; Peck, 1996a, b; Rubery, 1996).

In advanced economies, two distinct approaches to social polarization have been adopted (see Pinch, 1994; Williams and Windebank, 1995b). First, and most widely used, is the approach that examines inequalities in relation to employees in the employment place, such as in terms of widening income or earnings differentials (for example, Fainstein, 1996; OECD, 1993). Second is the approach that takes the household as the unit of analysis and examines the increasing disparities (for example, Gregg and Wadsworth, 1996; Myles, 1996; Williams, 2004f; Williams and Windebank, 1995b, 2003a). Whichever approach is adopted, the finding is the same. Neo-liberal nations witness social polarization to a much greater degree than more social democratic nations. One can thus only agree with Peck (1996a: 2) that, 'Contrary to the nostrums of neo-liberal ideology and neo-classical economics, the hidden hand of the market is not an even hand'.

There is also little evidence that some of the fundamental tenets of this ideology will have the impact laissez-faire theorists desire. Take, for example, the policy of stripping away the welfare state to encourage people to be more entrepreneurial and/or find employment. Numerous studies of the effects of reducing welfare benefits on the levels of unemployment conclude that decreasing levels of benefit (or withholding benefit) will not cause an increase in flows off the unemployment register (Atkinson and Micklewright, 1991; Dawes, 1993; Deakin and Wilkinson, 1991/2; Dilnot, 1992; Evason and Woods, 1995; McLaughlin, 1994). In an extensive review of the effect of benefits on (un)employment, McLaughlin (1994) concludes that the level of unemployment does have some impact on the duration of individuals' unemployment spells, but the effect is a rather small one. Following Atkinson and Micklewright (1991) and Dilnot (1992), she states that the level of unemployment benefits in the UK do not contribute to an explanation of unemployment to a degree that is useful when considering policy. Moreover, extremely far-reaching cuts would be required in benefit levels to have any significant impact on the duration and level of unemployment. The effect of such cuts would be to create a regime so different from the present one from which the estimates of elasticities (of unemployment duration with respect to out-of-work benefits) are derived that their predictive usefulness would be very suspect (Dilnot, 1992).

Neither will taking away the cushion of the welfare state simply allow people to flourish and display their entrepreneurial talents. To assume that people will simply adopt the attributes of the entrepreneur, discussed in Chapter 2, seems unfounded. Perhaps most importantly, however, this neo-liberal approach does not resonate with the wider political projects now being pursued by the vast majority of western economies. The overarching political project throughout the western world is not to legitimize the activities presently undertaken in the underground economy by reducing the regulations imposed on formal employment (the 'low road' approach) but rather, to adopt the 'high road' strategy of facilitating these entrepreneurs to join the legitimate economy as it exists in the here and now.

Evaluating Critically Laissez-faire Discourses on Underground Work

For many neo-liberals, underground work represents not only an indicator of the way forward for formal employment but a means by which the unemployed and marginalized are currently getting by in the advanced economies. As such, there is asserted to be little need for concern over the dismantling of the welfare 'safety net' (for example, Matthews, 1983; Sauvy, 1984). The problem, however, and as Part II of this book displayed, this is not the case. The unemployed engage in underground work to a lesser extent than the employed. Consequently, there are good reasons to suppose that if the formal labour market and welfare provision were further deregulated then the social and spatial inequalities would not be reduced and might even widen.

For example, the reason why many of the poor and unemployed conduct little underground work is not only because of institutional barriers (for example, the fear of prosecution) but also their lack of money, tools, social networks, skills and opportunities to engage in such work (Pahl, 1984; Williams and Windebank, 1993, 1994, 1995a, b, 2001a, 2003a). Consequently, even if a laissez-faire approach eradicates the institutional barriers to engagement, it will do little to help people tackle the other barriers that hinder their participation. For example, it would not enhance their skills or their social networks. Neither would it provide them with access to the tools and money necessary to engage in this form of work. All that such a move would do is to enhance their incentive to work on an underground basis in order to survive.

This alone, however, appears insufficient to tackle the barriers that prevent those excluded from the formal and/or underground labour market from participating in such work. As Gilbert (1994: 616) argues, 'The hope that it [underground work] can generate economic growth on its own, that the micro-entrepreneurs can go it alone, with a bit of credit and some deregulation, seem to be hopelessly optimistic'. Therefore, by adopting a laissez-faire approach which, for example, asserts that the way to solve poverty and unemployment is to take away formal welfare support, with little if any state assistance to facilitate the transition, the only possible reason that greater economic competitiveness and socio-economic equality would be achieved is because there would be a levelling down, rather than up, of material and social circumstances for the vast majority of the population.

As evidence of how deregulation of formal employment and the welfare system is insufficient by itself to enable poorer localities and regions to improve their circumstances, there are several lessons to be learned from Emilia-Romagna in Italy. As Amin (1994) identifies, the success of this region in turning itself into a competitive area is founded not only on underground enterprise and entrepreneurship but equally, on strong public sector support and co-ordination, such as industry-specific services to firms to foster task specialization and inter-firm co-operation to advertise the products of an area and to secure the long-term reproduction of sector-specific skills. This view that the success of this area is based on 'controlled deregulation' is reinforced by many other studies (for example Cappechi, 1989; Ghezzi, 2006; Warren, 1994). All find that the creation of contemporary Marshallian industrial districts in this region are the result of not only a particular 'cocktail' of conditions being present (for example, in inter-firm co-operation, structure of sociability, local 'industrial atmosphere' and 'institutional thickness') which have facilitated this transition but also strong state intervention in co-ordinating this transformation. On its own, therefore, deregulation is insufficient. Systemic support is required for this hidden enterprise culture along and across value-added chains.

CONCLUSIONS

In sum, the laissez-faire approach desires full employment and the creation of an enterprise culture but rather than bolstering what these neo-liberals see as the flagging edifices of 'diluted' or 'welfare' capitalism, they advocate 'undiluted' capitalism. The intention, in so doing, is to close the gap between formal employment and underground work by eradicating the regulations and constraints that currently hinder the achievement of full employment and enterprise culture. Consequently, although exponents see the already deregulated sphere of underground work as an exemplar of economic and social organization, they do not wish to promote or protect it in its present form. Instead, they seek to replace this dichotomy not by regulating underground work out of existence but by deregulating formal employment to a degree that renders underground work unnecessary.

Evaluating critically the implications of pursuing this approach, this chapter has argued that although deregulation of formal employment would reduce the magnitude of underground work which by definition is a product of the regulations imposed on formal employment, it is very doubtful that deregulation would enable people to improve their circumstances. On the one hand, the impact of such deregulation is to widen inequalities at a quicker rate in those nations that have pursued deregulation than in more social democratic countries. On the other hand, it has revealed that deregulation will not automatically allow marginalized groups and areas to solve their problems regarding their livelihoods.

Taken together, therefore, the last two chapters have reviewed the deterrence and laissez-faire approaches to underground work. As shown, the former is impractical and undesirable, while the latter would come at an extremely high price in terms of the levels of absolute and relative poverty. Instead, and as is becoming increasingly apparent, another path is required.

9. The enabling option

INTRODUCTION

Having reviewed the continuities and changes in thought on the underground economy, and elucidated how a more positive representation of the underground economy as a hidden enterprise culture has begun to emerge in western economies, it has been displayed in the last two chapters that neither a deterrence nor laissez-faire approach allows the potentially positive attributes of this hidden enterprise culture to be retained while dealing with its more negative impacts. For this to occur, this chapter will argue that an enabling approach is required that treats such enterprise and entrepreneurship as an asset but only if harnessed and transferred into the legitimate realm.

Here, therefore, the recognition of a hidden enterprise culture is not seen to provide a rationale for deregulating the formal economy (that is, turning formal employment into unregulated underground enterprise). Rather, the contention is that recognizing the underground economy as a breeding ground and platform for entrepreneurship and enterprise creation means that policies need to be pursued to legitimize such endeavour and move it into the formal sphere.

To introduce this policy option of harnessing enterprise and entrepreneurship in the underground economy, first of all, this chapter will review the arguments so far made regarding the nature of the underground economy and following this, the implications of pursuing the various policy options will be recapped so as to make the case for the third and final option of harnessing underground entrepreneurship by bringing it into the legitimate realm. How this might start to be implemented will be then briefly introduced.

REREADING THE UNDERGROUND ECONOMY

Throughout the majority ('third') world, the narrative that the underground economy is a hindrance to development has been gradually replaced over the past two decades or so by a discourse that represents this sphere as an asset that needs to be harnessed (for example, Cross, 2000; De Soto, 1989; Franks, 1994; ILO, 2002; Rakowski, 1994). From street-sellers in the Dominican Republic (for example Itzigsohn, 2000), South Africa (for example, Peberdy, 2000) and Somalia (Little, 2003), through underground garment manufacturers in India (for example, Das, 2003; Unai and Rani, 2003) and the Philippines (Doane *et al.*, 2003), to home-based micro-entrepreneurs in Mexico (for example, Staudt, 1998), the Transkei (Mahadea, 2001) and Martinique (Browne, 2004), the now widespread consensus is that enterprise and entrepreneurship in the underground economy needs to be transferred into the legitimate realm rather than simply eradicated (for example, Itzigsohn, 2000; Otero, 1994; Rakowski, 1994). The outcome is that a host of policy measures to facilitate the legitimization of such enterprises have been tried and tested. These include the provision of tailored education and training programmes for underground micro-entrepreneurs (for example, ILO, 2002; Unai and Rani 2003), micro-credit finance initiatives (for example, ILO, 2002; Jhabvala, 2003; Oladimeji and Ajisafe, 2003), business support services for off-the-books enterprises such as marketing, incubators and inter-sectoral linkages including subcontracting and consultancy services (for example, Das 2003; ILO, 2002; Maldonado, 1995), appropriate regulatory frameworks (for example, De Soto, 1989; Maldonado, 1995), and different ways of giving owners of underground micro-enterprises 'voice' (for example, Jhabvala, 2003). Indeed, a wealth of experience now exists of how in a majority world context underground micro-enterprises can be encouraged to make the transition to the formal economy.

Until now, however, the issue of harnessing underground enterprise in the context of the western world has received much less attention. This is because until recently, as highlighted in Chapter 7, the representation that dominated was of a sweatshop realm that hinders development and needs to be eradicated using deterrents. In the last few years, however, such enterprise in western economies has started to be similarly reconfigured as an asset that needs to be harnessed, not least in order to achieve fuller employment and foster an enterprise culture, and this has begun to result in calls for a change in how the underground economy is treated in public policy.

Until the 1970s, that is to say, the predominant representation of the underground economy was that of a primitive or traditional, stagnant, marginal, residual, weak, and about to be extinguished sphere. From the 1970s onwards, however, this representation came under considerable criticism as it was recognized that this was a large and growing rather than declining sphere in the majority world (for example, Hart, 1973; ILO, 2002; Rakowski, 1994). The result was a resurgence of interest in this sphere in a majority ('third') world context (for example, De Soto, 1989; Hart, 1973; Maldonado, 1995).

At this time, nevertheless, little consideration was given to the underground economy in western economies. This was to change from the 1980s onwards when the economic restructuring associated with the shift from Fordism to post-Fordism was seen to be resulting in the growth of underground work with the shift towards subcontracting and outsourcing under a post-Fordist regime of accumulation (for example, Castells and Portes, 1989; Sassen, 1997). The outcome was a swathe of studies documenting the magnitude of underground work in the western world and arguing that it was mostly marginal socio-economic groups providing such labour (for example, Blair and Endres, 1994; Button, 1984; Castells and Portes, 1989). As the 1980s progressed, however, empirical studies in western nations began to refute this 'marginality thesis', showing how underground work was concentrated in affluent rather than deprived populations (see Chapter 3). Put another way, a 'reinforcement' thesis came to the fore arguing that the socio-spatial contours of the underground economy mirrored those of the formal economy. However, in some specific populations such as West Belfast and Brussels, evidence was found to support the marginality thesis (for example, Kesteloot and Meert, 1999; Leonard, 1994, 1998a). The eventual outcome was a more embedded understanding that recognized how even if underground work is usually concentrated among the affluent, there are particular economic, political, cultural and/or geographical circumstances in advanced economies where this does not hold (for example, Kesteloot and Meert, 1999; Mateman and Renooy, 2001; Renooy *et al.*, 2004; Williams and Windebank, 1995a, 1998).

When representing the nature of underground work in the advanced economies, however, such refined and embedded understandings have been less prevalent. The recurring portrayal of the underground economy, reflecting the narrative of the post-Fordist literature, has been that enterprises engaged in such work are sweatshop-like businesses in which the marginalized work as off-the-books employees in low-paid exploitative conditions. In other words, this sphere has been commonly depicted as a new form of sweatshop work emerging in late capitalism as a direct result of economic globalization and a form of exploitative employment lying at the bottom of a hierarchy of types of employment with few benefits, low wages and poor working conditions (for example, Castells and Portes, 1989; Gallin, 2001; Portes, 1994; Sassen, 1997).

Recently, however, many have started to recognize that this sweatshop depiction does not tally with the widespread finding that underground work in advanced economies is usually undertaken by the formally employed and people living in relatively affluent localities. The result has been a questioning of this conventional representation. The way in which this has occurred is that a spectrum of types of underground work have been recognized ranging from 'organized' forms conducted by employees for a business that undertakes some or all of its activity on an off-the-books basis at one end to more 'individual' or 'autonomous' forms of underground work at the other (for example, Benton, 1990; Warren, 1994; Williams and Windebank, 1998). Following this recognition of both autonomous as well as organized underground work, a corpus of thought has emerged that has questioned whether this endeavour should always be viewed as a hindrance to development or whether greater emphasis needs to be placed on some of its more positive features, as earlier occurred in a majority world context.

Among the positive features of underground work so far identified in the advanced economies are that: it enables people to be active instead of being idle and losing motivation, and often becoming depressed and ill, which can be an effect of long-term unemployment; it provides a possible route into participation in the formal labour market, particularly for those with negative educational experiences, few skills and little experience; it reduces the burden on the benefit authorities in terms of individuals having to sign off and sign on as a fresh claimant each time they undertake a piece of work; and it reduces the possibility that individuals in poverty will resort to more serious crime in order to cope and survive (Evans *et al.*, 2004; Small Business Council, 2004; Williams, 2005a).

By far the most prominent positive feature of the underground economy so far recognized, however, is that this sphere is used by fledgling entrepreneurs as a launch pad for business ventures and as a test-bed for their enterprises and thus that this sphere represents an important platform for new enterprise creation and development (for example, Global Employment Forum, 2001; ILO, 2002; Jurik, 2005; Leonard, 1998a; Small Business Council, 2004; Tabak, 2000; Vaknin, 2000; Williams, 2004a, c, 2005a).

TOWARDS AN 'ENABLING' APPROACH

Given this more positive representation of the underground economy in western economies as a hidden enterprise culture, it is necessary to consider the implications of pursuing different policy approaches. First, and as discussed in Chapter 7, the recognition that much underground enterprise represents a hidden enterprise culture has led to a questioning of whether eradication through deterrence measures is the appropriate policy response (for example, Leonard, 1998b; Small Business Council, 2004; Tabak, 2000; Vaknin, 2000; Williams, 2004a, 2005a), following an earlier tradition in the majority world (for example, Franks, 1994; Otero, 1994; Rakowski, 1994). Such an approach is increasingly seen as undesirable because it seeks to deter precisely the enterprise culture that governments throughout the western world are seeking to foster. Second, therefore, there is the laissez-faire policy option. If pursued, however, not only will all of the negative impacts of the underground sector persist, but little if anything will be done to transfer such endeavour into the legitimate realm.

A third policy option, therefore, is to pursue an 'enabling' approach. Based on a recognition that the underground economy in the western world represents a hidden enterprise culture, this approach rereads this sphere as a potential asset to be harnessed or even a driver of economic development (for example, Global Employment Forum, 2001; ILO, 2002; Jurik, 2005; Small Business Council, 2004; Tabak, 2000; Williams, 2005a) and then seeks to develop enabling initiatives to bring such endeavour into the legitimate realm. One prominent organization adopting such an approach is the ILO (2002). Rather than view the underground economy in a purely negative light, this organization has begun to give prominence to its role as a breeding ground for the micro-enterprise system and to discuss 'harnessing' underground enterprise. As the ILO (2002: 8) assert, the key policy issue is 'how to move workers and entrepreneurs currently in the informal economy upwards along the continuum [*sic*] into formal decent jobs and how to ensure that new jobs are created in the formal and not in the informal economy'.

A similar shift is currently under way in the European Commission and many European Union member states. In the spring of 2003, the European Council decided that the eradication of underground work was to be one of its top 10 priorities for action with regard to employment reform in the member states of the European Union. No longer, however, was the aim simply to deter it. As Anna Diamantopoulou, Commissioner for Employment and Social Affairs, asserted in 2002 in a press release:

> Member states must increase efforts to quantify undeclared work, to cut it down and to *transform it into regular employment*. This is vital because of the direct link between combating undeclared work and hitting the Lisbon target of full employment by 2010 within a sound macroeconomic environment (European Commission, 2002: 1) [my emphasis].

Unlike in the past, therefore, where the objective was solely to eradicate such work, this new objective of transforming underground work into formal employment has led both policy-makers in the European Commission and the national governments in member states to reconsider whether deterrence is appropriate. What is emerging is the recognition that a new enabling approach is required.

Why, therefore, has this representational turn in how the underground economy is depicted taken place? What voices, in other words, are supportive of such a reconceptualization of the underground economy as a hidden enterprise culture rather than a sweatshop realm, and why? As will now be shown, depicting the underground economy as, in part, a hidden enterprise culture that needs to be harnessed appeals to values across the political spectrum (Goodin *et al.*, 1999).

First, and for social democratic governments, the growing pessimism about the ability of both the public sector and large businesses to produce sufficient jobs at liveable wages for citizens is resulting in a turn in economic policy towards harnessing this micro-enterprise sector in order to secure full employment and foster an enterprise culture, while in welfare policy such an enabling approach blends well with the shift from passive to active welfare measures, not least due to its potentially integrative role of incorporating the poor and economically marginalized into the market economy (Anthony, 1996, 1997; Balkin, 1989; Clinton, 1999; Desai, 2002; Ehlers and Main, 1998; Microcredit Summit 1997; Portes, 1997). This fostering of a hidden enterprise culture blends not only with social democratic economic and social policy but also second, with some conservative agendas for the privatization of government functions, whereby public benefits are restructured to reflect the principles of the marketplace. Calling for poverty alleviation through self-employment assistance rather than passive welfare programmes raises sentiments of individualism, appealing to long-held values of self-help, entrepreneurial spirit and pulling oneself up by one's bootstraps (Arnold, 1941; Auawal and Sighal, 1992). For green and bottom-up advocates, meanwhile, such an enabling approach is seen to facilitate a greening of capitalism by fostering a vision of local micro-enterprise development to challenge or at least balance corporate domination (for example, Herrold, 2003; Light and Pham, 1998; MacGillivray *et al.*, 2001; Westall *et al.*, 2000).

Recognizing and formalizing underground micro-enterprise is also supported by some feminists as part of the project of revaluing women's work and helping women to combine paid and unpaid work (Creevey, 1996; Servon, 1999). For yet others, it is seen as a first step in facilitating the development and formalization of ethnic entrepreneurship, much of which currently takes place in the underground economy (Ram *et al.*, 2002a, b, 2003).

From numerous perspectives, therefore, there is support for this representation of the underground economy as a hidden enterprise culture that needs to be brought into the formal realm. The question that now needs to be answered, however, is how this might be achieved.

POLICIES FOR FORMALIZING THE UNDERGROUND SECTOR

With the shift away from punishing those caught working on an underground basis and towards transferring this work into the legitimate realm, deterrence, although necessary, is no longer sufficient. Initiatives to help transfer such enterprise and entrepreneurship into the formal sphere are also required. Throughout the rest of this book, therefore, various incentives that could be provided to bring fledgling entrepreneurs and the established self-employed currently working in the underground economy into the formal sphere will be investigated. This does not mean, however, that an argument is being made for incentives alone to be used. Quite the opposite is the case. The provision of incentives is viewed as a precursor for even tougher punitive measures for those who persist in working on an underground basis. The reason for emphasizing the incentives in the forthcoming chapters is simply because until now, both governments and academic commentators have focused on investigating deterrence measures while relatively little attention in comparison has been given to considering positive incentives that might be provided alongside these deterrents. As such, it is solely due to the lack of attention so far paid to the incentives side of the coin, and for that reason alone, that the rest of this book focuses upon evaluating enabling measures. There is no intention to suggest that incentives can be used alone without deterrents in order to shift underground entrepreneurs and enterprise into the legitimate realm.

Furthermore, the emphasis in the rest of this book is only on what needs to be done about fledgling micro-entrepreneurs and the established self-employed working in the underground economy. Dealing with underground 'social' entrepreneurs who provide paid favours has been already analysed in-depth elsewhere (see Williams, 2004a) and what needs to be done about underground employees working for formal or wholly underground businesses will be the subject of a future book since a very different approach may well be required.

How, therefore, can fledgling entrepreneurs and the established self-employed working on an off-the-books basis be transferred from the underground to the legitimate realm? To understand how this might be achieved, a distinction is here made between 'push' and 'pull' measures, or what can be termed 'sticks' and 'carrots'. This differentiation is useful for it directly and explicitly displays how the current raft of deterrence initiatives constitute push measures and therefore only one side of the coin of what is required to legitimize the underground economy. It displays that unless such deterrents (that is, push measures) are complemented with enabling initiatives (that is, pull measures), public policy will be providing no help to those who may wish to legitimize their business.

Push Factors ('Sticks')

If the objective of public policy is merely to prevent underground work taking place and not to shift such work into the legitimate economy, push factors alone may well suffice. Punitive measures and increasing detection rates can be used as 'sticks' to deter businesses from engaging in the underground economy by ensuring that the expected cost of being caught and punished is greater than the potential economic benefits, thus changing the cost–benefit ratio. These measures might include:

- increasing sanctions for employers and/or employees;
- stepping up controls;
- increasing the level of punishments;
- increasing co-operation and data exchange between authorities;
- installation of co-operation networks at national, regional and local multi-disciplinary levels;
- field checks;
- introducing a fraud hotline;
- a centralized population register;
- increasing registration and identification requirements;
- arranging house visits or appointments with benefit claimants unannounced and/or during regular working hours;
- strict immigration policy;
- border controls; and
- excluding businesses having made use of off-the-books workers from public tenders.

Pull Factors ('Carrots')

If the objective is not only to eradicate this enterprise but also to encourage its transfer from the underground to the legitimate sphere, however, 'push' factors are necessary but insufficient. 'Pull' factors to help businesses legitimize their activity and transfer this work into the formal economy will be also required. These more positive measures, as will be discussed in-depth in Part IV, might include:

- VAT reductions on targeted goods and services;
- targeted direct tax incentives;
- benefit reforms;

- formalization vouchers;
- amnesties for off-the-books workers to declare themselves;
- subsidized formal employment;
- business start-up grants;
- coaching, training and advice (for employers and employees) in fulfilling formalities;
- greater flexibility in the 'self-employment' route-way on New Deal;
- anonymous telephone lines providing advice to people wanting to leave the underground economy;
- campaigns to change behaviour and attitudes; and
- greater co-ordination of government actions.

Deterrence, in consequence, might suppress engagement in underground work but does nothing to help those who may wish to legitimize their endeavour to do so. The argument here, therefore, is that 'carrots', which work in tandem with the existing 'sticks', are required to move economic activity from the underground into the legitimate economy. It is an evaluation of these 'carrots' that is the principal focus of the rest of the book.

CONCLUSIONS

Reviewing the evolution of thought on the underground economy, along with how this sphere has started to be viewed as an asset that needs to be transferred into the legitimate realm, this chapter has argued that neither the deterrence nor laissez-faire approach allows the positive features of underground entrepreneurship and enterprise to be retained while dealing with their more negative impacts. For this to be achieved, this chapter has argued that the most effective way of doing this is to adopt incentives that facilitate this transformation alongside deterrents rather than purely seeking to punish those caught engaging in underground work. In the following chapters, therefore, the range of possible incentives that might be used first, to encourage businesses to start up in a legitimate manner and second, to help enterprises to make the transition from the underground to the formal sphere will be reviewed and evaluated. Obviously, the initiatives to be reviewed in Part IV represent just a selection of the more positive measures that could be employed. There are doubtless many more. The point here, however, is not to provide a comprehensive listing. It is simply to show that many policy initiatives are already available that could be utilized by western governments wishing to take a more positive approach towards legitimizing underground entrepreneurs and enterprise.

PART IV

Harnessing the hidden enterprise culture

10. Helping enterprises start up in a legitimate manner

INTRODUCTION

If the underground economy is to be tackled, it is insufficient solely to adopt curative remedies to transform those enterprises and entrepreneurs currently operating on an underground basis into fully legitimate enterprises. Initiatives also need to be pursued to prevent future start-ups entering the world of underground work in the first place. While later chapters deal with the curative remedies required, the intention in this chapter is to identify ways of helping enterprises and entrepreneurs start up in a legitimate manner from the outset.

To help business ventures start up properly from the beginning, this chapter will evaluate five broad policy measures that might prevent new enterprises and entrepreneurs slipping into underground transactions. First, the issue of simplifying existing formalization procedures will be evaluated. Second, the idea of introducing new categories of legitimate economic activity so as to allow forms of endeavour currently conducted on an off-the-books basis to become legitimate will be considered. Third, the provision of direct and/or indirect tax incentives to help enterprise and entrepreneurs to start up legitimately will be reviewed. Fourth, the use of micro-enterprise development programmes (MDPs) to help micro-enterprises set up and develop in a formal manner will be examined and fifth and finally, a range of initiatives for smoothing the transition from claiming unemployment benefits to becoming self-employed.

The outcome will be an analysis of a range of policy measures that could be implemented in order to help enterprises and entrepreneurs start up legitimately rather than conduct some and/or all of their trade on an underground basis. Although many additional measures doubtless exist, the point here is to begin to identify at least a selection of initiatives that might be used. If this stimulates readers to consider further possibilities, then this is to be welcomed. There is absolutely no intention to suggest that the initiatives discussed below are the only possible ones available. The aim is merely to set in motion a fuller discussion of how enterprises and entrepreneurs might be encouraged to start up legitimately in future in western nations.

SIMPLIFYING REGULATORY COMPLIANCE

To encourage employers and employees to operate legitimately, the European Commission (2003a: 8) argue that prominence must be given to 'the creation of a legal and administrative environment which is favourable to the declaration of economic activity and employment, through simplifying procedures and by reducing costs and constraints which limit the creation and development of businesses, in particular start-ups and small undertakings'. At present, that is, start-ups might not fully adhere to the regulations that apply to them either intentionally or unintentionally. They may deliberately flout the regulations so as to cut costs, or they may engage in unintentional non-compliance (that is, not realizing that there are regulations to which they do not comply). For both groups, one option is to provide better advice on how to formalize within the existing rules and regulations. A second option is to simplify the regulatory compliance framework itself, as the European Commission recommend above. Until now, western governments have focused on the former. Much less emphasis has been placed on the latter option (OECD, 2003).

In the UK, for instance, regulatory compliance has been encouraged primarily by providing information to help people start businesses within the existing rules and regulations, such as the *Starting up in Business* campaign along with the Helpline for the newly self-employed and the provision of guides such as *The Right Way to Start Your Business*. Much less attention has been paid to changing the regulatory environment itself so as to help businesses start up legitimately. There has been little discussion, for instance, of whether the plethora of state rules and regulations with which new ventures must comply could be brought together under one umbrella agency rather than the current bewildering array of central and local government departments and agencies. This notion of creating a one-stop compliance agency composed of super-inspectors responsible for a fuller range of compliance measures will be returned to in Chapter 14.

Another way to make it easier for micro- and small enterprises to start up, grow and adopt the 'high road' strategy of working legitimately rather than on an underground basis is to simplify administrative procedures. One option is to consider whether the business regulation framework needs to lower the costs of establishing and operating a small business (for example, easier registration procedures, reasonable and fair taxation) and to increase the potential benefits of legal registration (for example, access to commercial buyers in the formal economy, more favourable credit markets, legal protection). If either or both were implemented, it is arguably the case that this will encourage businesses to start up formally and help micro- and small businesses start up legitimately from the outset.

How can this be achieved? For those of a neo-liberal persuasion opposed to regulation, the solution is to pursue deregulation as already seen in Chapter 8. As the World Bank (2004) reveal, some nations are far more 'business-friendly' (that is, deregulated) than others and if other nations are to compete, according to this narrative, then a similar process of deregulation needs to occur. Simplifying formalization procedures, however, does not necessarily equate to stripping away regulations. It can also mean improving rather than removing regulation and administrative procedures (see, for example, European Commission, 2004; OECD, 2004). Here, the problem is not defined as excessive regulation (see, World Bank, 2004) but as the costs of administrative compliance due to the complexity involved. Comparing the costs associated with first, taxes and second, administrative procedures, for example, the ILO (2002) conclude that the available research suggests that it is the latter which are often more burdensome. Legal and administrative requirements such as registration and licensing can become an obstacle to micro-businesses, where the transaction costs or costs of compliance per worker are higher than in larger firms due to their lack of internal resources (time, money, specialist expertise) to cope with regulation and their inability to spread the costs of compliance across large-scale operations (Chittenden *et al.*, 2002, 2003; Hansford *et al.*, 2003; Hart *et al.*, 2005; Michaelis *et al.*, 2001; OECD, 2000b). Where the costs of full administrative compliance are prohibitive, the finding is that compliance is low (see Adams and Webley, 2001; ILO, 2002; Matthews and Lloyd-Williams, 2001). Such administrative costs associated with regulatory compliance include form-filling, inspection (rather than advice), inconsistent application of the rules by different regulators or even different inspectors within the same regulator; and duplication of information requirements from different regulators.

A way forward beyond deregulation, therefore, is to reduce administrative costs, such as by simplifying tax administration for small businesses (for example, the number of tax forms and returns, pursuing an integrated approach to audit with a single visit to inspect records rather than separate inspections for different taxes) and improving support and education to improve the capacity of firms to comply. This is very different to deregulation. Simplifying existing formalization procedures does not necessarily mean stripping away regulations. It is about on the one hand, and as discussed above, streamlining both regulatory institutions and formalization procedures so as to make it more straightforward for businesses to start up legitimately. On the other hand, it might also be about evaluating the feasibility of offering exemptions (on a temporary or graduated basis) with respect to some areas of business regulatory compliance so as to encourage later compliance rather than force firms to start up on an underground basis.

Indeed, pursuing this latter approach of exemptions and graduated inclusion into the regulations would be nothing radical or new in most western economies. In the UK, for instance, Keter (2004) details how small firms are already exempt from a number of regulations. As he documents, the following exemptions have been either previously or currently applied to small firms:

Employment regulations
1. Current exemptions:
   a. Trade Union recognition – for firms with fewer than 21 workers;
   b. Maternity and parental leave – some exemptions for employers with less than five employees;
   c. Disability discrimination – until October 2004, firms with fewer than 15 employees were exempt;
   d. Consultation on collective redundancies – exemptions for firms with fewer than 20 employees;
   e. Statutory maternity pay – firms can recover 100 per cent of these payments and an additional 4.5 per cent compensation for administrative costs if their annual liability for Class 1 national insurance contributions is £45 000 or less;
   f. Written statement of disciplinary procedures – firms with fewer than 20 employees were exempt until 2004;
   g. Stakeholder pension – firms with fewer than five employees are exempt from the requirement to provide access;
   h. Health and safety – undertaking with less than five employees do not have to prepare a written statement on health and safety;
   i. Information and consultation – undertakings with less than 50 employees are not covered by the EU Directive on informing and consulting employees.
2. Previous exemptions:
   a. Unfair dismissal – people working for firms employing less than 21 employees had to wait two years before qualifying for protection against unfair dismissal, while those in larger firms had to wait only one year;
   b Sex discrimination – the 1975 Sex Discrimination Act excluded employment in private households and firms employing fewer than six people;
   c Redundancy rebates – when the redundancy payments scheme was introduced, employers were able to claim substantial rebates from the Redundancy Fund. Over time, these were reduced until they were abolished for all but firms with fewer than 10 employees. Today, all rebates have been abolished;
   d Statutory sick pay – small firms once received preferential access to recovering payments for employees on sick leave.

Other regulations
1. Tax:
   a VAT registration – firms with a turnover less than £58 000 do not have to register for VAT;
   b Zero rate on corporation tax – paid by companies and unincorporated associations on their annual profits. There are three rates: the starting rate, the small companies' rate and the main rate.
2. Rate relief – small businesses rate relief introduced from 1 April 2005 at 50 per cent for properties up to £3000 of rateable value and then declines on a sliding scale as rateable value increases;
3. Rate relief for rural shops – business in a rural village of less than 3000 can claim a 50 per cent mandatory reduction in the business rates bill;
4. Company audit and reporting – some small firms are exempt from the audit requirement and also reporting their accounts.

There are thus clear precedents in the UK, and in many other western nations, for simplifying formalization procedures for small firms to increase the likelihood that they start up legitimately. To determine which regulations require simplification, however, detailed research is required of which currently act as a barrier to setting up legitimately, as well as the consequences of using either graduated progression or exemption from them, so that decisions can be taken tailored to the needs of specific countries.

Before pursuing such a policy of exemptions for new ventures and micro-enterprises either on a temporary or graduated basis, however, there is a dire need to evaluate the relative extent to which regulation *per se* currently hinders formalization relative to other factors. One European study finds that 'administrative regulations' were reported by only about 10 per cent of all SMEs as the major business constraint over the previous two years (Observatory of European SMEs, 2004), with 'the purchasing power of customers' and 'lack of skilled labour' more frequently reported as constraints. There are thus grounds for perhaps not overexaggerating the importance of simplifying formalization procedures when seeking to facilitate the transfer of business from the underground to the legitimate realm.

Indeed, further evidence that simplifying formalization procedures should not be exaggerated comes from the UK. Using evidence of the impact of the National Minimum Wage and other employment regulations, a series of publications reveal that the law often exerts only a limited impact on owner-managers' decision-making and business competitiveness (Arrowsmith *et al.*, 2003; Edwards *et al.*, 2003, 2004; Gilman *et al.*, 2002; Ram *et al.*, 2001, 2003). In the main, business owners made adjustments to employment practices without causing major disruption to routine operations or undermining competitiveness. This is because either: the changes required were minimal or did not affect the business; the firm's market position was such that increasing employee pay (or incurring costs as a consequence of other regulation) did not seriously weaken the firm's competitive position; and the characteristic informality of many small firms' working arrangements allowed adjustments to working practices to be made at a relatively low cost. Where the business was in a vulnerable market position, the impact of regulation combined with market pressures aggravated an already difficult situation, pushing some businesses to the edge of legality or even out of the marketplace altogether (Ram *et al.*, 2001). But few businesses were in this situation. As Harris (2002) and Edwards *et al.* (2003) nevertheless argue, although individual regulations may not constitute much of a problem, their cumulative effect might still be highly problematic for small firm owners. For the moment, therefore, the jury must remain out on the importance of simplifying formalization procedures until it has been directly investigated in greater depth.

When assessing the extent to which regulation hinders formalization, so as to evaluate whether simplifying formalization procedures is an important priority, Hart *et al.* (2005) highlight how any evaluation will need to overcome at least three weaknesses of current compliance cost studies. First, most studies focus on those costs that can be easily quantified and exclude other types of cost (for example, psychological stress associated with discovering whether regulations apply and how best to meet regulatory requirements). Second, the benefits of regulation to small business owners are often excluded and third and finally, the narrow focus on compliance costs diverts attention from broader issues such as the extent to which business owners decide not to expand or formalize because of perceived regulatory constraints. Simply measuring compliance costs tells us nothing about these latter issues, nor does it demonstrate the importance of regulation relative to other factors.

A potential way forward, as in the UK, might be to introduce a Regulatory Impact Assessment (RIA) test for all proposed regulations. This could be extended, moreover, to include a Micro-Enterprises Impact Assessment test analysing the consequences for micro-enterprises. As Hart *et al.* (2005) highlight, however, there has been some criticism of such an approach. RIAs have been shown to vary in: the clarity with which policy objectives are expressed; their assessment of the risks; their use of stakeholder responses; their consideration of non-regulatory alternatives; estimates of the expected costs and benefits of the proposed regulations; and in their discussion of sanctions for non-compliance. Before proceeding further with the simplification of formalization procedures, therefore, in-depth research is required to identify the specific regulations that need to be targeted and impact assessments undertaken of the consequences of pursuing alternative options.

INTRODUCING NEW CATEGORIES OF LEGITIMATE WORK

Another means of encouraging businesses to start up in a legitimate manner is to introduce new categories of legitimate work so as to allow work currently, often by necessity, conducted on an underground basis to be transferred into the legitimate realm. For many years, similar to other western governments, the German state effectively shut its eyes to the fact that people occasionally undertake small jobs that they do not declare. Unlike other western nations, however, the German government decided to do something about this, creating a new 'mini jobs' category of employment so as to encourage people to legitimize these small underground jobs.

'Mini Jobs' (Germany)

Until 1999, 'minor employment' was allowed up to a certain income level (DM 630) and with a weekly working time cap of 15 hours. This work was exempt from social security payments for employers and employees alike. Employers had to pay a lump-sum tax of 23 per cent; employees had to pay no tax at all. This minor employment could be combined with normal employment and still be exempt from tax and social security contributions. At the start of 1999, there were over 6.5 million minor jobs, representing almost 70 per cent of all jobs in catering and 60 per cent of jobs in cleaning. In 1999, the government reformed the minor employment scheme, aimed at limiting its growth. This drove much of this work into the underground economy. In 2002, therefore, the German government introduced three new types of mini job:

1. *€400 jobs* – the income limit of the former DM 630 jobs was raised to €400. Within this income limit, mini jobs enjoyed reduced social security contributions of 23 per cent (12 per cent for the pension insurance system and 11 per cent for the health insurance system) and a lump-sum tax of 2 per cent. However, the 15 hours per week limited was lifted.
2. *Mini jobs in the household sector* – introduced to combat underground work in this sphere. The employer pays a levy of 12 per cent and can deduct a certain amount from their tax payments.
3. *Midi jobs* – to ease the transfer from minor to normal employment, a transition zone ranging between €400–800 was introduced, social security contributions for the employee rising gradually from around 4 per cent to the full 21 per cent.

Compared with 4.1 million employees in minor employment in September 2002, there were 5.5 million at the end of April 2003, one month after the introduction of mini jobs; a rise of 1.36 million. Some 1.21 million are people already in a formal job, about 580000 of which are estimated to have transferred their add-on job from the underground economy into the formal sphere (Baumann and Wienges, 2003).

Given the rigid labour market of Germany compared with the more flexible labour markets in other advanced economies, some caution is here urged with regard to the feasibility of transferring this approach more widely. Nevertheless, it is similarly the case that in many other advanced economies, people often feel they have no option other than to conduct such small jobs on an underground basis due to the perceived problems involved in declaring it. Creating a 'mini jobs' category might thus represent a significant breakthrough, especially for those people already in formal employment who are attempting to develop a fledgling business 'on the side' or who wish to declare their more established underground operations, a category of worker that the English Localities Survey identified as comprising a significant proportion of all underground entrepreneurs and enterprises (see Chapter 5). Indeed, given that those in formal employment who conduct small jobs 'on the side' on an occasional basis probably constitute the vast bulk of start-up entrepreneurs, it is perhaps more important to consider this option than most governments have so far realized. Unless such an initiative is adopted, micro-entrepreneurs might find themselves less able to start off on a formal footing than if such a category of employment existed.

DIRECT AND INDIRECT TAX INCENTIVES

A popular belief is that the most basic way to eradicate the underground economy is to reduce taxation. Indeed, many policy proposals reflect this belief. So far as encouraging micro-enterprises to start up legitimately, therefore, one way forward might be to reduce overall taxation, introduce a more graduated scheme, a flat rate of tax or change tax collection from direct to indirect collection methods.

The latter option of introducing a flat tax has been advocated ever since progressive income tax was first introduced. The problem is that it would provide the affluent with a very large tax cut. Another option, therefore, is to introduce a national sales tax on both goods and services. Of course, this already exists in many advanced economies in the form of VAT but exists alongside income tax. As Barlett and Steele (2000) report, however, there are proponents in the USA of shifting all tax revenue generation to sales taxes. Such a wholesale shift would result in a significant redistribution of those providing the tax revenue, resulting in a widening rather than narrowing of inequalities. Barlett and Steele (2000) highlight how IRS tax data for 1997 reveals that a total of 263 178 individuals and families reported incomes between $500 000 and $1 million. The average income in that range was $672 854. If they spent every cent on goods and services, a 15 per cent sales tax would yield $100 928. This is equivalent to a 49 per cent cut on their average income tax payment of $196 610. In short replacing the income tax with a 15 per cent sales tax would allow them to pocket an extra $95 682. For people with incomes of $40–50 000, there were 9 768 567 individuals and families with an average income of $44,713. If they again spent all their income, a 15 per cent sales tax would cost them $6707. They currently pay $4796 in income tax.

For Barlett and Steele (2000: 262–3), therefore, the way forward is to simplify the tax system in the following manner:

- eliminate all credits and deductions;
- treat all income the same, whether from wages or capital gains;
- institute withholding everywhere (on dividends, interest and the sale of capital assets);
- establish a dozen or more rates that rise as income goes up;
- cancel all existing tax code preferences; and
- remove tax offences from the criminal code and treat tax evasion and non-filing as a civil matter with draconian financial penalties that remove the incentive.

The problem with using general tax reforms to deal with the underground economy in general, and encourage new business ventures to start up in a legitimate manner more particularly, is that they have much broader impacts. Rather than considering reducing overall taxation levels, introducing more graduated schemes, flat rate tax or changing tax collection from direct to indirect collection methods, more targeted measures can be evaluated that directly address the issue at stake. One such measure is to be found in the Netherlands.

Rich Aunt Agatha Scheme (Netherlands)

It is well known that many people starting up in business find their venture capital not from formal but from informal sources such as family, friends and acquaintances. The resulting problem is that these loans are often made on a relatively informal basis and this perhaps helps create from the outset an attitude that informal practices are part of the culture of the enterprise that is being established.

In the Netherlands, therefore, and to make it easier for people to start their own businesses, it was formally recognized that this is how many entrepreneurs receive their venture capital. The introduction of the *Tant Agaath-Regeling* ('Rich Aunt Agatha Arrangement') was intended to not only provide an incentive to those providing such venture capital but also to help fledgling entrepreneurs who need starting capital and receive a personal loan from family and friends (Aunt Agatha) to start off on the right footing. By exempting these private moneylenders from some taxes, a major intention behind this scheme is that if such loans are put on to the radar screen of the tax authorities, this might help business start off on a more formal basis rather than see itself as engaged in informal arrangements, which might well carry over into everyday trading practices (Renooy *et al.*, 2004; Williams, 2004d).

So far as is known, no formal evaluation has been conducted of this scheme. Given that such an approach might well be applicable across many advanced economies, it is perhaps timely for such an evaluation to be conducted, particularly with regard to whether the formality involved carried over into other business practices for those benefiting from this scheme. This could be conducted by comparing the everyday business practices of new ventures making use of the Rich Aunt Agatha scheme with a control group of businesses who loaned money informally outside of this scheme in order to explore the variations in the degree to which they engaged in underground transactions in their daily practices. If it proves effective at helping business start off legitimately, then it could be more widely adopted across many other western nations.

MICRO-ENTERPRISE DEVELOPMENT PROGRAMMES (MDPS)

Another way of encouraging micro-enterprises to start up legitimately is to develop Micro-enterprise Development Programmes (MDPs) that provide micro-credit, advice, training and/or support to such ventures. Very small micro-enterprises, particularly when the entrepreneur is poor or a high-credit risk, often cannot gain access to loans or basic self-employment training (for example, Jurik, 2005). MDPs fill this void. MDPs usually waive collateral requirements and credit checks, lending on the basis of business plans or client character alone, even to clients with poor credit histories.

The goals of MDPs include some or all of the following: the alleviation of poverty through self-employment; the promotion of economic development in deprived areas; the empowerment of individuals, and collective empowerment through the mobilization of micro-entrepreneurs and their communities (Coyle *et al.*, 1994). Although some MDPs are lending-oriented and provide little or no training or additional support, others are more training- or advice-oriented and view lending as just one of a range of services (Jurik, 2005).

Following the apparent success of some high-profile MDPs in the majority ('third') world, such as the Grameen Bank, Americans for Community Cooperation in Other Nations (ACCION), the Foundation for International Community Assistance (FINCA) in Latin America and the Self-Employed Women's Association (SEWA) (Amin *et al.* 1998; Bhatt, 1995; Blumberg, 2001; Bornstein 1996; Counts, 1996; Remenyi and Quiñones, 2000; Rose, 1996; Wahid 1993; Wood and Sharif, 1997), MDPs have taken off in many advanced economies, complementing earlier micro-finance organizational forms such as rotating savings and credit associations (ROSCAs) and credit unions (for a review, see Jurik, 2005).

Evaluations of MDPs in advanced economies have on the whole been positive. They are found to be effective at promoting business growth, creating jobs and increasing clients' incomes, self-esteem and community involvement (Anthony, 1997; Auawal and Singhal, 1992; Balkin 1989; Edgcomb *et al.*, 1996; Himes and Servon 1998; Light and Pham, 1998; Servon 1999) as well as helping smooth the transition from unemployment to self-employment (Balkin 1989). Clark *et al.* (1999), for example, report that MDP clients in the USA have witnessed significant gains in household income of US$8484, rising from US$13 889 to US$22 374 over five years, while Himes and Servon (1998) find that ACCION's US programmes increased the average net income of clients by some US$450 or more per month.

What is not known, however, is whether MDPs are effective at helping fledgling micro-enterprises start up legitimately and existing underground micro-enterprises make the transition to the legitimate realm. In providing fledgling micro-enterprises with a formal source of micro-credit or venture capital rather than leave them reliant on informal sources from either loan sharks (who often charge extortionate prices) or family and friends, the hope, as intimated above in the context of the Rich Aunt Agatha scheme, is that this helps avoid from the outset of these enterprises the attitude that underground practices are part of the culture of the business that is being established. By providing formal loans, therefore, MDPs might well help businesses start off on a formal footing. If such formal loans from MDPs are then also coupled with advice, support and training, the likelihood of such ventures starting off on a formal footing could also be potentially further enhanced. It is not just start-ups, however, that might potentially benefit from MDPs so far as stemming the tide of underground work is concerned. As will be seen in the next chapter when the case study of a particular micro-finance organization, namely Street (UK), is reviewed, MDPs where they provide advice, support, loans and training, might also play an effective role in helping move existing underground micro-enterprises into the legitimate realm.

Until now, however, whether MDPs are effective at helping micro-enterprises start off on a formal footing (and helping existing underground enterprises move into the formal realm) has not been directly evaluated. First, therefore, and to evaluate whether MDPs help micro-enterprises to start up legitimately, a comparison is needed of the everyday business practices of new ventures making use of MDPs with a control group of new businesses who loaned money informally in order to explore the variations in the degree to which they engage in underground transactions in their daily practices. Such an evaluation, furthermore, could usefully compare lending-oriented MDPs with those offering a wider range of advice, support and training to explore the differences. Second, and on the issue of helping existing underground enterprise move into the formal realm, it is again the case that micro-enterprises aided by an MDP need to be compared with similar businesses operating outside of MDPs to evaluate the degree to which MDPs are facilitating the process of formalization. When conducting such evaluations, moreover, care must be taken not to repeat the errors of previous MDP evaluations that have usually relied solely on direct measures of success (for example, loan repayments), failed to include control groups and not attempted to engage in any longitudinal mapping of the outcomes (Jurik, 2005).

It is important, however, not to overemphasize the role of MDPs in stemming the underground economy since this directs attention towards individual self-help or agency-oriented solutions and away from changing the broader economic, social and political structures that often lead micro-entrepreneurs into the underground economy in the first place (for example, the tax system, overburdensome regulations, lack of acquiescence to the objectives of the state). MDPs, in other words, need to be complemented with the other initiatives discussed in this and the next four chapters if the underground economy is to be tackled effectively. Indeed, unless more positive incentives are provided for micro-enterprises to legitimize their affairs and changes take place in the broader business environment supportive of legitimate micro-enterprise development, MDPs may simply increase indebtedness among the poor (Adams and Von Pische, 1992; Berger, 1989). To believe that MDPs alone can encourage individuals to lift themselves out of poverty with hard work along with a little MDP credit or training is shortsighted (Rogaly, 1996), especially given that most MDPs not only currently fail to reach those running micro-enterprises who belong to the poorest sections of society (Bates and Servon, 1996; Clark and Hustom 1992; Edgcomb *et al.*, 1996; Himes and Servon 1998, Hulme and Mosley 1996; Mordoch 1999, 2000; Schreiner, 1999) but also quite deliberately 'cream off' those with the greatest chance of success due to the existence of an operational tension between running an effective MDP and meeting the needs of the most vulnerable micro-enterprises since operating costs increase unless they engage in 'creaming' processes (Blumberg, 1995; Ehlers and Main 1998; Howells, 2000; Jurik, 2005; Kidder, 1998). Last but not least, there is also a well-founded fear that with the shift from passive to active welfare policies, promoting MDPs serves to further legitimate the restriction of state responsibilities for welfare provision (Desai, 2002; Johnson 1998).

In sum, MDPs represent one potential way forward for helping businesses start off on a legitimate basis (and for helping existing underground enterprises to make the transition to the legitimate realm). However, before supporting such MDPs, an evaluation is required of the extent to which this is indeed the case and whether some types of MDP (for example, advice-oriented rather than lending-oriented) are more effective than others in facilitating this process.

SMOOTHING THE TRANSITION FROM UNEMPLOYMENT TO SELF-EMPLOYMENT

Despite the finding that the unemployed working on an underground basis often represent only a very small portion of the whole underground economy (for example, Jensen *et al.*, 1995; Leonard, 1998a; Pahl, 1984; Renooy, 1990; Williams, 2004a, b, c), one of the most active areas of public policy so far as tackling the underground economy is concerned, reflecting the shift towards active welfare policies, is to help smooth the transition from unemployment to self-employment. Here, just a few of the initiatives being used to do this are evaluated.

Ich AG's (Germany)

In Germany, a new business entity has been introduced to smooth the transition from benefits to self-employment, namely *Ich AG*'s or what I here call 'Me-PLC'. This is intended to help the unemployed wishing to start up their own self-employed business venture and enables them to receive a subsidy for the first three years equivalent to a maximum of 50 per cent of unemployment benefits.

Following a recommendation of the Hartz Committee in 2002 that sought to improve the functioning of the inflexible German labour market, in 2003, a new legal entity was created for unemployed people wanting to start up a one-person business (*Ich-AG*) or a family business (*familien AG*). They receive a monthly subsidy for three years. In the first year, they receive 50 per cent of the average unemployment benefit level, 30 per cent in the second year and 20 per cent in the third and final year. A start-up monitor shows that in 2003, over 93 000 long-term unemployed started a small business using this *Ich-AG* scheme. The German government expected around 20 000 start-ups (Renooy *et al.*, 2004).

Variants of this scheme to smooth the transition from benefits to self-employment are found in other western economies. In the Netherlands, for example, the Bbz (*Besluit Bijstandverlening Zelfstandigen*), meaning 'Decision Social Security Self-Employed', allows people who want to start their own business and self-employed people who want to temporarily earn less than the annual standard amount a person on social security receives, to apply for social security benefit while running their own business (Renooy *et al.*, 2004). In the UK, meanwhile, a variety of different schemes have been introduced.

'Test Trading' (UK)

This initiative to smooth the transition from unemployment to self-employment occurs at the New Deal options stage 3 and involves the participants test trading their business for up to 26 weeks. During the test-trading period, the participants receive an allowance equivalent to their previous benefit entitlements and in addition, a grant of up to £400 paid in equal weekly or fortnightly instalments. The money the business earns while in the test-trading period is either ploughed back into the business or stored in a special bank account until the test-trading period has ended. A mentor is provided to support participants during the test-trading period and for up to two years subsequently. During the test-trading period, New Deal for Young People participants are also required to undertake training leading to formal qualifications. An evaluation of the initiative concludes that:

> For many people entry into (and success in) self-employment remains a difficult and at times a precarious activity and hence there are considerations about how far policies should encourage potentially vulnerable groups to choose such a difficult route. For some, the consequences of self-employment failure can have financial and personal implications, although for others the experience may enhance their future chances of making successful and sustained moves into the labour force (Kellard *et al.*, 2002: 7).

However, whether this initiative does anything to reduce participation in underground work has not been evaluated. Those involved with clients 'on the ground' such as those working in Local Enterprise Agencies, nevertheless, widely believe that this is the case. As Williams (2005a) reports, practitioners involved with this initiative conclude that for 'test trading' to become more effective, the following needs to be considered:

- reducing the eligibility period (currently 18 months unemployment);
- elongating the current 26 weeks test-trading period to up to three years; and
- developing a graduated withdrawal from benefits (for example, 100 per cent of benefits guaranteed in first six months, 70 per cent in next 12 months and 40 per cent in last 12 months), as in the above initiative in Germany, and a parallel graduated release of the money earned by the business that is currently stored in a special bank account until test trading has ended.

Back to Work Bonus (UK)

The 'back to work bonus' was introduced in October 1996 with the aim of encouraging individuals and where relevant their partners to 'keep in touch' with the labour market by undertaking small amounts of work while still claiming Income Support (IS) or Jobseekers Allowance (JSA). The rationale was that this would provide an incentive for claimants to move from unemployment into paid work. In effect, it became a measure to condone underground work. It works in a complex way by the accrual of a bonus if the claimant's earnings from part-time work reduce the amount of JSA or IS they are paid. They can then claim the Bonus (a tax-free lump sum of up to £1000) if and when they move off benefits and into work proper. The bonus is accumulated from 50 per cent of the declared earnings above the 'earnings disregard' (normally £5) but this can only commence after 91 days of being on JSA/IS. It also has to be claimed within 12 weeks of leaving benefit (otherwise it is lost) and it can only be paid if the claimant starts work within two weeks of leaving benefits. It cannot be accrued by people over 60 claiming IS although men aged 60–64 on JSA can join the scheme. If a claimant is on IS, the earnings of the claimant's partner are taken into account in the calculation of the bonus, but this is not the case for claimants on JSA.

Evaluations of the scheme have been carried out, albeit not directly in relation to its effectiveness at reducing the underground economy (Ashworth and Youngs, 2000; Department for Work and Pensions, 2003c, d; Thomas *et al.*, 1999). Research is thus required with participants on whether this initiative facilitates a shift of work from the underground to the formal economy.

'Twin Track' (UK)

'Twin track' is a DWP pilot initiative running in two Government Office Regions (Wales and the North West), whereby under certain conditions a 'lighter touch' is taken with people working while claiming benefit in an effort to get them into formal work via contact with a Personal Adviser. This is one way in which a level of tolerance in government policy has been displayed towards those making the transition from benefits to work via the underground economy. So far, no public results have been made available of any evaluation. Given that the unemployed provide only a very small proportion of all underground work, however, it is unlikely that such an initiative alone would have any significant impact on the size of the underground economy. It is, nevertheless, potentially useful as one initiative in a barrage of measures to help some people make the transition from the underground into the formal economy.

In sum, such initiatives to smooth the transition from unemployment to self-employment are popular in many advanced economies. It needs to be recognized, however, that since the registered unemployed usually constitute only a very small proportion of those working on an off-the-books basis, such initiatives will have only very marginal impacts on both helping business start off on a formal footing and shifting the hidden enterprise culture into the legitimate realm.

CONCLUSIONS

In order to encourage enterprises and entrepreneurs to start off on a formal footing rather than conducting a portion or all of their trade on an underground basis, this chapter has considered several measures. First, the notion of simplifying existing formalization procedures has been introduced. Until now, most western nations have on the whole sought to tackle the underground economy by providing advice on how to formalize within the existing rules and regulations. Few have considered whether this might be insufficient and if it might be also necessary to simplify compliance procedures. Here, therefore, the need for such an idea to be taken more seriously has been introduced with some suggestions as to the way forward.

A second means of encouraging businesses to start up legitimately might be to introduce new categories of legitimate work so as to allow forms of endeavour currently conducted on an off-the-books basis to become legitimate. To see how this might be achieved, the ways in which this has been pursued in Germany has been here reviewed. A third way of helping enterprises and entrepreneurs to start up legitimately is to provide either direct and/or indirect tax incentives to help them do so. Although many general modifications to taxation have been proposed in the past, the focus here has been upon more targeted measures that do not have so many wider impacts and more directly encourage new business ventures to start up on a formal footing, notably the Rich Aunt Agatha scheme in the Netherlands. Fourth, this chapter has introduced the notion of using Micro-enterprise Development Programmes (MDPs) to help businesses start off on a legitimate basis (and micro-enterprises make the transition to the formal realm) and finally, initiatives to smooth the transition from claiming unemployment benefits to becoming self-employed have been reviewed.

Although there are doubtless many additional measures that could be considered to help enterprise and entrepreneurs start up in a legitimate manner rather than conduct some and/or all of their trade on an underground basis, this chapter has at least begun to identify and evaluate a selection of the possibilities. If this stimulates consideration of further possibilities, then this is to be welcomed. For the underground economy to be tackled, however, it will be insufficient to solely adopt measures that stop new enterprises and entrepreneurs entering the underground economy. Curative remedies are also needed to transform those currently operating on an underground basis into legitimate ventures. It is to this that attention now turns.

11. Moving underground enterprise into the mainstream: supply-side initiatives

INTRODUCTION

The last chapter reviewed measures to help business ventures start up legitimately from the outset. If the underground economy is to be tackled, however, curative remedies are also required. Until now, as highlighted in Part III, the predominant way in which public policy throughout the advanced economies has sought to deal with those currently working in the underground sector is by using deterrents ('sticks') to push enterprise out of the underground sphere. Although perhaps appropriate if the sole intention of governments was to eliminate such work, this is no longer the case. As shown earlier, increasingly, they also want to shift this work into the formal economy, not least so as to move nearer to full employment and promote the development of an enterprise culture (see European Commission, 2002, 2003a, b; ILO, 2002; Small Business Service, 2004).

There is a growing appreciation, in consequence, that deterrence measures are necessary but insufficient. To transfer such work into the formal economy, the emerging recognition is that deterrents ('push' measures) need to be supplemented with enabling ('pull') initiatives that help underground businesses legitimize their operations (Copisarow, 2004; Copisarow and Barbour, 2004; Evans et al., 2004; ILO, 2002; Small Business Council, 2004; Williams, 2004a, b). In the next chapter, demand-side incentives will be evaluated. In this chapter, the focus is upon supply-side measures to help underground suppliers make the transition to the legitimate economy.

Three broad types of supply-side initiative will be here evaluated. First, the use of society-wide amnesties will be explored. Second, the use of voluntary disclosure, or what might be seen as individual-level 'amnesties', as a first step towards legitimization will be analysed. And third and finally, the provision of tailored business support and advisory services to help enterprises make the transition from the underground to the legitimate realm will be evaluated.

SOCIETY-WIDE AMNESTIES

In many advanced economies, society-wide amnesties have been used not only to tackle the underground economy but also non-compliance in many other spheres of social life (for example, gun ownership). A previous overview of whether society-wide amnesties are an effective means for tackling the underground economy concluded that this was not an appropriate measure. This report by Lord Grabiner (2000) written for Her Majesty's Treasury so as to determine the approach of the UK government towards the underground sector rejected the use of society-wide amnesties on several grounds. First, there is the practical difficulty of defining the amnesty precisely enough to make it workable and second, there is the question of whether to treat all kinds of underground work in the same manner (for example, benefit fraud is normatively seen as worse than income tax fraud in many advanced economies and an amnesty on VAT fraud would be problematic since it has already been collected from customers).[1] Grabiner (2000) also suggests that the evidence from advanced economies is that amnesties are not effective in practice. For example, in the 1980s, several states in the USA used them as well as France, Italy and Ireland. They were perceived as unfair, as a free lunch for those who had not met their responsibilities at the expense of the honest taxpayers. Holding an amnesty, moreover, tended to create an expectation of further future amnesties that in turn reduced the incentive for tax-evaders to come forward immediately. These factors were thus seen to undermine public confidence in amnesties, and even encourage honest taxpayers to become more fraudulent. Finally, the revenue generated by amnesties was argued by Grabiner (2000) to be exaggerated. The net return (that is, the revenue that would not have been collected without an amnesty, less the costs of operating the amnesty) was asserted to be low. One reason for this is because amnesties appear to be more effective when they are accompanied by tougher enforcement measures. It is thus likely that much of the revenue collected and attributed to amnesties would have been collected by enforcement alone (Grabiner, 2000).

The outcome of this evaluation was that the UK government decided to reject their usage. Whether such a negative approach should be more widely adopted, however, remains open to question, especially given that few data sources were given by Grabiner to justify his stance. Indeed, society-wide amnesties continue to be used in many nations. In Italy, for example, an amnesty in 2003 resulted in some 703 000 illegal immigrants coming forward, 48.6 per cent of whom were women employed in underground work as domestic workers and care givers (Ghezzi, 2006). There thus appears to be a need for western governments to conduct a thorough evaluation of the effectiveness of society-wide amnesties before rejecting their usage.

Importantly, moreover, any such evaluations must consider the way in which amnesties might work alongside 'push' measures. Society-wide amnesties, for example, might offer a precursor for legitimizing the use by government of tougher enforcement ('push') measures.

Amnesties, in consequence, should not necessarily be written off as a measure to transfer underground enterprise into the formal economy. It is by no means certain that society-wide amnesties are unworkable, as revealed for instance in Spain (see LópezLaborda and Rodrigo, 2003). What is apparent, however, is that rather than use amnesties alone, they need to be used as part of a package of push and pull measures.

INDIVIDUAL-LEVEL VOLUNTARY DISCLOSURE

Besides using society-wide amnesties, another approach is to offer amnesties on an individual basis to those voluntarily disclosing that they have been operating wholly or partly on an underground basis. To explore how this more person-centred approach operates in practice, two initiatives are here explored. The first is the Italian regularization campaign and the second is the 'offer in compromise' system used in the USA.

Regularization Campaign, 2001–3 (Italy)

In October 2001, the Italian government implemented a law known as the Regularization Campaign (L.383/2001) that ended in February 2003. This allowed underground workers and enterprises to regularize their situation with respect to tax, labour, safety, social security contributions, land use irregularities and so forth. In exchange, they paid reduced taxes and social contributions for three years, as well as reduced pension contributions for the past, so as to enable them to adapt. Underground workers were given two options: to declare their irregularities and pay immediately all (reduced) taxes and contributions to be paid, or to engage in gradual regularization, in which a regularization plan was submitted, including deadlines to solve an irregularity, to an ad hoc committee. If the plan was then not followed and the deadlines not met, they would be penalized by having to pay 100 per cent of the tax and contributions owed rather than the reduced amount.

In total, this campaign produced some 1794 declarations and 3854 new regularized workers (Meldolesi, 2003). Superficially, therefore, this outcome might suggest that the campaign was unsuccessful. The Italian government expected a much higher-level of declarations. However, and as Meldolesi (2003) points out, although it failed to attain its targets, unprecedented media coverage produced a process of 'indirect regularization' in that between October 2001 and October 2002, a period of economic stagnation, 385 000 additional workers registered nationally. This is because although small businesses were reluctant to submit the regularization form (generally perceived as a dangerous form of self-incrimination), they did regularize indirectly resulting in a process of 'silent' formalization (Meldolesi, 2003). Evaluated in terms of the process of indirect formalization that ensued, therefore, this regularization campaign can be viewed as more of a success than when solely direct formalization is considered.

'Offer in Compromise' Approach (USA)

To encourage individual-level voluntary disclosure of underground enterprise in the USA, if taxpayers are unable to pay a tax debt in full, and an instalment agreement is not an option, they may be able to take advantage of the 'offer in compromise' (OIC) programme. Generally, the OIC is seen as a last resort after taxpayers have explored all other available payment options. The Internal Revenue Service (IRS) has the authority to settle, or 'compromise' federal tax liabilities by accepting less than full payment. A tax debt can be legally compromised where there is either: doubt as to liability; doubt as to feasibility of being able to collect the debt; or for effective tax administration purposes. The objective of the OIC programme is to accept a compromise when it is in the best interests of both the taxpayer and the government, and the OIC promotes voluntary compliance with all future payment and filing requirements.

Such a system can be used as an incentive to come clean about past misdemeanours and to facilitate voluntary compliance in the future. If a person comes forward who has been working on an underground basis, an OIC could be in some circumstances offered. Encouraging voluntary disclosure using such a person-centred OIC system is one way forward in other advanced market economies. Indeed, according to Bajada (2002), when Revenue Canada introduced a voluntary disclosure policy, this resulted in voluntary disclosures quadrupling. Again, and similar to society-wide amnesties, however, it is perhaps the case that its importance lies in the fact that it allows much tougher punishments to be adopted once a voluntary disclosure programme has been offered.

Such an OIC programme, moreover, would probably work most effectively in enabling formalization if it was used in conjunction with other enabling programmes. With this in mind, attention turns towards the use of advisory and support services as a further supply-side measure for helping underground enterprise to make the transition to the legitimate realm.

ADVISORY AND SUPPORT SERVICES

In the last chapter, using Micro-Enterprise Development Programmes (MDPs) to help businesses start off legitimately was discussed. Here, a similar approach is explored but for enabling underground enterprise to make the transition to the legitimate economy. In recent years, the development of advice and support-oriented MDPs that provide a bespoke local advisory and support service to businesses seeking to formalize their operations has started to be widely discussed in public policy circles both in Italy (for example, Bàculo, 2005; Caianello and Voltura, 2003; Meldolesi and Ruvolo, 2003), the UK (for example, Evans *et al.*, 2004; Small Business Service, 2004; Williams, 2005a), the European Commission (Mateman and Renooy, 2001; Renooy *et al.*, 2004) and the USA (for example, Jurik, 2005).

It is now widely recognized that the kind of business advice and support required by those seeking to transfer their current business ventures into the formal economy is very different to the advice and support required by start-up or growth businesses who wish to go through a formal business planning process (for example, Caianello and Voltura, 2003; Copisarow, 2004; Copisarow and Barbour, 2004; ILO, 2002; Meldolesi and Ruvolo, 2003; Small Business Council, 2004; Williams, 2005a). It is also acknowledged that support and advice is generally not widely available at present to wholly underground enterprises and businesses conducting a portion of their work on an underground basis about how they might resolve their situation (Copisarow and Barbour, 2004; ILO, 2002; Small Business Council, 2004; Williams, 2005a). The development of a 'formalization service', therefore, is viewed as necessary to bridge this gap between the wealth of business advice and support available to formal businesses and its absence for those who operate wholly or partially on an underground basis.

In order to move from the underground to the formal economy, micro-entrepreneurs and businesses require help and support on issues such as tax and benefit rules, insurance, credit, loans, book-keeping, marketing, regulations and so forth. There is thus a need to tailor business advisory and support services to the needs of underground micro-entrepreneurs and businesses than is currently the case. Two examples of MDPs in advanced economies that have tailored their provision to helping micro-enterprises make the transition from the underground to the formal realm are first, the Naples CUORE initiative in Italy and second, Street (UK) in the UK.

The Naples CUORE Initiative

CUORE (Centri Operativi per la Riqualificazione Economica), or Operative Urban Centre for Economic Upgrading, started in 1998 with an agreement between the municipality of Naples and the University Frederico II to research the local business environment. This research revealed that the principal local labour market problem in Naples was not unemployment but the underground economy. Today, CUORE ('cuore' is the Italian word for heart, courage and passion) consists of a network of neighbourhood service centres for entrepreneurs and would-be entrepreneurs. Each local CUORE centre services a low-income neighbourhood and their target group is small and micro-sized underground entrepreneurs with the potential for growth. Once identified, CUORE centres offer information and advice to aid formalization (Bàculo, 2001, 2002, 2005).

Following a request by the entrepreneur, CUORE operators devise custom-made regularization and development paths. The project workers closely monitor each step in the process to make sure that the entrepreneur follows the agreed path towards regularization and that the path still suits the entrepreneur's needs. Project workers tend to be familiar with the neighbourhood. In total, according to Bàculo (2005), some 141 underground businesses have received counselling and 168 problems have been solved; 80 additional enterprises have received support to set up legitimately.

Besides providing advice and support to help businesses formalize, attempts have also been made to provide incentives for businesses that may wish to do so. One of the principal ways in which this has been achieved is by establishing business consortia that provide promotional aid, training, arrange trade fairs, help protect the originality of their labels and provide aid with the internationalization of their markets. The intention, in so doing, is to give them positive reasons for legitimizing their business that allow them to compete on grounds other than labour cost (so as to reduce the necessity for underground practices). This has resulted in a set of opportunities for businesses joining these clusters and negated their perceived need to continue on an underground basis (Comitato per l'emersione del lavoro no regolare, 2003c).

Since this Naples experiment, this initiative has started to be replicated elsewhere in Italy, such as in Lazio, Toscana, Pulia, Abruzzo, Calabria and Apulia, especially the idea of outreach workers who work in neighbourhoods and identify such underground entrepreneurs. One of the innovative aspects of the *cuore* centres, that is, is that project workers directly approach entrepreneurs by visiting companies and have no central office that the underground entrepreneur needs to visit. Since this initiative, the idea of 'formalization mentors' has thus started to spread more widely with such mentors now being used in many other regions of Italy. Until now, unfortunately, no known independent evaluation of the effectiveness of the Naples *cuore* initiative has been undertaken.

Street (UK)

Street (UK) was set up in 2000 to offer loans, advice and business support to self-employed people and micro-enterprises wishing to formalize their business. Their clients fall into two main categories. On the one hand, they include people claiming benefits, such as disability benefit. On the other hand, they include those not claiming benefit but who are either not declaring or under-declaring income from their enterprise activity. Street (UK)'s approach is to provide them with the tools necessary to make the transition into the formal economy. Their activities cover three areas: providing tailored financial services and business development support tools; offering a back-office loan administration and system support service for other community loan funds; and undertaking research, policy recommendation and advocacy work.

By March 2004, Street UK had served around 200 clients. A range of case studies of specific individuals who have been helped can be found both on their web site (www.street-uk.com) and in recent internal reports from this organization (Copisarow, 2004; Copisarow and Barbour, 2004). What is important to highlight here is the strategy that Street (UK) adopts. Since Street UK clients include a wide variety of people at different stages of development of their enterprises, the approach is to monitor progression of clients in each of the following 12 areas:

- moving from part-time to full-time work;
- moving from home to business premises;
- keeping basic level records;
- keeping higher-level accounts;
- purchasing public liability and employer's liability insurance;
- hiring employees on a PAYE basis;
- using a bank account for their business transactions and/or opening a separate business bank account;
- obtaining the required licences and permits to operate the business (for example, health and safety inspection certificates, driver instructor licence);
- graduating of all non-work benefits;
- graduating from majority cash revenues to majority invoiced revenues;
- incurring formal business tax liability; and
- becoming VAT registered.

Street (UK) attempts to ensure that in any 12-month period, at least three of these steps are taken with each client although the order in which they are taken is tailored to the specific business.

In its first three years of operation, Street (UK) disbursed 259 loans worth £606 000, with the average loan being around £2300, and by March 2004, it had just over 100 current clients, with many borrowers taking successive incremental loans. Loan repayment rates range from 12–26 per cent (Copisarow, 2004). Business advice and ongoing support, meanwhile, has been provided to well over 1000 clients most of whom are 'one-person-band' businesses run by sole traders. So far, for every 10 businesses to which loans have been made, four businesses (40 per cent), which would very likely have been liquidated within the next 12 months, have been safeguarded, and four businesses (40 per cent), which would very likely have not been liquidated within the next 12 months, have been able to grow and create new jobs. The average number of new jobs created by these 'growth' businesses since they first became Street UK clients is 2.5. Remembering that the average loan is around £2300, Street UK has found that its clients create one full-time job for every four loans (Copisarow, 2004). In sum, this community development finance initiative (CDFI) is a relatively small-scale initiative to provide loans, support and advice to help businesses make the transition from the underground to the legitimate economy. Third sector community-based finance, support and advisory services, therefore, are one possible model for developing a 'transition service' infrastructure.

Creating a 'Transition Service': Alternative Options

The CUORE initiative in Italy and Street (UK) thus represent two options of how a specialized 'transition service' could be provided (for which public funding could be made available and targets set). Besides such independent third sector community-based business support networks, such a transition service could also be embedded within the public sector. In the UK, for example, this might occur by extending the Inland Revenue's Small Business Support Teams, establishing a separate offshoot of Business Links or extending the remit of Jobcentre Plus advisers. An independent third sector transition service might attract more clients, however, than a transition service embedded within state institutions, due to such a service being seen as relatively detached from the state. Whichever mode of delivering this transition service is adopted, nevertheless, full consideration might be given to the establishment of 'one-stop formalization shops' for the provision of business support and finance as well as legal, tax, debt and benefit advisory services that would take a business through each and every step from the underground to the legitimate realm.

Indeed, such a transition service could well be set up in conjunction with an individual-level voluntary disclosure initiative along the lines of the OIC system discussed above. If this partnership working between the state (for example, IRS in the USA and HMRC in the UK) and this third sector transition service were adopted, then it would provide a key incentive for underground businesses approaching such a transition service. It might be the case, for example, that businesses approaching the transition service and agreeing to follow a plan to move from the underground to the legitimate realm might be given an offer in compromise concerning their tax liabilities so long as they continue to keep to the tailor-made formalization plan constructed for the business by the transition service.

Formalization Tutors

Although developing a transition service is necessary, there is also a need for more informal first points of contact for such enterprises from which they might graduate to these transition services. In this regard, the development of a system of formalization tutors, or what might be termed mentors or 'outreach workers', may be a way forward.

This has been used in Italy since November 2001. Here, a network of regional tutors has been established to support companies who want to leave the underground economy by providing help and support, as displayed in the example of CUORE. These tutors are independent professionals with backgrounds in socio-economic disciplines (for example, labour and fiscal consultants, economic and urban planners, lawyers), and who understand the labour market situation in the region in which they operate. They have a freelance contract as a government consultant, meaning that they are not state employees. Set up under the auspices of the *Comitato per l'emersione del lavoro no regolare* (Committee for the Exposure of Underground Work), this national committee temporarily hires them on a freelance basis. These tutors have no central office where the underground entrepreneur goes for information. Instead, the tutors directly approach entrepreneurs by visiting companies (Comitato per l'emersione del lavoro no regolare, 2003a). By December 2003, there were 44 tutors employed by the Italian government (Comitato per l'emersione del lavoro no regolare, 2003b).

In other advanced economies, formalization tutors could be developed as an extension of existing volunteering initiatives, be incorporated into the portfolio of community development workers or alternatively, the 'business mentoring' systems that exist in many countries could be extended to incorporate such a function. In the UK, for example, there is a national mentoring system operated by the Business Volunteer Mentor Association, which is led by the National Federation of Enterprise Agencies. The Prince's

Trust has demonstrated that there is a market of available mentors and that having a mentor assist start-up businesses has a direct impact on its longevity and success (Meager *et al.*, 2001; Westall *et al.*, 2000). Extending this mentoring system to cover formalization mentoring is thus one way forward, especially when it is used in conjunction with the development of transition services and an OIC-type programme.

CONCLUSIONS

This chapter has reviewed supply-side incentives to move underground enterprise into the legitimate economy. First, societal-wide amnesties have been analysed, second, person-centred amnesties and third and finally, transition services. Here, the argument has been that these measures should not be used or seen in isolation. Given the plethora of reasons for the hidden enterprise culture, it has been stressed that each of these initiatives might be most effective when used in conjunction with others. Before pursuing these measures, however, detailed evaluation of existing examples is required before any firm decision can be taken on whether to extend their usage beyond their existing milieu.

It is certain, however, that the current deterrence approach cannot continue. Given that governments in advanced economies now view the hidden enterprise culture as an asset to be harnessed, existing push initiatives need to be complemented by pull initiatives to help such enterprises make the transition to the formal economy. Here, a range of supply-side initiatives have been introduced that could facilitate such a transfer. Targeting the underground entrepreneurs themselves, however, is not the only approach. Other measures, as the next chapter details, target the demand-side of the equation.

NOTES

1. Interestingly, however, HM Customs and Excise had prior to Grabiner (2000) already operated an amnesty scheme to encourage VAT registration. If they came forward, and were compliant for 12 months, their penalties were mitigated. Several thousand businesses came forward as a result of this amnesty (personal communication with HM Customs and Excise).

12. Moving underground enterprise into the mainstream: demand-side initiatives

INTRODUCTION

Public policy in most western economies has predominantly relied on supply-side deterrence measures to tackle the underground economy. In the last chapter, it was revealed that complementing deterrents with the provision of incentives to suppliers might encourage formalization. In this chapter, the other side of the coin is considered, namely demand-side measures to encourage customers to acquire goods and services on a legitimate rather than underground basis. To commence, therefore, this chapter recaps how public policy in western economies has predominantly adopted a supply-side deterrence approach towards the underground economy and how this has resulted in little attention being given to either demand- or supply-side incentives. Following this, a range of possible demand-side incentives is evaluated. First, targeted indirect tax measures to persuade customers of underground enterprise to use formal employment are evaluated, second, targeted direct tax measures and third and finally, voucher schemes that seek to shift demand into the formal economy. This will reveal that if the hidden enterprise culture is to be brought out of the shadows, then public policy in western economies will need to give greater attention to supplementing supply-side deterrents not only with supply-side but also demand-side incentives so as to facilitate its transfer into the legitimate realm.

FROM SUPPLY- TO DEMAND-SIDE PUBLIC POLICY APPROACHES

As shown in Chapter 7, western governments have focused on using deterrents to curtail those either already engaged in underground work or considering participation. Relatively under-emphasized so far in public policy are, on the one hand, incentives to encourage suppliers to work formally rather than on an underground basis (considered in Chapter 11) and on the other hand, demand-side measures both of a deterrence and incentives variety. Given the growing desire of western governments to transfer underground work into the formal economy in order to move nearer to fuller formal employment and the creation of an enterprise culture, deterring suppliers is necessary but insufficient. Encouragement to suppliers and consumers to transfer their underground transactions into the formal economy is also required. In this chapter, the concentration is on demand-side measures to 'pull' consumers away from using underground labour and encourage them to use formal labour instead.

To explore the feasibility of using demand-side incentives to legitimize the hidden enterprise culture, this chapter reviews a range of innovative economic experiments that have been taking place in numerous western countries, most of which have targeted domestic services and the home maintenance and improvement sphere. As shown in Chapter 5, these are sectors where underground labour is rife and also spheres in which a large share of all underground work takes place. Although tackling underground work in these spheres will not eliminate all underground enterprise and demand-side incentives dealing with other sectors will be required, an evaluation of these initiatives at least starts to highlight the range of options available. In what follows, in consequence, answers will be sought to the following questions wherever possible. How does each initiative encourage consumers to use formal rather than underground labour? What is the magnitude of the scheme? Who engages in it? Is it effective at transferring work from the underground to the legitimate sphere? And what, if any, problems have been witnessed and how have these been overcome?

TARGETED INDIRECT TAX MEASURES

A first way of encouraging consumers (and businesses) to use formal rather than underground production is to reduce Value-Added Tax (VAT) on specific goods and services where the underground economy is rife, such as in the household repair, maintenance and improvement (RMI) sector (see Chapter 5). This strategy has been used in numerous countries. In France, a directive of 25 May 1999 reduced VAT on both services and goods related to the improvement, transformation and organization of household maintenance work. In Italy, similarly, the 2000 Finance Act decreased VAT from 20 per cent to 10 per cent on services related to ordinary and extraordinary household repairs. These reductions were a result of European Directive 99/85 and more recently, alterations to EU directive 77/388/EEC allow further modifications. Previously, this latter directive only allowed member states to reduce VAT on the supply, renovation and alteration of housing where it was provided as part of social policy. The 2003 amendment to this directive (COM(2003) 397 final, 16.7.2003), however, deletes 'provided as part of social policy' and instead adds 'repair, maintenance and cleaning of housing'. This opens the way for EU member states to reduce VAT on all RMI work.

Whether VAT reductions might lead to a formalization of underground work, however, is open to debate. Although early academic research argued that the introduction of VAT had little effect on the size of the underground economy (Bhattacharyya, 1990; Feige, 1990; Frey and Weck, 1983; Macafee, 1980), there have been few contemporary evaluations on whether this is the case. Here, therefore, one of the few evaluations of the impacts on the underground economy of reducing VAT is reported.

Impacts of Reducing VAT on the UK Household Repair, Maintenance and Improvement (RMI) Sector

The RMI sector is not small. According to Capital Economics (2003), RMI in the UK private housing sector totalled £12.8 billion in 2002 in current prices, which represented 15 per cent of total construction output (£84 billion). Indeed, the Department of Trade and Industry (DTI) estimate that the value of RMI output in the underground economy in 2002 was some £7 billion. In order to investigate the implications of reducing indirect taxes on underground work, Capital Economics (2003) conducted a feasibility study that evaluated the implications of reducing VAT to 5 per cent on RMI as well as combining this with the introduction of a 5 per cent VAT rate on new house-building.

To do this, Capital Economics (2003) provide various calculations based on the assumption that the proportion of RMI that is currently conducted on an underground basis lies somewhere between 10 and 60 per cent. Since a lower rate of VAT encourages firms to move into the formal economy, they argue that a reduction could boost VAT revenue. At present, firms escape paying VAT either by illegally failing to become a VAT registered company despite being over the VAT threshold, or by registering for VAT but then suppressing turnover by doing some underground work. Their argument is that by reducing VAT from 17.5 to 5 per cent, underground work would reduce due to the smaller price differential between legitimate and underground prices for customers. Indeed, it might even boost the volume of work taking place. Capital Economics (2003) report the results of an experiment on the Isle of Man, where VAT on RMI was reduced to 5 per cent for three years, which was found to lead to 40 per cent of traders saying that customers were having more work undertaken.

To estimate the decrease in revenue to the UK government following a VAT reduction to 5 per cent, they first make the conservative assumption that the RMI industry does not change in terms of activity or structure in response to this change (see Table 12.1). That would imply a loss of £1.6 billion, as shown in row 2 of the table. Rows 3 to 6 then display the impact on VAT receipts if 10 per cent, 50 per cent, 75 per cent or 100 per cent of underground work shifts into the formal economy. At best, this reduces the revenue loss to £1.3 billion. However, these figures gloss over two important issues. First, in practice the gain in tax revenue from formalization would be less since anyone previously in the underground economy would not have been able to reclaim VAT when purchasing materials. Once VAT registered they could do so. Second, these figures assume that all transferred underground work comes from wholly underground businesses rather than from under-reporting businesses.

Rows 7 to 10 then adjust the numbers given in rows 3 to 6 to take into account any extra revenue received in the form of income tax and social security contributions, using the assumption that there are 282 000 construction workers in the underground economy, all of whom are working in the RMI sector. To estimate the extra revenue from income tax and national insurance, Capital Economics (2003) use the average tax paid by a full-time male worker in 2002, namely £5673. Row 10 shows that, even without an increase in RMI output, if 100 per cent of all underground work shifted into the formal economy, once the increase in tax and national insurance contributions is taken into account, HM Treasury would actually receive about £400 million more in tax receipts despite the reduction in the rate of VAT.

Moreover, as the Isle of Man experiment mentioned above shows, a reduction in VAT might increase the amount of RMI activity, resulting in a rise in the amount of VAT and other tax revenue. The impact on revenues will depend on how far this demand is sensitive to changes in price – the price elasticity. If the price of such work falls by 12.5 per cent, demand could increase by 12.5 per cent, thereby leaving the total spent on this sphere unchanged (that is, the elasticity would be 1). However, the elasticity could be higher or lower. The effect of assuming an elasticity of 1 is shown in rows 11 to 14. If 75 per cent of work done in the underground economy were to switch to the formal sphere, then when the increases in income tax and national insurance contributions are taken into account, HM Treasury would break even. If 100 per cent of underground work were to switch to the formal realm, and output increased by 12.5 per cent, HM Treasury would make an extra £500 million (see row 14). Given that the increase in output in rows 11–14 might be too conservative, rows 15–18 show what would happen if output increased by 40 per cent in response to a reduction

Table 12.1 The impact on tax receipts of a reduction in VAT, £ billion

	Formal economy			Underground economy	Total		
	Output	VAT receipts	Other tax receipts	Output	Output	Tax receipts	Net tax gain
1. Base scenario	12.8	2.24	–	7.0	19.8	2.24	–
2. VAT rate reduced to 5%	12.8	0.54	–	7.0	19.8	0.64	-1.6
Shift from the underground to the formal economy							
3. 10% shift	13.5	0.58	–	6.3	19.8	0.68	-1.6
4. 50% shift	16.3	0.32	–	3.5	19.8	0.82	-1.4
5. 75% shift	18.1	0.91	–	1.8	19.8	0.91	-1.3
6. 100% shift	19.8	0.99	–	0.0	19.8	0.99	-1.3
Add receipts of income tax and NI							
7. 10% shift + income tax and NI	13.5	0.68	0.16	6.3	19.8	0.84	-1.4
8. 50% shift + income tax and NI	16.3	0.82	0.80	3.5	19.8	1.62	-0.6
9. 75% shift + income tax and NI	18.1	0.91	1.20	1.8	19.8	2.11	-0.1
10. 100% shift + income tax and NI	19.8	0.99	1.60	0.0	19.8	2.59	+0.4
Add receipts from extra work							
11. 10% shift + extra work + 12.5% growth	15.2	0.76	0.16	6.3	19.8	0.92	-1.3
12. 50% shift + extra work+ 12.5% growth	18.3	0.92	0.80	3.5	19.8	1.72	-0.5
13. 75% shift + extra work + 12.5% growth	20.4	1.02	1.20	1.8	19.8	2.22	0.0
14. 100% shift + extra work + 12.5% growth	22.3	1.12	1.60	0.0	19.8	2.72	+0.5
Assume an even stronger response							
15. 10% shift + extra work + 40% growth	18.9	0.95	0.16	6.3	25.2	1.21	-1.0
16. 50% shift + extra work + 40% growth	22.8	1.14	0.80	3.5	26.3	1.94	-0.3
17. 75% shift + extra work + 40% growth	25.3	1.27	1.20	1.8	27.1	2.47	+0.2
18. 100% shift + extra work + 40% growth	27.7	1.39	1.60	0.0	27.7	2.99	+0.8

Source: Capital Economics (2003: Table 1)

in price of 12.5 per cent. The maximum extra revenue that the Treasury would gain is £800 million, including the VAT on the extra work, additional income tax revenue and national insurance contributions.

Of course, there are a myriad of unintended consequences not considered by this model regarding such a tax reform. For instance, given that RMI work is to some extent a substitution for moving house, it could be argued that if RMI output were to increase, not so many homeowners would move. The reduction in housing transactions and consequent saving in time and resources consumed in moving could be beneficial. But the effect would also be to reduce the Government's revenue from stamp duty. However, the impact of this factor is likely to be minor.

Implications of Reducing Indirect Taxation

This study by Capital Economics (2003) is one of the few known attempts to estimate the implications of reducing VAT on the underground economy and more particularly, on government revenue. If raising government revenue is the objective underpinning formalization, then reducing indirect taxes is by no means certain to achieve this objective. Of course, there are many other rationales for legitimizing off-the-books work, including the benefits for individual off-the-books workers, for formal firms, for workers in underground enterprises, for customers and for society itself (see Chapter 7 for a review). Nevertheless, there are two reasons for adopting a cautious approach towards formalizing underground enterprise and entrepreneurship using VAT reductions.

On the one hand, stripping away taxes so as to tackle the hidden enterprise culture has the potentially dangerous consequence of kick-starting a 'race to the bottom'. Generally, reducing tax in one nation might encourage other nations to follow suit. Although this might not be the case with indirect taxes, especially in relation to the domestic RMI sector, there remains the possibility that deciding to reduce indirect taxes to formalize underground work will then cause attention to turn to reducing direct taxes. Following this logic, the net outcome would be little different to the proposal of the neo-liberals. There would be a steady stripping away of taxes (and perhaps other regulations) resulting ultimately in a process of deregulation.

On the other hand, this approach of reducing indirect taxes is based on the mistaken mono-causal explanation that higher taxation always leads to a growth in the underground economy and, *vice versa*, that lower taxation reduces its size. There is no evidence that this is always and everywhere the case, as displayed in Chapter 6. For these reasons, in sum, a cautious approach to using VAT reductions is recommended. At best, it should be adopted as one of a barrage of measures.

TARGETED DIRECT TAX MEASURES

To encourage consumers to employ formal rather than underground labour, a diverse range of direct tax measures can be used. Although some might argue for general reductions in the rates of income tax, this has very wide societal implications (see Chapter 6). Here, therefore, more targeted strategies will be evaluated. As Chapter 5 revealed, some three-quarters of the underground economy is concentrated in first, the RMI sphere and second, other domestic services (for example, household cleaning, gardening, child-care) in western nations. Here, therefore, initiatives to tackle underground work in these spheres are focused upon.

One option is to give straightforward income tax relief, claimed on (self-assessed) tax returns, to customers using formal labour to do specific household tasks (for example, roof maintenance, outside painting, household cleaning). In the RMI sphere, for example, tax rebates on home maintenance expenses have been available in France since 2000, along with tax reductions for house repairs in Italy and Luxembourg. As the European Commission (1998: 14) conclude with regard to these initiatives, 'tax-deductions and subsidies for refurbishing and improvements of houses have been particularly successful in encouraging more people to use the opportunity to repair their houses legally, and had the effect of moving work which might have been done informally to the formal and registered sector'. In relation to other domestic services (for example, household cleaning, gardening), meanwhile, similar targeted direct tax measures have been introduced in countries such as Finland and Germany to encourage household work (for example, cleaning, gardening) to be carried out in the formal rather than underground sector.

Here, however, attention shifts away from using general tax rebates in relation to specific RMI tasks and domestic services and towards some experiments that are even more tailored direct tax measures to encourage consumers to use formal rather than underground labour. These are the Home Services Scheme in Denmark and the Melkert initiatives in the Netherlands. Each is now considered in turn.

Home Service Scheme (Denmark)

The Danish Home Service Scheme (*hjemmeserviceordningen*) began in 1994 as a pilot project and was made permanent three years later in 1997. Its aims are first, to compete with the underground economy, second, to promote the development of formal enterprises that provide household services and third and finally, offer job opportunities to low-skilled jobseekers. Once businesses register with the Danish Commerce and Companies Agency

(DCCA) – *Erhvervs-og Selskabsstyrelsen* – to participate in the scheme, they can provide services to households for which the government reimburses a portion of the cost. From January 2000, for example, shopping for daily goods, cleaning, cooking and washing up, doing the laundry and other kinds of common domestic work were subsidized at 50 per cent of the salary cost by the government. If the household buys other services from these firms, including bringing home the children from school, this is also subsidized at 50 per cent of the cost. The reimbursement for gardening and other outdoor maintenance, however, has been reduced from 50 per cent in the early days of the scheme to 35 per cent latterly. Among the services not now subsidized are window cleaning (which used to receive a subsidy of 50 per cent), walking the dog and RMI work. The company submits the claim to the DCCA. It is a prerequisite that a licensed company conducts the work. It is not possible for individuals to perform the subsidized service for one another.

In 1998, 3506 companies were registered with the DCCA, 91 per cent of which were one-person micro-enterprises. Of these, 1500 specialized in domestic services and the rest (some 2200) performed domestic services as part of other activities. Not all companies, however, participate to the same extent. Indeed, just 10 per cent of the registered companies earn more than 50 per cent of the total payments made through the Home Service Scheme. Households find information on the companies they can hire within the scheme at their town hall and each household is allowed to spend a maximum of €7000 on such services per annum. In 1998, one in eight Danish households used the Home Service Scheme, an average of five times per year. Almost 90 per cent of consumers were very satisfied with the company and its services. In 1997 alone, more than 2000 jobs were created; by 2000, it had grown to 3700 full-time equivalent jobs (Renooy *et al.*, 2004). According to one study that interviewed 375 customers, it was found that 85 per cent of customers were buying cleaning services (cited in Platzer, 2002).

Analysing the impact of the Home Service Scheme on the underground economy, it has been estimated that such work in Denmark has reduced in size by 10 per cent since the introduction of the Home Service Scheme (Platzer, 2002; Sundbo, 1997). Perhaps due to this success, since 2000, the government has not only reduced the subsidies for specific tasks but also narrowed the range of tasks included in the scheme, as detailed above. Platzer (2002) draws attention to the gendering of this process. Window cleaning, a male task when conducted professionally, was removed. Other typically male tasks such as gardening and other outdoor activities had their subsidy cut from 50 to 35 per cent. The 50 per cent subsidy for services associated traditionally with women remained unchanged. And another service, namely bringing home children, was introduced. This channelled the Home Service Scheme, in consequence, much more towards social reproductive work for which women are deemed responsible. Indeed, in 2004, households could claim a maximum subsidy of DKK 15000 per quarter for work carried out by the same company.

Leaving aside this political decision by the Danish government to orientate this scheme towards underground labour conducted by women (see Platzer, 2002), this initiative displays that it is wholly feasible to use demand-side measures to transfer underground work into the formal realm on a large society-wide scale.

Melkert Initiatives (Netherlands)

According to a 1995 survey, one Dutch family in three needed more help at home, especially with cleaning as well as washing and ironing clothes (Cancedda, 2001). Under the Melkert Plan, a programme was implemented to subsidize the wages of declared domestic cleaners so that they could compete with their underground counterparts. Under this Cleaning Services for Private Persons Arrangement (RSO, *Regeling Schoonmaakdiensten Particularien*), a subsidy of not more than 19000 NLG was granted for every long-term unemployed person hired by a private cleaning company. The government, in effect, was paying the difference between formal and underground wage rates as an active welfare policy designed to shift from paying the unemployed for their inactivity to paying them to work. By 1997, however, only 250 jobs had been created. In 1998, changes were made to the scheme. Cleaning companies, nevertheless, had problems finding workers since they are required to have been unemployed for at least one year, which excludes many women who would like such work but have not been registered as unemployed people (Renooy *et al.*, 2004). The Melkert Plan also created subsidized jobs in other spheres, including home help services and child-care. In the realm of home help, however, some of the jobs created were replacing regular formal jobs. Nevertheless, some 1700 Melkert jobs were created in the sphere of child-care by the end of 1998 (Cancedda, 2001). These Melkert schemes were thus not as successful as originally expected.

Similar to other demand-side approaches, therefore, the Melkert initiatives sought to combine the objective of seeking to legitimize underground work with the additional objective of creating formal work for the (long-term) unemployed, perhaps based on the assumption that these two objectives are interrelated. Put another way, they erroneously assume underground work to be concentrated among the unemployed. There is no reason, however, why these two objectives should be always combined when pursuing demand-side approaches. As the Melkert initiatives display, limiting formal jobs to the unemployed severely curtails them. Opening up demand-side initiatives by not limiting participation to the registered unemployed thus seems to be necessary in future initiatives if the underground economy is to be effectively tackled.

VOUCHER SCHEMES

The use of voucher schemes to encourage customers to employ legitimate rather than underground labour has become ever more popular, especially in Europe. Here, four such initiatives are evaluated: the Local Employment Agency and Service Voucher schemes in Belgium, and the *Cheque Emploi Service* and *Titre Emploi Service* schemes in France.

Local Employment Agencies (Belgium)

In the mid-1990s, *Plaatselijke Werkgelegheidsagentschappen* (PWA), or what are here referred to as Local Employment Agencies, were introduced in most Belgian municipalities. These bring together the supply of labour of the long-term unemployed and the demand for labour in the community services sphere. The PWA is a non-profit association, with local politicians and social partners on the executive board. It issues vouchers that can be bought by citizens, government bodies and firms. One voucher, with which one can pay for one hour of work, costs €7.45. When a household, government body or private firm needs a job done (for example, odd jobs), it makes its demand known to the PWA. The agency then searches its files for a suitable supplier. The worker receives the vouchers as payment and then exchanges them for money at the PWA. The worker receives €4.10 per voucher/hour. The difference between the buying and selling price covers the overheads and insurances involved. The long-term unemployed who conduct the work for the PWA and earn the money can keep it as extra earnings alongside their unemployment benefits. There is no reduction in their benefit payments.

Not all unemployed people, nevertheless, are entitled to work in this scheme. It is reserved for unemployed people: over 45 years old and more than six months unemployed; under 45 years old and longer than two years unemployed, and people with no unemployment benefit, but living on a minimum social security grant. In practice, it has been mainly unemployed women involved in the scheme, reflecting the wider societal gender divisions regarding domestic work. In 1997, 82.6 per cent of the participants in PWE activities were women (17.4 per cent men) and people participated on average for 26 hours per month (ILO, 2004). For those participating in this scheme for the average number of hours, therefore, their monthly income was bolstered by an average of €106.60.

As the PWA initiative developed, the Belgian government moved closer towards obliging the unemployed after two years of unemployment to register with the PWAs and then either to accept the jobs offered to them or to have their benefits cut (this was introduced in 1994). Although the protection of the unemployed worker in the PWA has improved from the point of view of employment legislation, one consequence of this shift towards compulsion is that the jobs offered are not seen as 'proper' formal employment. Indeed, the unemployed person participating still has the official status of being unemployed, but is allowed to top-up unemployment benefit through this scheme. As the ILO (2004) put it, nevertheless, the obligatory aspect is applicable solely to the registered long-term unemployed who must be available for the labour market anyway and are called upon only as a last resort, if nobody voluntarily wishing to conduct a task is available. Moreover, the work must be a 'suitable activity'. The suspension of the right to unemployment benefits, furthermore, is only temporary. Indeed, until now, only one unemployed person has been suspended, for a four-week period, following the refusal to carry out a suitable activity within the PWE.

What services, therefore, can customers request? Over time, the answer to this question has changed, similar to the Danish Home Services scheme discussed above, and there is also a great deal of local autonomy in determining the basket of tasks included. Analysing what occurs in practice, in 1997, some 51.52 per cent of the hours spent working consisted of providing domestic household assistance, 3.60 per cent garden maintenance, 0.99 per cent the accompaniment of children and patients, 0.05 per cent administrative formalities and 43.84 per cent mixed activities (ILO, 2004).

An evaluation of this scheme found that customers previously sourced some 44 per cent of the work now conducted in PWAs on an underground basis, and 84 per cent of users of the PWA were glad to no longer have to turn to the underground economy (de Sutter, 2000). As such, it appears that PWAs have acted as an effective means of transferring underground work into the legitimate realm. However, this is not to say that PWAs have completely eradicated the underground economy either in the society at large or even in their own internal operating environment. On the latter issue, the PWA worker can raise his/her earnings by doing part of the work for vouchers and part of it on an underground basis. Indeed, and as Renooy *et al.* (2004) state, through the PWA system, demand and supply are actually brought together to facilitate such underground transactions in a way that would not have occurred without the existence of the PWA. The extent to which this occurs in practice, however, has not been evaluated.

Neither is it likely to be evaluated in the future. At the end of 2003, and because many unemployed people decided to stay in this scheme rather than seek formal jobs, the Belgian government decided to transfer the vouchers sold to private households into a new 'service vouchers' scheme. The other purchasers of vouchers, however, namely government bodies and firms, remain in the PWA scheme.

Service Vouchers (Belgium)

In this scheme, households can purchase subsidized vouchers to pay for 'local community services' (for example, childcare or household tasks such as cleaning). Like the PWA system, this scheme was primarily created with the aim of combating underground work in the household and community services sector. A household buys vouchers for a price of €6.20 (for an hour of work) with which it purchases services from a certified business. These companies hire the unemployed at first on flexible contracts but after six months, the business has to offer them a permanent contract of at least a 50 per cent full-time equivalent post.

An employee of a certified company is allowed to do at least the following activities: house cleaning; washing and ironing; sewing; errands; and preparing meals. The rationale for choosing this range of core tasks is on the one hand, that the service vouchers scheme will then not act as a substitute for formal firms since the proportion of these tasks conducted on a formal basis is currently relatively minor and on the other hand, that these are tasks where the use of underground labour is rife when it is conducted on a paid basis. As such, this service vouchers scheme adopts a targeted approach to combating underground work. Indeed, it gives municipalities flexibility with regard to the tasks they include so as to enable them to respond to local circumstances *vis-à-vis* the underground economy.

The household purchasing such services from registered companies pays with the vouchers. The cost price of a voucher is €19.47 (to be indexed from 2005). The difference is paid to the company by the federal government. Households can recover 30 per cent of the price of a voucher in their tax return. So for them the price of a voucher is €4.34, which is well below the price paid in the underground economy for such services (Rubbrecht and Nicaise, 2003; Smets, 2003). In total, more than 40 000 users have bought 1.7 million vouchers from 600 certified companies, which has created 4200 jobs (Renooy *et al.*, 2004). Given that some 44 per cent of work in the PWA scheme (which includes government departments and private firms as well as households) was previously conducted in the underground economy, this means that the equivalent of at least 1848 jobs have been transferred from the underground into the formal realm. In reality, however, and given that households are more likely to have sourced services underground than government agencies and private firms, the total number of jobs transferred from the underground to the formal economy by this service vouchers scheme will be higher.

To finance the creation of 25 000 jobs in this scheme, the federal government allocated to it €91 million in 2004 rising to €354 million by 2007. Due to the recovery of some of these costs through tax and social security contributions, the real costs for the government are limited to €17 million in 2004 and €163 million in 2007 (Rubbrecht and Nicaise, 2003).

In sum, although the use of service vouchers is relatively new and the detail rapidly evolving, the initial reports suggest that this initiative has been successful in stemming the use of underground labour in the domestic and community services sphere in Belgium. Although the decision on whether to replicate this scheme elsewhere should perhaps wait until the full evaluation conducted in late 2005 has been published, the preliminary evaluations suggest that it might well be considered by other western nations for adoption.

Cheque Emploi Service (France)

To combat underground labour in the domestic services sphere (for example, as cleaners), the French government in 1993 introduced the *Cheque Emploi Service* (CES) scheme. To simplify the process of hiring and paying a domestic worker and making social security contributions in a country infamous for its bureaucratic red tape, anybody can now legally employ a domestic worker without complying with the extensive administrative procedures and labour contracts usually required in French law. This is achieved by paying his or her salary using a system of cheques, which can be purchased at the local bank. The benefit for the purchaser is that they can claim an income tax reduction that amounts to 50 per cent of the sum spent on purchasing the cheques. For the supplier, meanwhile, the salary cannot be less than the national minimum wage, plus a 10 per cent indemnity for paid leave.

This is thus a targeted response to the notion that the regulations and legislation required in order to employ formal workers resulted in many people employing somebody on an underground basis. It targets household services in which underground work is rife, and simplifies the formalization procedures in order to shift work from the underground into the formal economy. By the end of 1995, just one year after its introduction, there were 250 000 permanent users of CES registered, 160 000 being new customers of domestic services (Finger, 1997). According to Labruyere (1997), moreover, after one year of experimentation through 1995, it was used by nearly 25 per cent of household employers and at the same time contributed to their increasing numbers. However, by May 1996, according to Finger (1997), the CES had created only approximately 40000 full-time equivalent jobs (if the number of jobs are divided by the 39 hours normal working week at the time) for a loss of €91.5 million (600 million FF) in taxes. Even the €65.5 million increase in social security contributions (430 million FF) was asserted to not compensate the public deficit of some €1200 per job created. At first glance, therefore, these early studies seemed to intimate that the CES was producing poor results.

The more recent figures, however, are far more positive. As Table 12.2 displays, participation has rapidly grown and by 2002, the number of households legally using domestic service workers was some 765411 while the number of full-time equivalent jobs created was just under 88000 FTEs (Adjerad, 2003). As such, it appears that this scheme either has commodified domestic services previously conducted on an unpaid basis (for example, by household members) and/or has legalized some of the domestic service provision that used to take place on an underground basis. The reality is probably a mix of the two.

Table 12.2   The development of the Cheque Emploi Service *scheme*

Year	No. of employers	Employers aged over 70	No. of employees	Hours worked	Full-time equivalent (FTE) employees
1998	469000	170000	370261	100963905	50482
1999	556000	193000	344389	124739193	62370
2000	564757	217282	369433	138993000	69497
2001	666228	251036	381993	153756612	76879
2002	765411	252585	425845	175542612	87771

Source: Adjerad (2003)

On the whole, consumers in this scheme tend to be the relatively affluent, leading to an accusation that this is a tax break for the wealthy when employing domestic cleaners with all of the issues regarding social divisions that result from this assertion. As Le Feuvre (2000: 1) concludes, 'The CES service cheques proved to be highly successful, particularly with the highly skilled, two-income households and the active and relatively affluent elderly population'.

Nevertheless, their impact on the underground economy in domestic services has been impressive. An estimated 20 per cent of those working in the underground economy are now officially employed (Le Feuvre, 2000). Indeed, by 2002, 53 per cent of all formal employers of domestic workers used the CES scheme (Adjerad, 2003) and this scheme is continuing to bring into its fold those formal and underground domestic workers previously outside of it. The CES, nevertheless, has not perhaps resolved the problem of quality control in this sphere, nor has it contributed to the creation of a commercial market, as the CES only settles transactions between private individuals.

Titre Emploi Service (France)

In 1996, a similar scheme was thus created to the CES, namely the *Titre Emploi Service* (TES) scheme. The essential difference between the TES and the CES is that the private person does not employ the domestic worker. Instead, the worker is employed by a business that acts as a service provider. The worker receives the TES from his or her employer as part of their salary. Hence, unlike the CES, the TES is not for sale in a bank. Instead, TES vouchers can be obtained through work councils, regional and local authorities and welfare associations. These institutions provide the vouchers to their employees and members to enable them to hire formal domestic help. In consequence, rather than directly hiring domestic workers, as in the CES, in the TES, they are indirectly employed and this system is viewed as offering better guarantees both to workers (who receive support from the organization) and users (who are guaranteed better quality since the organizations that provide services are subject to government approval), thus overcoming the quality control and commercial market issues raised at the end of the review of the CES scheme.

As Table 12.3 displays, six years after its introduction, in 2002, a total of 1.3 million TES had been used, representing a value of €15.7 million, which is roughly equivalent to the creation of 1000 full-time equivalent jobs in this domestic services sphere (Adjerad, 2003). The TES, however, is much less used than expected and it has not generated the volume of regular work that had been assumed. Indeed, it is just 5 per cent of the initially expected 20 000 full-time equivalent jobs.

One of the principal reasons for the slower than expected expansion of the TES scheme is that it has been difficult to identify sufficient service providers. In other words, there is a supply-side problem. This is because in the domestic services sector in France, provision is fragmented with few organized businesses in this sector. The outcome is that organizations wishing to use the TES scheme have had problems finding providers and even when identified, there have been problems identifying both the services that they propose to deliver as well as the services which organizations within the scheme wish to receive (Guimiot and Adjerad, 2003).

Table 12.3   Growth of the Titre Emploi Service *(TES)*

	Number of vouchers sold	Value (€)	Average value €
1999	557081	5776160	10.37
2000	863889	9485949	10.98
2001	999970	11425633	11.43
2002	1255148	15668315	12.48

Source: Adjerad (2003)

Furthermore, it has not been the case that this more macro-level approach has guaranteed a better quality of work than the one-to-one relationship promoted under the CES scheme. This is because the direct relationship between the supplier and customer established under the CES scheme has in practice proven more flexible with regard to the content of the work conducted and better nurtured a relationship based on mutual trust, which is important in the case of domestic service provision (for example, Renooy, 1990). The TES scheme has been unable to replicate the nurturing of this more informal side of the exchange relationship. The result is that TES service providers have had difficulties meeting certain needs on the demand side, such as urgent household support arising from hospitalization or small emergencies involving household maintenance. The formalization of the competencies requested by service providers is not conducive to the nurturing of the flexible employment contracts sometimes required in domestic services.

One of the intentions underpinning the creation of the TES scheme was to provide access to formal domestic services for those groups who would not normally use such provision. TES, however, has not been effective in generating demand from this group. A main reason is the cultural barrier to using formal domestic services among these groups and that the most frequently offered service, cleaning activities, is not a priority demand for them. Diversification of the breadth of service provision will be thus required to fulfil the needs of this category. For example, basic home improvement and maintenance tasks might be included within the TES scheme in order to meet the needs of this client group.

Finally, there remains an awareness issue concerning such schemes. As Le Feuvre (2000) points out, there remains an ignorance of both the CES and TES schemes as well as the financial advantages of using them. This lack of awareness results in households opting for self-provisioning rather than availing themselves of the available commercial services. This issue of raising awareness will be returned to in the next chapter.

Subsidy Schemes in Other Nations

Although these voucher schemes in Belgium and France have been heralded as 'best practice' in reports to the European Commission (Mateman and Renooy, 2001; Renooy *et al.*, 2004), subsidy schemes in other countries have not met with the same level of success. It is important, therefore, to consider why this might be the case.

In Finland in October 1997, an experiment began to subsidize domestic work in the form of lower taxes for customers. Originally, it was anticipated that some 10 000–12 000 new jobs would be created. However, only 208 full-time equivalent new jobs were created in 1998 and fewer than 400 in 1999. About 24 000 households used the scheme. By April 1999, only 17 million FIM had been used out of the 200 million FIM allocated to the first two years of the programme. A principal reason for its lack of success was that the subsidy was insufficient to make formal domestic services cheaper than underground services (Cancedda, 2001: 29). The lesson, therefore, is that unless governments make the incentive sufficient enough to encourage households to formalize provision, then such demand-side experiments will be ineffective. This, of course, raises problematic issues for governments. There is a need to calculate the real cost of the initiative by calculating the cost of the incentive and the return in terms of additional taxes paid and reduced social security payments. The tendency will be to keep the cost to a minimum by providing as low an incentive as possible. The problem, however, as seen in Finland, is that the incentive offered can sometimes be too low to encourage consumers to make the transition.

In Germany, the same problem occurred when a 'maid's concession' was introduced which allowed families to employ domestic workers and deduct from their taxes the cost of doing so up to a maximum of DM18 000. This measure did not produce the predicted 100 000 new jobs in the sector. In fact, only 1200 additional individuals were employed because the subsidy was again insufficient, except for families in the highest tax band. Household cheques were also another failed experiment in Germany. Instead of the 500 000 expected jobs, only 4500 cheques were used in 1997. This is because the cheques were only designed to guarantee social security benefits, and did not allow workers to receive a net wage comparable to their earnings in the underground economy (Cancedda, 2001). In consequence, the price of vouchers must be set at a level that gives clear advantages not only for customers but also for suppliers shifting from the underground to the formal sphere. Unless this is done, voucher schemes are likely to be unsuccessful.

When calculating the incentive required to move work from the underground to the formal economy, moreover, intranational geographical variations in the level at which it is set might be needed. This is because there may be regional and/or local variations in the differential wage rate for underground and formal labour, not least due to the overheating of demand and/or supply shortages in particular areas. Some regional and/or local flexibility in the level of incentive, wherever possible, might therefore need to be built into the design of such demand-side incentive schemes.

Until now, furthermore, demand-side incentive schemes have concentrated on transferring a relatively narrow range of domestic services from the underground to the legitimate realm. It might be useful if such schemes are implemented elsewhere to consider both the range of activities included and whether the activities for which vouchers are available need to be tailored to suit local, regional and national circumstances. On the range of activities covered, for example, there is perhaps an argument for extending demand-side incentives to the RMI sector where underground work is concentrated. Before doing so, however, further research is required to estimate the proportion of work in particular aspects of the RMI sphere that is conducted on an underground basis, so as to evaluate whether it is appropriate to extend such a voucher scheme to these sectors of the economy and which sub-sectors in particular. There is also a need to evaluate the geographical variations in the propensity to conduct such RMI activities in the underground economy.

CONCLUSIONS

This chapter has revealed how incentives can be offered to customers of underground work to encourage them to source formally. These include both indirect and direct tax measures. Of particular note are the service voucher schemes that in France and Belgium appear to have made strong inroads into stemming the use of underground labour.

Some of the problems arising with these schemes, moreover, need not be repeated if implemented elsewhere. Local Employment Agencies in Belgium, for example, have been criticized for obliging the unemployed to work on such schemes and can thus be read as a form of 'workfare'. If such an initiative is promoted primarily to eradicate the underground economy, however, there is no reason why participation should be compulsory for the unemployed or even suppliers only selected from the long-term unemployed. After all, underground work is not concentrated among the unemployed, as believed in the marginality thesis, but is instead a form of enterprise and entrepreneurship more often than not conducted by the employed and already self-employed. Nor is there any reason why the list of tasks in such schemes should not significantly expand to incorporate for example, a range of home improvement and maintenance services. If this occurred, then the suggestion is that a more representative range of socio-economic groups might demand services from these schemes. What seems certain from France, moreover, is that the more flexible CES scheme based on one-to-one exchanges is more popular and successful than the TES scheme that attempts to add further layers of formalization into the design. Finally, when deciding on the incentive necessary to transfer work from the underground to the formal economy, some consideration is required of the need for intranational geographical variations in the level at which the subsidy is set. This is because there may be regional and/or local variations in the differential wage rate for underground and formal labour, not least due to the overheating of demand or supply shortages in some localities relative to others.

In sum, even if supply-side deterrents have been predominantly used in most western economies to tackle underground work, there is no reason why in future measures should continue to be confined to this narrow approach. It is now perhaps time that other advanced economies started to consider extending the types of method they use. Indeed, unless they do so, it is highly unlikely that they will achieve their objective of moving the hidden enterprise culture into the legitimate realm.

13. Raising awareness: towards high commitment societies

INTRODUCTION

The previous three chapters have reviewed first incentives to help business start off legitimately and then demand- and supply-side incentives to encourage the transfer of underground work into the formal realm. This chapter argues not only that it is important to raise awareness of these measures for them to be effective but also that it is necessary to deal with the low tax morality that prevails in many western societies if the hidden enterprise culture is to be formalized.

This chapter deals with the need for each form of raising awareness in turn. First, a brief review is provided of the need to promote among target groups the existence of both the deterrents and incentives available to encourage underground work to be transferred into the legitimate realm. Second, the need for broader awareness-raising campaigns about the costs of underground work and benefits of legitimizing such activity are considered. The argument here will be that although introducing direct control methods in the form of incentives to encourage compliance is a way forward, this could be usefully supplemented with indirect control methods that seek to develop a 'high commitment society' by relaying more on internal control from the individual themselves and the wider society to elicit participation in the legitimate rather than underground economy. If pursued, this would use similar techniques to elicit behaviour change to those currently being employed in post-bureaucratic organizations that seek to win the hearts and minds of people.

RAISING AWARENESS OF EXISTING INITIATIVES

There is little point providing incentives to help businesses start off legitimately along with demand- and supply-side measures to encourage underground participants to transfer their activity into the formal realm if people are unaware of these initiatives. Where it has been researched, a lack of awareness of these initiatives is frequently identified. This prevents schemes from being as effective as might otherwise be the case. For example, a principal reason for the lack of success of the CES service voucher scheme in France is that some segments of the population, especially lower income groups, do not know about its existence (Le Feuvre, 2000). It is doubtless similarly the case with many other initiatives.

In this chapter, therefore, the first intention is to highlight the importance of raising awareness of specific initiatives to encourage the transition from the underground to the legitimate economy. Unless this occurs, such initiatives will have little impact on the overall size of the underground economy. This, however, is not the only, or even the major, way in which awareness needs to be raised in order to tackle the underground economy.

RAISING AWARENESS ABOUT THE IMPACTS OF UNDERGROUND WORK

On a broader level, awareness raising and information campaigns are also required with regard to the costs of underground work and benefits of transferring such work into the formal economy targeted at underground enterprises and entrepreneurs, their customers as well as the society at large. Until now, this has been achieved by focusing upon the use of publicity as a tool for deterring engagement in the underground sphere.

Awareness campaigns, recommended by the ILO (2002) as good practice, may be about some and/or all of the following:

- informing underground workers of the costs and risks;
- informing underground workers of the benefits of being formal;
- informing potential users of underground labour of the risks and costs; and/or
- informing potential users of the benefits of employing formal labour.

Such campaigns can be either general awareness-raising initiatives or targeted at particular sectors. Such publicity can have the double effect of highlighting the risks involved in underground work and the benefits of formality, as well as strengthening trust in the system by taxpayers. Both effects are essential, since compliant taxpayers must be confident in the ability of the state to prevent tax evasion, while underground workers must recognize the risks involved and benefits of formalization.

Until now, however, most publicity campaigns have tended to focus upon the costs of participating in underground work rather than the benefits of formality. Such campaigns include:

- The 'targeting fraud' pilot initiative in the North West of England between May and October 2000 that sought to publicize sanctions and encourage people to report fraud. TV and radio commercials were used presenting case studies, supported by newspaper advertising and billboards. Little emphasis was put on the benefits of working formally, however, merely the risks of working underground. No results are known.
- *'Illegal ist unsozial'* (illegal is unsocial) was a campaign in Germany to encourage the population to declare their underground work by highlighting the costs of participating in such work.
- *'Zwartwerk is broodroof'* ('black work is taking the bread out of someone else's mouth') in the Netherlands, organized by the National Institute of Social Insurance, targeted the general public between 1996–8 and consisted of billboard, radio and television commercials and newspaper advertisements. An evaluation shows that the majority of the target audience knew of the campaign and what it was about. The impacts of this attempt to depict the negative consequences of underground work, however, have not been evaluated.
- In France, a campaign was run on the risks to households of using underground labour in the home improvement and repair industry where there is no recourse against any defects in the work carried out or when using such labour means that there is no cover against the risk of burglary or damage.

In many awareness-raising and information campaigns, therefore, the emphasis has been upon the costs and risks of underground work.

Here, however, it is considered that such campaigns should perhaps emphasize the benefits of working formally rather than the costs of working on an underground basis. This is because, as Thurman *et al.* (1984) highlight, publicizing the adverse consequences of underground work are unlikely to be effective because individuals neutralize their guilt about engaging in underground transactions in one or more of the following ways:

- *Denial of responsibility*. The individual will regard the adverse consequences arising from the underground economy to be the result of others, who could even possibly be big players in the underground economy. It is not a product of their own actions.
- *Denial of injury*. The individual disagrees that their activity could have adverse consequences on others and may rationalize their actions by arguing that without their activities and endeavour, the community may pay a higher price or even be unable to get such services provided.

- *Denial of victim.* The individual accepts the adverse consequences their actions may have on the community but believes that the victims deserved it.
- *Condemnation of condemners.* The individual may believe that the law, the lawmakers and law enforcers are to blame for an unjust system that burdens the community at large and believe that the community should not succumb to these laws and evade them if possible.
- *Appeal to higher loyalties.* The individual justifies their action as the result of 'non-conventional social order', believing that similar and across-the-board behaviour justifies their actions.
- *Metaphor of the ledger.* The individual contemplating evasion believes that their actions, although they may be bad, are not reflective of their true and good nature, and regards these actions as temporary deviations from otherwise good behaviour.
- *Defence of necessity.* The individual justifies their actions to be the result of personal circumstances that have led to non-compliance.

For these reasons, it is here advocated that awareness raising and information campaigns should in future preferably focus upon the benefits of formal work, not the risks and costs of underground work.

These campaigns to highlight the benefits of formal work can be targeted at either employers or suppliers of underground work, and either be of a general variety or targeted at specific sectors where the underground economy predominates (for example, home improvement and repair as well as domestic services). To take just one example, in the UK, one could extend the recommendations of the 2002 Davies Review of 'Enterprise and Economy in Education' to include discussion of ethical issues for and against underground work as well as the benefits of paying tax, using for example, the 'Red Box' educational game developed by the Inland Revenue in citizenship classes.

It is important to realize, however, that not all awareness raising and information campaigns need to be conducted by the public sector. Governments, for example, can also work in partnership with other groups. For formal businesses undercut by underground enterprises and who lose market share to these underground enterprises, there is a strong rationale for wanting them transferred into the legitimate sphere. There are also numerous trade associations who have an interest in dealing with this problem. Given that consumers are also affected by the underground economy, another way forward is for government to work with national consumer protection groups (for example, the Consumers Association in the UK) in order to raise awareness of the benefits of sourcing goods formally. Until now, furthermore, there has been no attempt to involve local governments despite their interest in developing local micro-enterprise and meeting community needs. There is also a role for trade union involvement in these issues. For trade unions, the underground economy is a problem because it reduces union membership and leads to a race to the bottom. In sum, although national governments have a role to play in raising awareness, they are not the sole interested party.

FROM COMPLIANCE TO A 'HIGH COMMITMENT' SOCIETY

For awareness-raising campaigns to be effective, it is perhaps insufficient to solely highlight the current benefits of working formally. There is also a need to complement deterrents with incentives to encourage people to transfer their endeavour into the legitimate realm. After all, positive reinforcement of 'good' behaviour is more effective than negative reinforcement of 'bad' behaviour in eliciting behaviour change. The current public policy emphasis in this sphere on punishing bad behaviour rather than rewarding 'good' behaviour is thus perhaps surprising when all of the evidence clearly displays that punishing people for doing something wrong (that is, negative reinforcement) is a less effective way of changing behaviour than rewarding good behaviour (that is, positive reinforcement). Indeed, there is now a vast body of research on this in fields ranging from how to motivate employees and provide effective leadership in organizations (for example, Prewitt, 2003; Romero and Kleiner, 2000), through such diverse subjects as effective toilet training (Cicero and Pfadt, 2002), smoking cessation (Glautier, 2004) and effective personal management of diabetes (for example, Parra-Medina *et al.*, 2004), to the mitigation of anti-social behaviour in schools and classrooms (Beaman and Wheldall, 2000; Luiselli *et al.*, 2002). In all these fields and a vast range of others, it is rare to find punishments rather than rewards being used to elicit behaviour change. Yet, until now, the field of underground work appears oblivious to what is elsewhere viewed as common knowledge.

To change behaviour, therefore, one can envisage campaigns on the benefits of working formally being coupled with the incentives discussed in the previous three chapters. Even this type of positive reinforcement approach, however, although necessary, is perhaps still insufficient. Analysing contemporary management theory and practice, it quickly becomes apparent that such an incentives approach is in many organizations now part of a much wider project to engender commitment. Rather than seek to control behaviour through direct control methods, the common approach is to use indirect control methods by seeking to win hearts and minds in order to engender self-policed compliance. Known by a variety of names including 'post-bureaucratic management', 'high commitment' management and 'soft' human resource management (HRM), this approach has been so far confined almost entirely to organizations. Here, however, this idea is to extend it to creating 'high commitment' societies, achieved by drawing upon the 'hearts and minds' approach towards organizations and engaging in what might be seen as 'societal-level human resource management' (a so far uncharted territory).

To chart what a 'high commitment society' approach might look like if applied to tackling underground work, a very brief review is here undertaken of contrasting hard and soft HRM and bureaucratic and post-bureaucratic management approaches so as to reveal the shift towards the construction of 'high commitment' workforces. In so doing, the intention is to make the novel proposition that if these contemporary models were extended to the societal level and used to manage society (rather than organizations), then perhaps this would provide a more effective means of stemming participation in the underground economy.

Management studies is currently fascinated with the supposed transition from a bureaucratic to a post-bureaucratic style of management which calls for managers to combine the subjective and emotional aspirations of their employees with the strategic goals of the organization. Viewed through the lens of HRM, Legge (1995) characterizes this as a shift away from the 'hard' or 'utilitarian-instrumentalism' HRM model and towards the 'soft' or 'developmental humanism' HRM model. This soft model is characterized by a movement away from behavioural compliance to employee commitment, resulting in enhanced performance via programmes of culture change. Put another way, and as Table 13.1 highlights, while the conventional industrial relations approach sought to directly control behaviour, a soft HRM or high commitment approach seeks to capture the hearts and minds of people in order to ensure self-policed compliance. Table 13.2 provides a summary of a similar tendency associated with a shift from direct control of people from the outside to control from the inside or what can be again viewed as a shift from compliance to commitment.

In these contemporary management models, therefore, there is a shift from externalized to internalized control relying on acceptance of values and peer reinforcement rather than rule following. Consequently, while compliance was conventionally sought and maintained by externally imposed bureaucratic control systems, generating reactive rather than proactive behaviours, the intention now is to seek commitment through internalized belief, generating constructive proactivity on the part of people (for example, Guest 1987; Legge, 1989, 1995). As Watson (2003: 109) states, 'the single feature that distinguishes what are called HRM management approaches from non-

Table 13.1   High commitment workplace: industrial relations versus HRM

Dimension	Industrial relations	Human resource management
Psychological contract	Compliance	Commitment
Behaviour referent	Norms, customs and practice	Values/mission
Relations	Low trust, pluralist, collective	High trust, unitary, individual
Organization and design	Formal roles, hierarchy, division of labour, managerial controls	Flexible roles, flat structure, teamwork/autonomy, self-control

Source: Kochan and Osterman (1998: Table 15.1)

Table 13.2   Direct and indirect approaches in the pursuit of management control in work organizational design

Direct control approaches	Indirect control approaches
Close supervision and monitoring of activities	Empowerment and discretion applied to activities
Tight rules	Loose rules
Highly prescribed procedures	Flexible procedures
Centralized structures	Decentralized structures
Low commitment culture	High commitment culture
Low trust culture	High trust culture
Adversarial culture	Culture of mutual interest
A tightly bureaucratic structure and culture	A loosely bureaucratic structure and culture

Source: Watson (2003: Table 5.2)

HRM ones is its concern with developing a high level of psychological and social commitment towards the employing organization on the behalf of the workforce'. Or as Bunting (2004: 115) puts it, 'Employees are subjected to mission statements, vision statements, brand values, all of which are designed to capture their hearts, minds and souls'.

Surveillance is still used to exercise control but as Edwards (1979) comments, managerial practices have moved away from the coercive control of the late nineteenth century and the later technological control (like the assembly line) followed by the bureaucratic control methods of the mid-twentieth century. Post-bureaucratic control is now about instilling emotions, values and world views congruent with the interests of the organization so as to generate internal control from both the individual themselves and the team of people surrounding them (Wilkinson and Wilmott, 1995). The use of rewards is one tool used to generate this internal control. How this might be achieved beyond the organization and at the societal level in the policy sphere of tackling underground work is now considered.

TACKLING UNDERGROUND WORK: DIRECT AND INDIRECT CONTROL METHODS

Public policy towards underground work has so far used direct control methods to deter engagement. Little consideration has been given to indirect control methods. To engender a shift from compliance to commitment, the first step is to reward 'good' behaviour, namely formal employment, rather than punish 'bad' behaviour. At the simplest level, this necessitates the emphasis in awareness-raising campaigns to be transferred away from deterring bad behaviour and towards encouraging good behaviour. It necessitates advertising the benefits of engagement in formal employment rather than the disadvantages of participating in underground work. All sticks and no carrots, as is well known in so many other spheres of public policy, seldom provides an effective means of achieving the desired outcome and there is no reason why combating underground work is any different.

The objective in so doing, however, must not be simply to employ an external locus of behaviour control through direct approaches or bureaucratic controls. After all, it would be relatively easy to envisage a shift in direct methods of control away from the less effective punitive measures that seek to push people away from underground work and towards direct rewards or incentives to pull them into the formal economy. Instead, a more significant and wholesale rethinking of public policy towards the underground economy is required if this realm of public policy is to reflect contemporary management thought on eliciting behaviour change. This requires a shift from direct to indirect control, from compliance to commitment.

How is this to be achieved? To answer this, it is necessary to adopt a more critical lens towards the contemporary management literature than adopted until now in this chapter. Reading this literature, it is often the case that the direct and indirect management control methods are seen as mutually exclusive, even as descriptive of some linear and uni-dimensional evolution of management thought whereby the trajectory of managerial practice has been universally from direct to indirect control. Here, however, and in line with the more refined understanding that is emerging, the argument is that such a view of direct and indirect methods as either mutually exclusive or some evolutionary trajectory so far as managerial practices are concerned, is far from the reality. In practice, direct and indirect management methods are often practised alongside each other in order to elicit behaviour change in organizations. One outcome of this recognition has been that a great deal of contemporary discussion has revolved around the emergence of hybrid forms of managerial practice (for example, Du Gay, 2005; Reed, 2005; Thompson and Alvesson, 2005). Thompson and Alvesson (2005), for example, argue that bureaucracy has never been a single or static phenomenon and that contemporary organizational changes are not in the main 'post-bureaucratic' but rather, tend towards a re-configuration or 'hybridization' of bureaucratic forms.

Here, however, I wish to question whether hybridity is resulting in the contemporary period or whether it is more the case that the ideal-types variously referred to as bureaucracy versus post-bureaucracy, hard versus soft HRM and industrial relations versus high commitment approaches created by business school academics and gurus were ever descriptive of the lived experience of organizations. What they are now identifying as hybrids of the ideal-types may well have always been there but uncaptured by these oversimplistic dichotomies. If this is the case, then the issue for public policy towards underground work is not to consider how a 'high commitment society' might be created where indirect methods are employed to tackle underground work but rather, how direct and indirect methods can both be used alongside each other to tackle the underground economy.

Indeed, it takes only a moment's reflection with regard to policy towards the underground economy to recognize that direct and indirect control methods are far from mutually exclusive options and, that if combined, will be perhaps more effective. Using direct compliance methods or bureaucratic controls, whether punitive measures to prevent 'bad' behaviour or direct incentives (outlined in Chapters 10–12) to elicit 'good' behaviour, are necessary to change behaviour. However, there is no reason that these cannot be employed alongside and in combination with more indirect methods to capture the hearts and minds of the population with regard to the benefits of formal work and costs of underground work. Indeed, if direct methods are combined with indirect techniques, then direct controls are much more likely to be effective. After all, to pursue purely indirect control, without at the same time offering rewards for those seeking to transfer their underground practices into the formal economy and punishing those continuing to work on an underground basis is unlikely to be as effective as using direct and indirect methods combined. Direct and indirect management control methods, therefore, are not mutually exclusive. It is not an either/or choice but rather, a both/and approach that is necessary if such work is to be effectively transferred into the formal realm.

Indeed, such a combined approach would be perhaps nothing new. Although contemporary management studies, to repeat, has interpreted their combination in organizational control methods as some new hybrid, so far as public policy towards underground work is concerned, a combination of direct control methods to elicit behaviour change (albeit mostly in the form of punitive measures) has for some time been combined with indirect management methods to change people's hearts and minds concerning engagement in such work. What would be new in the proposal here is the shift towards rewarding good behaviour rather than punishing bad behaviour using both direct and indirect control methods.

CONCLUSIONS

This chapter has shown it is insufficient to develop initiatives to help business start off legitimately and demand- and supply-side incentives to encourage underground participants to transfer their activity into the formal realm. If the underground economy is to be effectively tackled, it is also necessary to raise awareness not only of the various measures currently available but also the benefits of working formally and costs of engaging in underground work.

Analysing how this might be achieved, the argument here has been that it is more effective to highlight the benefits of working formally and the positive rewards available for those who choose this route. However, akin to contemporary managerial thought with regard to eliciting behaviour change in organizations, it has been here argued that the intention should not be purely to use direct controls to ensure compliance but rather, that indirect control methods also need to be introduced. Moreover, rather than view direct and indirect control methods as mutually exclusive, this chapter has revealed the feasibility of combining direct and indirect control methods with an emphasis on rewarding good behaviour so as to engender the shift towards what I have here called a high commitment society that relies more on internal control from the individuals themselves and the wider society to elicit participation in the legitimate rather than underground economy.

14. Co-ordinating government thought and action

INTRODUCTION

Besides providing incentives to help businesses start off on a formal footing and transfer underground work into the legitimate realm, and engendering commitment to the benefits of formal employment, it might be assumed that the final piece required in the public policy jigsaw is the co-ordination of government strategy and operations if the underground economy is to be effectively tackled. In other words, there is a common assumption that the presence of disjointed and fragmented policy approaches across government is less effective in dealing with the underground economy than co-ordinated government thought and action (for example, Caianiello and Voltura, 2003; Grabiner, 2000; Meldolesi and Ruvolo, 2003; Small Business Council, 2004). This chapter evaluates the evidence of whether this is the case.

To do this, two national governments with starkly contrasting approaches so far as 'joining up' their strategy and operations when tackling the underground economy are evaluated. First, there is the UK with an institutional infrastructure composed of a multitude of disjointed agencies and, which despite recent attempts to improve co-ordination, remains essentially a 'silos' approach with only limited co-operation between the plethora of government institutions involved. Other social partners, moreover, are largely absent. Second, and the polar opposite so far as joined-up thought and action is concerned, is the case of France where there is a highly co-ordinated approach to both thought and action with regard to the underground economy and full integration of a wide array of social partners at both the national, regional and local levels. In this chapter, taking these contrasting case studies, an evaluation is undertaken of the value of pursuing joined-up strategy and operations. The finding will be that a distinct lack of evidence exists that joining up thought and action necessarily leads to a more effective approach and until such time as evidence is provided, the pursuit of more joined-up policy approaches should not be given priority with regard to tackling underground work.

A CASE STUDY OF DISJOINTED THOUGHT AND ACTION: THE UK

At the outset of this book, the underground economy was defined as involving the paid production and sale of goods and services that are unregistered by, or hidden from the state for tax, benefit and/or labour law purposes but which are legal in all other respects. As such, three broad types of underground work were identified:

- evasion of both direct (that is income tax) and indirect (for example VAT, excise duties) taxes;
- benefit fraud where the officially unemployed are working while claiming benefit; and
- avoidance of labour legislation, such as employers' insurance contributions, minimum wage agreements or certain safety and other standards in the workplace (for example, hiring labour off-the-books or subcontracting work to small firms and the self-employed asked to work for below minimum wages).

In the UK, responsibility for each of these segments lies with different central government departments (see Williams, 2004b). Until recently, the Inland Revenue (IR) primarily concerned itself with the evasion of direct taxation and Her Majesty's Customs & Excise (HMCE) with the evasion of indirect taxation (VAT and excise duties). In 2005, these two departments merged to form Her Majesty's Revenue and Customs (HMRC), which now deals with both. The Department for Work and Pensions (DWP), meanwhile, focuses on those 'working while claiming' while the primary emphasis of other government departments (OGDs) is upon various facets of the third aspect of the underground economy. For example, the Department of Food and Rural Affairs (Defra) concentrates on organized providers of underground labour in agriculture and fisheries (known as 'gang masters'), the Home Office on illegal workers, the Health and Safety Inspectorate with health and safety standards in the workplace and the Department of Trade and Industry (DTI) and Small Business Service (SBS) with regulatory compliance in the workplace.

Departmental Responsibilities

Each government department, in consequence, focuses upon, and has responsibility for, a particular segment of the underground economy. The result is that this sphere has different meanings to various departments and what is of interest to one department is not to another. Claiming benefits while working as a pay-as-you-earn (PAYE) employee, for example, is of interest only to the DWP. If claiming benefits while working on a 'cash-in-hand' basis, however, this is also of interest to the HMRC. Similarly, an illegal worker using a falsified NI number to gain formal employment is of interest to the Home Office but not the HMRC because they pay their taxes. Here, in consequence, the various UK central government departments responsible for various facets of this sphere need to be briefly identified along with their approach.

Department for Work and Pensions (DWP)

For the DWP, the principal focus is upon those 'working whilst claiming' and tackling the underground economy is seen as part and parcel of the wider issue of error and fraud in the payment of welfare benefits (DWP, 2003a, b, 2004a, b, c). Combating such underground work is thus incorporated within its Public Service Agreement (PSA) target to reduce the level of fraud and error on Income Support (IS) and Jobseeker's Allowance (JSA). By 2002–3, 6.4 per cent (£1.15 billion) of total expenditure was lost due to fraud (DWP, 2004c), a 29 per cent reduction against the 1998 baseline figure of 9 per cent of total benefit overpaid. Its target is to reduce loss for customers of working age from IS and JSA by 50 per cent by March 2006 (DWP, 2003a, 2004a, b, c).

Only a segment of this fraud and error is related to those 'working while claiming' and an even smaller proportion is related to those claiming while working on an underground basis. No figures, so far as is known, have been published on the proportion of fraud and error that is due to working while claiming, but it is estimated that only some 30 per cent of those caught working while claiming are engaged in underground work (DWP, 2004a). The majority are engaged in formal employment. The interests of the DWP, in consequence, overlap only at the margins with those of HMRC (previously IR and HMCE) in relation to tackling the underground economy.

Inland Revenue (IR)

The IR is primarily interested in those not reporting or under-reporting their income tax liabilities. In 2001–2, the IR spent £428 million on activities to tackle non-compliance and achieved an overall yield-to-cost ratio of 8.3:1. Over 80 per cent of these resources are deployed on compliance work by the 500 local tax offices grouped into 65 geographical areas, who have considerable autonomy of how they decide to go about conducting targeted enquiries on tax returns. These generate a yield-to-cost ratio of 3.6:1 in additional settlements and penalties. The remainder is spent on compliance activities by specialist IR offices, which deal with enquiry work on large and specialist businesses and on tax credits, and the Special Compliance

Office (SCO) whose main role is to investigate serious fraud and complex non-compliance and who in 2001–2, recovered 12 times their costs (Select Committee on Public Accounts, 2003).

For the IR, therefore, tackling the underground economy is part of the wider objective of ensuring tax compliance. A distinction is made between 'ghosts' (that is, wholly underground enterprises) and 'moonlighters' (that is, those doing a proportion of trade off-the-books) or put another way, between non-reporting rather than under-reporting. In 2003/4, IR investigations identified 2441 people who had not declared any of their income and 9837 people who had failed to declare income from part of their activities. The tax in charge resulting from these investigations totalled £30 million (Select Committee on Public Accounts, 2004).

Her Majesty's Customs and Excise (HMCE)
The interest of HMCE in the underground economy is in the non- or under-payment of VAT and excise duties and this is part of the wider issue of fraud and error in VAT and excise duties. The merger in April 2005 of HMCE with IR to form HMRC combines the two departments who respectively target the evasion of direct (that is, income tax) and indirect (for example VAT, excise duties) taxes. In practice, however, this might be far from smooth since in contrast to the IR, which gives considerable discretion to local offices, HMCE is very much a top-down department that gives little autonomy to local operations.

Dept of Environment, Food and Rural Affairs (DEFRA)
DEFRA's main involvement in combating the underground economy is on a sectoral level and concerns the use of illegal gangmasters in agriculture and fishing. The drowning in Morecambe Bay of illegal workers who were cockle picking has recently resulted in concerted action by DEFRA in this realm through some joint initiatives which will be discussed below. For DEFRA, therefore, the focus is upon the third aspect of the underground economy, particularly labour providers who do not comply with labour law legislation in the agriculture and fisheries sector.

Home Office
Similarly, the Home Office's major interest in the underground economy again relates to the flouting of labour law, particularly where illegal workers are employed. Indeed, during 2004, legislative action was taken to tighten the laws preventing illegal working using secondary legislation in relation to section 8 of the Asylum and Immigration Act 1996, the main preventive check on the use of illegal labour by employers. This strengthens the types of document that employers are required to check at the point of recruitment

to comply with section 8 and makes it easier for the Immigration Service to identify and prosecute non-compliant employers. An employer can now be fined up to £5000 for each employee who has no right to be employed.

Other Government Departments (OGDs)

Beyond these principal departments tackling the underground economy, a host of other government departments have to varying extents become involved. The Department of Trade and Industry (DTI) and Small Business Service (SBS), the latter not being a policy-making department, both focus upon regulatory compliance issues, increasingly from a viewpoint that provides advice and incentives rather than punishments to ensure compliance and views this sphere as a seedbed for entrepreneurship that needs to be harnessed (Small Business Council, 2004; Williams, 2004b, 2005a). The Office of the Deputy Prime Minister (ODPM), meanwhile, has a policy interest in the role of the underground economy in tackling joblessness in deprived neighbourhoods (Evans *et al.*, 2004). HM Treasury, meanwhile, also has a developing interest in this sphere, not least as a means of filling the current 'black hole' in public finances and the Office of National Statistics (ONS) in measuring the size of this sphere.

In sum, the meanings of the underground economy vary across government departments. The result is a fragmented and disparate approach towards tackling the underground economy. Each department has its own particular segment of the underground economy that it is keen to eliminate and focuses upon this rather than other aspects. Recently, however, a view has emerged across government that if departments worked together, they might be more effective in achieving their ultimate common aim of eradicating underground work in its totality (for example, Grabiner, 2000; Select Committee on Select Committee on Environment, Food and Rural Affairs, 2004; Select Committee on Public Accounts, 2003, 2004). Below, how departments have begun to do this is documented. For the purposes of clarity, the moves towards greater co-ordination at the level of operations and strategy are distinguished.

Co-ordinating and Crosscutting Operations

Recently, there has been a move away from a pure 'silos' approach where different government departments work autonomously to combat the segments of the underground economy in which they are interested. The stimulus for joint working so as to facilitate effective compliance has come from two sources. First, the Chancellor of the Exchequer, in part motivated by a desire to reduce the above-mentioned 'black hole' in public finances, commissioned the Grabiner report on the underground economy (Grabiner,

2000). Its recommendations emphasized the need for greater co-ordination across government, resulting in the establishment of the 'Grabiner Steering Group', now renamed the 'Informal Economy Steering Group' (IESG) to formulate and co-ordinate cross-departmental actions. Second, the events at Morecambe Bay where illegal immigrants working as cockle-pickers died, as well as media stories of gang masters in the agricultural sector exploiting vulnerable groups, heightened the political will for more effective action, necessitating that the IESG step up its action. All the initiatives outlined below have arisen out of the work of this Steering Group to join up this fragmented and disparate policy sphere.

Joint Shadow Economy Teams (JoSETs)
To co-ordinate action, the 'Grabiner Steering Group' formed in March 2000 set up Joint Shadow Economy Teams (JoSETS) bringing together officers from the DWP, IR and HMCE to tackle four priority sectors: construction and building services; taxi operators and couriers; catering, including takeaways, licensed restaurants and tenanted public houses; and hotels and guest houses. Two other priority sectors were given separate initiatives discussed below. By March 2001, 200 staff worked jointly in these area-based teams. The first five JoSETS were located in Coventry, Gloucester, Derby, Luton and Plymouth. By September 2001, 650 previously unregistered VAT traders had been identified with a VAT yield of £5.5 million and 900 business previously not notified for tax purposes. Some 15 additional teams were then established in Chelmsford, Woking, Swansea, Widnes, Shipley, Kensington, Salford, Newcastle-upon-Tyne, Wolverhampton, Maidstone, Belfast, Glasgow, Cambridge, Oxford and Croydon.

These 20 JoSETs employ 199 staff: 87 from HMCE, 59 from IR and 53 from DWP (Select Committee on Public Accounts, 2004). According to DWP (2004c), JoSETs brought in direct tax yields of £2.4 million in 2003–4 along with additional VAT of £26.5 million. DWP investigators recovered benefits overpaid or terminated false claims amounting to £1.7 million. Nevertheless, relative to number of staff employed in individual departments and the volume of activity they uncover, JoSETs still represent only a very minor segment of total compliance activity.

Joint Fashion Industry teams (JoFITs)
Akin to JoSETs in the above four sectors, JoFITs target the clothing and fashion industry. The first team was located in London and a second team was established in Leicester in 2001. Their aim when launched by the Paymaster General, Dawn Primarilo, was to provide a service to business, reduce fraud and improve regulatory understanding and compliance through a multi-agency approach comprising officers from the IR, HMCE, DWP and the

Health and Safety Executive. Until now, little evidence has been made public regarding their effectiveness relative to conventional departmental-level compliance work or even the level of work that they have uncovered.

The Multi-Agency Team (MAT) project
The MAT pilot project in Wolverhampton was set up in October 2000, staffed by HMCE, DWP, IR, Jobcentre Plus and the Child Support Agency. Its objective is to improve tax, benefits and employer compliance across a wide range of businesses and customers so as to: increase direct and indirect tax yield; reduce benefits abuse against central and local government, and reduce child poverty. The only publicly available evaluation of MAT combines its outcomes with those of the two JoFITs. By the end of February 2003, they had recorded 34 sanctions, 78 adjustments to benefit, 47 overpayments and two collusive employers had been prosecuted. The total value of adjustments to benefit and overpayments was £80 000 (Select Committee on Public Accounts, 2004). These initiatives thus represent only a very small proportion of all compliance work, displaying the very limited degree to which joint action has been seriously taken on board until now.

Operation gangmaster
The sixth priority sector identified by the 'Grabiner Steering Group' (now IESG) was the agriculture and fisheries sector for which a separate cross-government initiative – 'Operation Gangmaster' – was established to tackle illegal labour providers who organize the supply of labour to employers requiring short-term (often seasonal) labour such as crop-pickers (gangmasters). The Gangmasters (Licensing) Act 2004 establishes the Gangmasters Licensing Authority to set up and operate a licensing scheme for labour providers operating in the agriculture, shellfish gathering and associated processing and packaging sectors. Operation Gangmaster has been initiated through regional forums that collate intelligence from all participating departments and agencies. In March 2004, there were 10 'live' operations under Operation Gangmaster at various stages in the planning/operational cycle and in 2003/4, the specialist teams settled 51 investigations identifying additional liabilities of £4.7 million (Select Committee on Environment, Food and Rural Affairs, 2004: 3). Again, in consequence, this initiative constitutes a relatively small segment of all non-compliance identified by government.

Data matching and sharing exercises
Besides these 'on-the-ground' teams, further co-ordinated operations have taken place around data sharing and matching. Legal authority is needed before government departments and agencies can share data and any legally

authorized data exchange must accord with the Data Protection Act 1998 and the requirements of the Human Rights Act 1998. Take, for example, the Social Security Fraud Act 2001. Government was unwilling to give provision in this Act for DWP to obtain information from banks and other financial institutions on benefit claimants judged to be at high risk of committing fraud. Instead, the power was limited to cases where reasonable grounds for suspicion of fraud exist.

Within such confines, nevertheless, the legal gateways to enable data sharing between departments have expanded considerably since the turn of the millennium. DWP, for example, sources data on National Insurance contributions and tax credits from IR as well as on hidden capital that may affect benefit entitlements. It also sources data held by banks and other financial institutions in relation to those considered to be at high risk of committing fraud. Joint computer audit teams are based in Edinburgh, the West Midlands, London, Reading and Manchester.

On the frequency of data matching, some 72 different runs take place and the intervals between each run range from weekly to six monthly. Some 34 data-matching runs take place weekly to identify anomalies (for example, customers claiming IS while their partner is working, children being claimed for by more than one customer and a customer claiming JSA while in employment). The frequency of each run is largely dependent on the refresh rate for the data and the capability of the data provider to supply data strips. Such runs produce a significant number of inconsistencies. Between April 2003 and February 2004, for example, 217 510 inconsistencies in data for further investigation were identified by the DWP data-matching service with a total saving of £39 million, not all of which related to 'working while claiming' (DWP, 2004a).

Co-ordinating Strategy Across Departments

It is not only at the operational level that co-ordination across departments has occurred. There now exists a multitude of cross-departmental and inter-agency committees, forums, steering groups, working groups and co-ordinating groups, each of which addresses various strategic aspects of the problem or have wider strategic responsibilities. Figure 14.1 provides a structure of the various groups and the interrelationships between them in the form of an organizational chart.

The role of each group, documented in evidence provided to the Select Committee on Environment, Food and Rural Affairs (2004), is as follows:

- *Illegal Working Steering Group* set up in November 2002 and focused upon illegal workers, it is chaired by a Minister of State in the Home

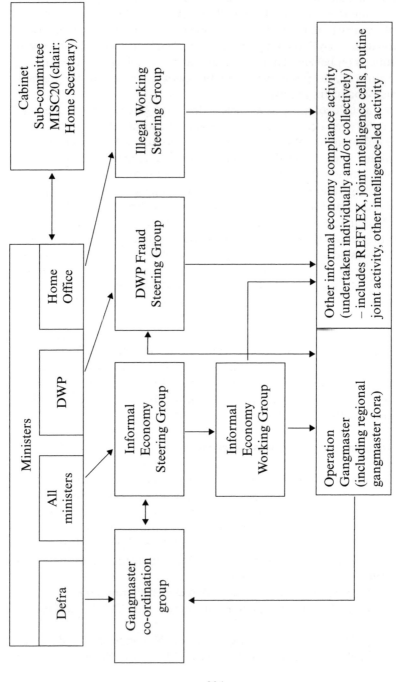

Figure 14.1   Co-ordinating actions on the underground economy: an organizational chart of the UK

Office. Bodies represented on the group are: the Confederation of British Industries; Trades Union Congress; Health and Safety Executive; Commission for Racial Equality; Government Small Business Service; National Farmers' Union; Construction Skills Certification Scheme; Recruitment and Employment Confederation; British Chambers of Commerce; British Hospitality Association; NHS Employment Branch, and J. Sainsbury.

- *Informal Economy Steering Group (IESG)* established in March 2000 to implement the recommendations of the Grabiner report. It is chaired by the Inland Revenue, and includes officials from HMCE, DWP, DEFRA and the Home Office. Operation Gangmaster reports to the Steering Group. The recommendations of Grabiner have now been fully implemented and IESG is turning its attention to other strategic issues.
- *Informal Economy Working Group (IEWP)* supports and reports to the IESG, and is concerned with operational issues. It is chaired by HMCE, and attended by IR, DWP, the Home Office and DEFRA.
- *Gangmaster Coordination Group* set up at the behest of the IESG in July 2003 as a specific forum for the discussion of policy and enforcement issues relating to agricultural gangmasters. It is chaired by a DEFRA official, reports to the Minister for Food and Farming, and attended by senior officials from DEFRA, DWP, Home Office, IR, DTI, HMCE, the Cabinet Office and the Health and Safety Executive.
- *Regional Gangmaster fora* to consider and share intelligence, and make decisions about the initiation of multi-agency enforcement actions under the Operation Gangmaster banner. The DWP is responsible for the fora, and chairs all eight of them. Attendance at the regional fora varies, but core participants are IR, HMCE, DEFRA, DTI, the Health and Safety Executive, local authorities, the National Asylum Support Service, UK Immigration Service, the National Criminal Intelligence Service and the police.
- *The DWP Fraud Steering Group* chaired by a Minister from the Department, a regular monthly meeting held between the DWP Minister with responsibility for fraud matters and his/her senior officials.
- *Reflex* chaired by the National Crime Squad, includes the National Crime Squad, the National Criminal Intelligence Service, the Immigration Service, the Foreign and Commonwealth Office, intelligence agencies, and certain key police forces.

Although no evidence was provided to the Select Committee on the role of the MIS20 Cabinet sub-committee chaired by the Home Office Minister, this Committee is believed to deal with illegal workers in the underground economy, particularly illegal migrants. There are also various *ad hoc* committees, meetings, workshops and focus groups on the underground economy that at any time bring together relevant civil servants from various government departments to discuss specific strategic issues (for example, on harnessing entrepreneurship of the underground economy; tackling the underground economy in deprived neighbourhoods; data sources on the underground economy).

Following the provision of this organizational chart in May 2004 in evidence to the Select Committee on Environment, Food and Rural Affairs, a good deal of concern was expressed about the complexity of the organizational framework. As the Select Committee on Environment, Food and Rural Affairs (2004, 5) commented:

> we are concerned that the complex structures put in place are likely to hinder rather than help a successful multi-agency response. ... There are four obvious deficiencies. First, there are simply too many different working groups, steering groups and other bodies; greater coherence in the overall structure is essential. Second, the membership of the fora and working groups is inconsistent: Defra has no role in Reflex, for example. Third, the chairmanships [*sic*] of the various groups are split between Departments and agencies. It cannot be easy, therefore, for those involved to be clear which is the 'lead' Department. Fourth, three Ministers of State – from the Home Office, Department for Work and Pensions, and Defra – have responsibilities for different, sometimes overlapping, aspects of the matter. This again makes it impossible to judge who is in charge. Given the range of Departments and agencies which have an interest in illegal working this complicated structure is perhaps not surprising. But it is wholly unsatisfactory.

Further discontent was expressed in the House of Commons the day after its publication. In a Commons debate on this report, Hansard on 21 May 2004 in columns 1217–18 records the following comments: 'I think that the Minister is indicating that he is a little concerned about its complexity ....'; 'enforcement continues to be held back to an extent by ... an absence of coordination', and 'there is still a very complex enforcement framework, and the Government needs to do much more to bring it together'. How this might be achieved is now considered.

Future Possibilities for Joined-up Thought and Action

Even if some efforts have been made to join up action and thought, there remains a considerable gap between the present situation and a fully co-ordinated approach. Here, in consequence, some possibilities for further bridging this gap are made. To do this, three separate but closely interrelated actions are considered, namely joining-up data, strategy and operations.

Joining up data

There is currently only limited data sharing across central government departments. No centralized database brings together all relevant data necessary to engage in data-matching exercises so as to identify possible individuals and businesses engaged in underground work. A way forward is to develop the Inter-Departmental Business Register (IDBR) by government departments adding their data (notwithstanding the changes in legislation that might be necessary) to provide a 'data bank' for all government departments to undertake data-matching exercises. Such a recommendation is in accordance with the recent evaluation of the future potential of the IDBR by Dugmore (2004), which makes the case for incorporating a multiplicity of data sets, such as data from the Valuation Office (rateable value, floor space and land use), new company details and company tax returns, the data from *Yellow Pages*, VAT records, PAYE and income tax records. This would provide a valuable and powerful tool for data-matching exercises so as to identify individual businesses in need of further investigation.

Joining up strategy

There is growing evidence that 'mixed messages' are coming out of government concerning their approach towards the underground economy (Small Business Council, 2004, Williams, 2005a). Not least, this is because some UK government departments are moving away from purely a deterrence (push) approach and towards a (pull) approach that is also seeking to provide advice and incentives to join the formal economy (see Evans *et al.*, 2004; Small Business Council, 2004; Williams, 2004a, 2005a), similar to other nations (for example, Global Employment Forum, 2001; ILO, 2002; Tabak, 2000; Williams, 2004b, 2005a). A joined-up and co-ordinated approach to strategy seems ever more necessary. As the Select Committee on Environment, Food and Rural Affairs (2004: 5) concludes:

> The organizational charts above confirm that there is no one Minister in charge of policy and enforcement in this area. We are convinced that the overly complicated structure of bodies put in place to deal with this cross-departmental issue hinders rather than helps a coherent response to the problem .... We recommend that the Government rationalize and streamline the steering groups, working groups and other bodies that operate in this policy area. Currently coordination of activities appears only to take place on the ground: we recommend that a single coordinating body for illegal working and the underground economy be established. We again recommend that a single Minister be made clearly responsible for the issue.

On this issue of one minister and/or department having responsibility for co-ordinating strategic and/or operational issues, given that 'working while claiming' constitutes only a small fragment of the underground economy (Renooy *et al.*, 2004; Williams, 2004a), while compliance with labour laws is fragmented across many departments, none of whom would define tackling the underground economy as one of their core objectives, the proposal here is that the newly formed HMRC might take overarching responsibility for this issue.

Joining up operations
How operations are co-ordinated depends on decisions with regard to joining-up strategy. The two are interrelated. Expanding the current area-based sectoral approach is one potential incremental way forward. Another, and one that would complement the strategic proposal for one department and minister being made responsible, is to establish a single compliance agency in central government. This 'employment-place compliance agency' would take responsibility for tackling the underground economy and bring the disparate range of compliance activities out of their existing departmental silos and into one agency. One outcome might be to reduce the number of separate labour law inspections of workplaces, perhaps using super inspectors and consideration could be given to creating one return for all aspects of direct and indirect taxation. Perhaps HMRC might be the appropriate location for such an agency and in deciding on its objectives and structure, lessons could be learned from the Multi-Agency Team (MAT) pilot project in Wolverhampton, although no evaluations have been made public to be able to establish its efficacy. It is certain, however, that the current level of joined-up operational work is dwarfed by unilateral action by individual departments working in their silos.

Critical Reflections on Joining up Strategy and Operations

In the UK, unilateral action by individual government departments remains the norm rather than collective co-ordinated action. Although the post-Grabiner period has resulted in greater co-ordination both at the strategic and operational level, there remains a large gap between the present situation and a fully joined-up approach. Here, various recommendations have been made of how to further join up strategy and operations, including: transcending the current situation of data-sharing on what is normally a bi-lateral basis to a situation where there is a national database for data-matching purposes; moving away from the current fragmented approach towards strategy and giving one department and minister overarching responsibility (possibly HMRC); and creating an employment-place compliance unit/agency within HMRC responsible for all operational aspects related to the underground economy.

Indeed, following the publication of the Small Business Council report on tackling the underground economy (Small Business Council, 2004), and the welcoming of its recommendations by the Chancellor of the Exchequer in his pre-Budget speech November 2004, along with a request to report on the feasibility of implementing its recommendations, the IESG has been busily engaged in identifying which of its measures to take forward. On the whole, it appears that less emphasis has been put on the various incentives (discussed in Chapters 10–12) and awareness-raising measures (discussed in Chapter 13) and more on joining up thought and action.

This may well be a mistake. Whether greater co-ordination will improve the effectiveness of government remains very much open to question. Despite the apparent presumption that this is the case, reflected in how the IESG is perhaps taking forward the recommendations of the Small Business Council (2004) report, there is little evidence to support such an assumption. Indeed, the returns on many of the current co-ordinated operations appear, if anything, lower than conventional departmental operations. In practice, therefore, such co-ordination could prove to be very expensive. Before pursuing any of the above recommendations, in consequence, it is crucial that pilot studies are conducted to evaluate the marginal net benefits in terms of improved tax recovery and/or reduced benefit fraud of both the existing and proposed joint initiatives for it is by no means certain at present that greater co-ordination at the operational level will be more effective than the currently predominant silos approach.

AN EXEMPLAR OF A JOINED-UP APPROACH: THE CASE OF FRANCE

Unlike the UK, France has since 1997 developed a highly co-ordinated approach not only at the level of national government but also at the local and regional scales, and has in addition involved social partners at all spatial levels. Here, a brief overview of the French system of governance with regard to underground work is provided, along with a search for evidence on whether this is a more effective means of combating the underground economy than the UK system.

Architecture of Governance in France for Tackling Underground Work

In stark contrast to the fragmented and disjointed organizational collage of institutions that characterizes UK governance in this realm, France has a more cohesive and integrated approach. Since 11 March 1997, a law has been in place that created a coherent architecture of governance. This ensures not only full co-operation between the numerous central government departments with responsibilities for tackling underground work but also provides a key role for regional and local government, as well as trade union and employer organizations at all spatial scales (ACOSS, 2004; DILTI, 2002, 2004a, b). As Figure 14.2 displays, unlike the UK where no one minister or government department is responsible, in France, overarching responsibility for policy towards underground work lies with an Inter-Ministerial Committee to Combat Underground Work (*Le comité interministériel pour la lutte contre le travail illégal*) which is chaired by the Prime Minister and involves all ministers of departments with a responsibility for tackling underground work. This provides the overall co-ordinating role in all government matters surrounding underground work.

Inter-Ministerial Committee (chair: Prime Minister

The National Commission (chair: Ministry of Employment, Work and Social Cohesion)

Délégation Interministérielle à la Lutte contre le Travail Illégal (DILTI)

Départment commissions (chair: mayors)	COLTIs (chair: magistrates)

Figure 14.2   Architecture of governance towards underground work in France

Underneath this is the National Commission for Combating Underground Work (*La commission de lutte contre le travail illégal*). This is composed of senior civil servants in central government departments and agencies involved in combating underground work along with representatives from a range of social partners including national employer and employee federations, and representative organizations of various professions. Its role is to co-ordinate the actions decided by the ministers in the Inter-Ministerial Committee.

To provide the overarching co-ordinating function in both strategic and operational matters, there is the Inter-Ministerial Delegation to Combat Underground Work (*Délégation Interministérielle à la Lutte contre le Travail Illégal*, DILTI). This is the secretariat of the National Commission and co-ordinates all administrative departments and units with responsibility for tackling underground work. The Minister of Work and Employment is responsible and reports direct to the Prime Minister. This delegation composed of 40 or so civil servants from seven Ministries (justice, employment, interior, defence, finance, transport and agriculture), communicates the policy decisions to regional and local functionaries, as well as the various social partners, charged with responsibility for tackling underground work. Three-quarters of the employees in DILTI work in Paris, a quarter in Marseille and the rest in Toulouse. Its co-ordinating role involves: attending to the implementation of policy measures; providing assistance to the control services and magistrates, including the provision of specialized documents, reference books and periodical publications; providing a central institution for the analysis of all information concerning underground work; developing partnerships with professional organizations that represent the sectors touched by underground work; and presenting to public authorities measures that would improve the efficiency of the fight against underground work.

Recognizing that underground work is a geographically diverse phenomenon and that it is necessary to tailor policy towards local circumstances, the 1997 law provided for the establishment of local institutions that take the co-ordinating role at the local level. In each and every department, Departmental Commissions (or what are in effect local DILTIs) have been set up to bring together governmental actors and social partners to tackle underground work. Their role is to implement at the local level the programme of the national DILTI, taking into account their local knowledge. They are also responsible for producing annual reports of the situation in their domain of competence and producing plans for action.

In addition to these more strategic Departmental Commissions are local units whose function is to co-ordinate the operational side in the fight against underground work. Known as COLTIs (*Comités opérationnels de lutte contre le travail illégal*), these bring together those interested in compliance issues and ensure that the various agencies act in a co-ordinated manner. The permanent secretary of the COLTI is responsible for ensuring that the agencies share information, disseminates technical information and organizes the co-ordination of operations. S/he also provides technical detail on new civil and administrative penalties for different activities, priorities and so forth that feed down from central government. In 2002, moreover, a further spatial scale was introduced when 'regional action units' (*groupements d'intervention régionaux*, GIRs) were created in all regions.

Having outlined this institutional infrastructure, it is important to note that its creation has not resulted in a multitude of new edicts, programmes and policies being cascaded down from the centre to the localities and regions. Indeed, after 1998, the National Committee did not meet again until June 2004 when it drew up a new plan of action for underground work. This 2004 plan adopted a sectoral targeting approach that focuses on four industries, namely live and recorded entertainment, agriculture, construction and civil engineering, and the hotel, café and restaurant sector. Across all these sector initiatives, the relevant trade union and employer organizations are now working with DILTI at the national, regional and local levels in partnership-based arrangements, although central government takes the lead role. There is also an emphasis on data sharing both within and between the national, regional and local levels as well as on a cross-border basis with other EU member states. Whether detection has improved since 1997, however, is not known. Indeed, there have been no evaluations, for example, of the relative costs of detection pre- and post-1997 made public so far as is known or any other type of evaluation of the marginal net benefits in terms of improved tax recovery and/or reduced benefit fraud of such a joined-up approach.

CONCLUSIONS

This chapter has revealed that in stark contrast to the fragmented and disjointed UK institutional infrastructure for dealing with underground work where no minister or government department takes responsibility, France adopts a highly co-ordinated approach not only at the national scale but also at the local and regional levels of government that, in addition, involves social partners at all spatial scales. Until now, there has been a presumption that joining up thought and action, as found in France, is a precursor for a more effective approach.

However, there is no evidence that such a joined-up approach is more effective at tackling underground work. Indeed, examining the marginal net benefits of the few joined-up initiatives pursued in the UK in terms of how they improve tax recovery and/or reduce benefit fraud identifies that it is far from conclusive that joining up actions results in a more effective approach. As such, there is currently a lack of supporting evidence for joining up thought and action and until such time as this is evaluated, caution is urged with regard to putting emphasis on this aspect of public policy when seeking to harness the hidden enterprise culture.

15. Conclusions

INTRODUCTION

At the outset of this book, the following questions were posed. How many enterprises and entrepreneurs start up in business conducting a portion or all of their trade on an off-the-books basis? And how many continue to conduct a portion of their trade in such a manner once they become more established? What should be done about them? Should governments adopt ever more punitive measures to eradicate this form of risk-taking enterprise and entrepreneur from the economic landscape? Should a laissez-faire approach be adopted towards them? Or should these underground entrepreneurs be recognized as a hidden enterprise culture and policies pursued to help them legitimize their business ventures? If so, how might this be achieved? What can be done to help those currently working on an off-the-books basis to move towards formalizing their business operations? And what preventive measures can be taken to ensure that in future, enterprises start up in a legitimate manner? In this concluding chapter, the overall findings are reviewed so as to summarize the arguments.

ENTERPRISE CULTURE AND THE UNDERGROUND ECONOMY: THE MISSING LINK

Part I of this book highlighted how few have so far identified the relationship between enterprise culture and the underground economy in the western world. In Chapter 2, it was shown how the wealth of literature on entrepreneurship and enterprise culture has only adopted a very partial representation of these concepts by always viewing them through the lens of the legitimate economy. In this literature, there is little, if any, discussion of the underground economy and the central role that it can and does play in enterprise creation, entrepreneurship and the operation of enterprise culture. It then proceeded to argue that whether narrow or broader definitions of entrepreneurship and enterprise culture are adopted, understanding the underground economy is central to advancing knowledge on these subjects and that it is wholly possible to conceptualize enterprise and entrepreneurship in the underground economy as representing a 'hidden enterprise culture' that has so far remained out of sight in the vast majority of business and management studies texts.

Chapter 3 then charted the continuities and changes in thought on the underground economy in the western world over the past three decades or so. This displayed how the vast majority of the literature on the underground economy has focused upon its negative attributes and, as such, viewed it as a form of work that needs to be eradicated using deterrence measures. In very recent years, however, it was revealed that there has begun to slowly and gradually emerge a caucus of thought that is beginning to highlight some of the more positive features of this sphere, notably how it acts as a platform for enterprise creation and seedbed for entrepreneurship, and that this is leading to a view of the underground economy as an asset that needs to be harnessed rather than a hindrance to development. Moreover, it was shown that this emerging view of the underground economy as an asset to be harnessed is very different to the much earlier neo-liberal strand, encapsulated in the writings of neo-liberals, which argued that the formal economy should be deregulated. Instead, it was revealed that this new perspective is adopting a high-road strategy of exploring how underground work can be transferred into the formal economy. With this review in hand that identifies how the relationship between the underground economy and enterprise culture is often missed, attention then turned towards an investigation of the extent and nature of the underground economy.

EXTENT AND NATURE OF UNDERGROUND ENTERPRISE

To begin unpacking the anatomy of the underground economy in the western world, Chapter 4 reviewed the wide range of methods employed to investigate this phenomenon, ranging from direct survey methods to indirect methods that seek statistical traces of the underground economy in data collected for other purposes, including non-monetary proxy indicators, monetary proxies and income/expenditure discrepancies. The outcome was to display how measurements of its size and growth are heavily dependent on the technique used and that there is a need for great caution when reading-off data on this phenomenon. Nevertheless, the conclusion was that whatever techniques are employed, nearly all display that the underground economy is large and growing relative to the formal economy.

Chapter 5 then provided a portrait of underground enterprise. Reporting not only secondary evidence but also fresh empirical data from the UK on the characteristics of this sphere, it revealed for the first time the extent to which entrepreneurship and self-employment prevails in this sphere, displaying how the vast majority of off-the-books work (some 70 per cent) is conducted by micro-entrepreneurs and the self-employed on an own account basis, often as part of a strategy to help them establish a new business venture. First-hand case study accounts of enterprise and entrepreneurs working in the underground economy were then detailed so as to provide a richer more textured understanding of this heterogeneous hidden enterprise culture.

In order to explain why entrepreneurs and enterprise engage in this hidden enterprise culture, Chapter 6 showed how there are no general universal causes for its existence and development. Instead, it was shown as brought about by a complex interplay of variables, displaying the need to move beyond simplistic solutions calling for reductions in the general rate of income tax and so forth.

WHAT SHOULD BE DONE ABOUT UNDERGROUND ENTERPRISE? POLICY OPTIONS AND THEIR IMPLICATIONS

Before identifying specific policy initiatives to deal with the multiplicity of factors that lead people to join the hidden enterprise culture, Part III addressed what should be the overarching goal of policy interventions. Is the primary goal to eradicate underground entrepreneurs? Is it to adopt a laissez-faire approach so that they might flourish? Or is it to actively intervene so as to enable them start up on a legitimate basis and help those already working in this sphere to make the transition to the formal realm?

Here, three contrasting policy options towards this hidden enterprise culture were evaluated, namely a deterrence, laissez-faire and enabling approach. Reviewing in Chapter 7 how the policy approach that dominated until very recently was one which sought to eradicate the underground economy using deterrence ('push') measures that increase the probability of detection and rack up the punishments in order to change the cost-benefit ratio confronting potential participants, this chapter reviewed the implications of pursuing such a policy agenda. The argument was that although the eradication of the underground economy is an appropriate goal, given the negative impacts of this sector on consumers, suppliers, formal businesses and society, deterrence alone is inappropriate. Instead, it was shown that there is an emerging recognition that this sector represents an asset to be harnessed rather than a hindrance to development and that this recognition calls for 'deterrence' ('push') measures to be combined with more enabling ('pull') measures to bring this enterprise and entrepreneurship into the formal economy.

In Chapter 8, therefore, the laissez-faire option was evaluated critically that until recently was the preferred choice of those who recognized the presence of entrepreneurship in the underground economy. Evaluating the implications of pursuing their preferred policy option of deregulating the formal sphere, this revealed that the net result would be a levelling down rather than up of material and social circumstances in western societies. In sum, rather than deregulating the formal economy (that is, turning formal employment into unregulated underground work), this chapter began to argue that the opposite is required; this entrepreneurship and enterprise needs to be moved into the legitimate realm (that is, formalized) using high- rather than low-road strategies. Indeed, it was shown that this is now also the view of most western governments.

Chapter 9 then introduced the policy option of harnessing enterprise and entrepreneurship in the underground economy, making clear that 'harnessing' underground enterprise and entrepreneurship does not refer to a strategy of cultivating greater engagement in underground work but, rather, transferring underground enterprise into legitimate endeavour. An important aspect of this chapter was to highlight the growing momentum across western governments and supra-national agencies towards this approach that recognizes underground enterprise and entrepreneurship as an asset that needs to be harnessed.

HARNESSING THE HIDDEN ENTERPRISE CULTURE

Part IV of the book then turned towards identifying the specific ways in which such an enabling approach could be implemented.

Helping Enterprise Start Up in a Legitimate Manner

To help business ventures start up properly from the beginning, Chapter 10 evaluated a host of initiatives that have been tried and tested in particular western nations, including: the simplification of existing formalization procedures rather than just providing advice on how to formalize; introducing new categories of legitimate work; direct and indirect tax incentives such as the 'Rich Aunt Agatha' scheme in the Netherlands; micro-enterprise development programmes; and initiatives to smooth the transition from benefits to self-employment, including *Ich AGs* in Germany, and test trading, back to work bonus and twin-track in the UK. The finding was that these are just some of the preventive measures that can be taken to stop enterprises entering the underground economy in the first place. To tackle enterprises already participating in the underground economy, however, a host of more curative remedies were argued to be required.

Moving Underground Enterprise into the Mainstream: Supply- and Demand-side Initiatives

To begin to explore how underground enterprise and entrepreneurs can be moved into the legitimate realm, Chapter 11 evaluated a host of supply-side measures which encourage those supplying underground work to make the transition to the formal realm. This included a review of: societal-wide amnesties; person-centred voluntary disclosure measures such as the 'offer in compromise' approach in the USA and the regularization campaign in Italy; advisory and support services such as Street (UK) and the Naples 'cuore' experiment in Italy; and the use of formalization tutors.

Besides supply-side measures that encourage enterprise and entrepreneurship to make the transition to the legitimate realm, another set of measures are those on the demand-side that encourage customers to acquire goods and services from legitimate rather than underground sources. How this might be achieved was the subject of Chapter 12. Reviewing the range of experiments that have been conducted throughout the advanced economies to encourage customers to use the formal rather than underground sphere, this chapter focused upon three types of demand-side initiative: targeted indirect tax measures, including experiments with reducing VAT; targeted direct tax measures such as the Home Service Scheme in Denmark and the Melkert initiatives in the Netherlands; and a host of voucher schemes including Local Employment Agencies and service vouchers in Belgium and the *Cheque Emploi Service* and *Titre Emploi Service* schemes in France. This revealed that if underground enterprise and entrepreneurship is to be transferred into the legitimate realm then deterrents alone are insufficient. Such deterrents will need to be coupled with a range of incentives or enabling initiatives that facilitate underground enterprises and entrepreneurs to make the transition to the formal realm.

Raising Awareness: Towards High Commitment Societies

However, it is insufficient to purely develop initiatives to help business start off legitimately and use demand- and supply-side incentives to encourage underground participants to transfer their activity into the formal realm. If the underground economy is to be effectively tackled, it is also necessary to raise awareness not only of the various measures currently available but also the benefits of working formally and costs of engaging in underground work.

Analysing how this might be achieved, the argument in Chapter 13 was that it is more effective to highlight the benefits of working formally and that the provision of positive rewards is one way of achieving this. However, akin to contemporary managerial thought with regard to eliciting behaviour change in organizations, it was also argued that the intention should not be purely to use direct controls to ensure compliance but rather, that indirect control methods also need to be introduced. Rather than view direct and indirect control methods as mutually exclusive, especially with regard to underground work, this chapter displayed the feasibility of combining direct and indirect control methods with an emphasis on rewarding good behaviour so as to elicit not only compliance but also a shift towards a high commitment society that relies more on internal control from the individual themselves and the wider society to elicit participation in the legitimate rather than underground economy.

Co-ordinating Government Thought and Action

Reviewing the degree to which different countries have pursued 'joined-up' co-ordinated government thought and action when tackling the underground economy, Chapter 14 highlighted considerable cross-national variations. In the UK, for example, this chapter reveals an institutional infrastructure that is composed of a multitude of disjointed agencies and although there have been recent attempts at joining up thought and action, a 'silos' approach remains prevalent and only limited co-operation between the government institutions involved. Other social partners, moreover, are shown to be absent from both the strategic and operational sides. The polar opposite was shown to be France where there is a highly joined-up approach to both thought and action with regard to the underground economy with the full integration of a wide array of social partners at both the national, regional and local levels. In this chapter therefore, the range of models available for joining up strategy and operations was evaluated so as to provide pointers as to the way forward. The finding was that despite the emphasis in some countries on this type of measure, there is currently little evidence of the effectiveness of joining up either thought or action with regard to the underground sphere. Caution was thus urged with regard to giving this measure too much emphasis until such time as evaluations have been conducted so as to show the marginal net benefits in terms of generating tax revenue or reducing benefit fraud.

CONCLUSIONS

This book has provided the first detailed account of the hidden enterprise culture that pervades western economies including an analysis of its extent, nature and reasons for its existence using both large-scale data sets and first-hand accounts from participants. Showing how western governments are currently with one hand destroying through their deterrence approach towards the underground economy precisely the enterprise culture that with another hand they are seeking to foster, it has been contended that the way to resolve this troubling contradiction is by adopting a new policy approach towards the underground economy that seeks to help such enterprise make the transition to the legitimate realm. Scanning the advanced economies and well beyond for policy measures that can be used to achieve this, a coherent set of tailored initiatives have been proposed that can help enterprise start up in a proper manner and encourage both fledgling entrepreneurs and more established enterprises who are currently embedded in the underground economy to legitimize their operations. The outcome is a lucid guide as to how this hidden culture of enterprise can be brought into the legitimate realm. It is now up to western governments to take this forward.

Bibliography

ACOSS (2003), *L'Evaluation de l'Economie Souterraine: un recensement des études*, Paris: ACOSS.

ACOSS (2004), *Lutte Contre le Travail Illégal: bilan 2003*, Paris: ACOSS.

Adams, C. and P. Webley (2001), 'Small business owners' attitudes on VAT compliance in the UK', *Journal of Economic Psychology*, **22**(2), 195–216.

Adams, D.W. and J.D. Von Pische (1992), 'Microenterprise credit programmes: déjà vu', *World Development*, **20**(10), 1463–70.

Adjerad, S. (2003), *Dynamisme du Sectuer des Employs Familiales en 2002*, Paris: DARES Premieres Informations.

Ahn N. and S.D.L. Rica (1997), 'The underground economy in Spain: an alternative to unemployment?', *Applied Economics*, **29**(6), 733–43.

Aitken, J. (1967), *The Young Meteors*, London: Secker & Warberg.

Alden, J. (1982), 'A comparative analysis of moonlighting in Great Britain and the USA', *Industrial Relations Journal*, **13**(1), 21–31.

Allingham, M. and A. Sandmo (1972), 'Income tax evasion: a theoretical analysis', *Journal of Public Economics*, **1**(2), 323–38.

Alonso, J. (1980), *Lucha Urbana y Acumulacion de Capital*, Mexico City: la Casa Chata.

Amado, J. and C. Stoffaes (1980), 'Vers une socio-economie duale', in A. Danzin, A. Boublil and J. Lagarde (eds), *La Societe Francaise et la Technologie*, Paris: Documentation Française.

Amin, A. (1994), 'The difficult transition from informal economy to Marshallian industrial district', *Area*, **26**(1), 13–24.

Amin, R., S. Becker and A. Bayes (1998), 'NGO-promoted microcredit programs and women's empowerment in Bangladesh: quantitative and qualitative evidence', *Journal of Developing Areas*, **32**(2), 221–36.

Amin, S. (1996), 'On development: for Gunder Frank', in S.C. Chew and R.A. Denemark (eds), *The Underdevelopment of Development*, London: Sage.

Anderson, B. (2001a), 'Why madam has so many bathrobes: demand for migrant domestic workers in the EU', *Tijdschrift voor Economische en Sociale Geografie*, **92**(1), 18–26.

Anderson, B. (2001b), 'Different roots in common ground: trans-nationalism and migrant domestic workers in London', *Journal of Ethnic and Migration Studies*, **27**(4), 673–83.

Aniello, V. and P. Coppola (2003), *The Colours of Undeclared Work*, Rome: Comitato per l'emersione del lavoro no regolare, accessed at www.emersionelavororegolare.it/catania/index.php.

Anthony, D. (1996), *Working: a Report on the Impact of the Working Capital Program*, Cambridge, MA: Working Capital.

Anthony, D. (1997), 'Micro-lending institutions: using social networks to create productive capabilities', *International Journal of Sociology and Social Policy*, **17**(2), 156–78.

Apel, M. (1994), 'An expenditure-based estimate of tax evasion in Sweden', RSV Tax Reform Evaluation Report No. 1, Stockholm.

Armstrong, P. (2005), *Critique of Entrepreneurship: People and Policy*, Basingstoke: Palgrave Macmillan.

Arnold, T. (1941), *The Folklore of Capitalism*, Garden City, NJ: Blue Ribbon Books.

Arrowsmith, J., M. Gilman, P. Edwards and M. Ram (2003), 'The impact of the National Minimum Wage in small firms', *British Journal of Industrial Relations*, **41**(3), 435–56.

Ashworth, K. and R. Youngs (2002), 'Prospects of part-time work: the impact of the back-to-work bonus', Department of Work and Pensions research report no. 115, London.

Atkins F.J. (1999), 'Macroeconomic time series and the monetary aggregates approach to estimating the underground economy', *Applied Economics Letters*, **6**(9), 609–11.

Atkinson, A. and J. Micklewright (1991), 'Unemployment compensation and labour market transitions: a critical review', *Journal of Economic Literature*, **29**(8), 1679–727.

Auawal, M.A. and A. Singhal (1992), 'The diffusion of the Grameen Bank in Bangladesh', *Knowledge*, **14**(1), 7–28.

Bàculo, L. (2001), 'The shadow economy in Italy: results from field studies', paper presented at the European Scientific Workshop on The Shadow Economy: Empirical Evidence and New Policy Issues at the European Level, Ragusa, Sicily, 20–1 September.

Bàculo, L. (2002), 'The shadow economy in Italy', paper presented at conference on Unofficial Activities in transition countries: Ten Years of Experience, Zagreb, accessed at www.ijf.hr/UE_2002/program.html.

Bàculo, L. (2005), 'Harnessing entrepreneurship in the shadow economy: the Naples cuore experiment', paper presented at Public Administration Committee Conference, University of Nottingham, Nottingham, September.

Bajada, C. (2002), *Australia's Cash Economy: A Troubling Issue for Policymakers*, Aldershot: Ashgate.

Bajada, C. and F. Schneider (2003), 'The size and development of the shadow economies in the Asia Pacific', University of Linz Department of Economics discussion paper, Linz.

Balkin, S. (1989), *Self-Employment for Low-Income People*, New York: Praeger.

Barlett, D.L. and J.B. Steele (2002), *The Great American Tax Dodge: How Spiralling Fraud and Avoidance are Killing Fairness, Destroying the Income Tax, and Costing You*, Los Angeles: University of California Press.

Barrientos, A. and S. Ware Barrientos (2003), 'Social protection for informal workers in the horticulture industry', in F. Lund and J. Nicholson (eds), *Chains of Production, Ladders of Protection: Social Protection for Workers in the Informal Economy*, Durban: University of Natal School of Development Studies.

Barthe, M.A. (1985), 'Chômage, travail au noir et entraide familial', *Consommation*, **3**(1), 23–42.

Barthe, M.A. (1988), *L'Economie Cachée*, Paris: Syros Alternatives.

Barthelemy, P. (1991), 'La croissance de l'économie souterraine dans les pays occidentaux: un essai d'interpretation', in J-L. Lespes (ed.), *Les Pratiques Juridiques, Economiques et Sociales Informelles*, Paris: PUF.

Bartlett, B. (1998), 'The underground economy', National Center for Policy Analysis, accessed at www.ncpa.org/ba/ba273.html.

Bates, T. and L. Servon (1996), 'Why loans won't save the poor', *Inc Magazine*, **18**, 27–8.

Baty, G. (1990), *Entrepreneurship in the Nineties*, London: Prentice Hall.

Baumann, A. and S. Wienges (2003), 'Policies on undeclared labour in Germany', paper presented at Conference on Undeclared Labour, Malmo, November.

Baylina, M. and M. Schier (2002), 'Homework in Germany and Spain: industrial restructuring and the meaning of homework for women', *GeoJournal*, **56**(4), 295–304.

Beaman, R. and K. Wheldall (2000), 'Teachers' use of approval and disapproval in the classroom', *Educational Psychology*, **20**(4), 431–46.

Beatson, M. (1995) *Memories of Class*, London: Routledge.

Begley, T.M. and D.P. Boyd (1987), 'Psychological characteristics associated with performance in entrepreneurial firms and smaller businesses', *Journal of Business Venturing*, **2**(1), 79–93.

Bender, D.E. (2004), *Sweated Work, Weak Bodies: Anti-sweatshop Campaigns and Languages of Labor*, New Brunswick: Rutgers University Press.

Benton, L. (1990), *Invisible Factories: The Informal Economy and Industrial Development in Spain*, New York: State University of New York Press.

Berger, M. (1989), 'Giving women credit: the strength and limitations of credit as a tool for alleviating poverty', *World Development*, **17**(8), 1017–30.

Bernabe, S. (2002), 'Informal employment in countries in transition: a conceptual framework', Centre for Analysis of Social Exclusion, paper no. 56, London School of Economics, London.

Bhatt, E. (1995), 'Women and development alternatives: micro- and small-scale enterprises in India', in L. Dignard and J. Havet (eds), *Women and Micro- and Small-Scale Enterprise Development*, Boulder: Westview.

Bhattacharyya, D.K. (1990), 'An econometric method of estimating the hidden economy, United Kingdom (1960–1984): estimates and tests', *The Economic Journal*, **100**, 703–17.

Bhattacharyya, D.K. (1999), 'On the economic rationale of estimating the hidden economy', *The Economic Journal*, **109**(456), 348–59.

Bhide, A. and H.H. Stevenson (1990), 'Why be honest if honesty doesn't pay?', *Harvard Business Review*, **68**(5), 121–9.

Biggs, T., M.D. Grindle and D.R. Snodgrass (1988), 'The informal sector, policy reform and structural transformation', EEPA discussion paper no. 14, Harvard Institute for International Development, Cambridge, MA.

Blair, J.P. and C.R. Endres (1994), 'Hidden economic development assets', *Economic Development Quarterly*, **8**(3), 286–91.

Blanchflower, D.G. and B.D. Meyer (1991), 'Longitudinal analysis of young entrepreneurs in Australia and the United States', National Bureau of Economic Research working paper no. 3746, Cambridge, MA.

Blumberg, R.L. (1995), 'Gender micro-enterprise, performance and power', in C. Bose and E. Acosta-Belen (eds), *Women in the Latin American Development Process*, Philadelphia: Temple University Press.

Blumberg, R.L. (2001), '"We are family": gender, microenterprise, family work, and well-being in Ecuador and the Dominican Republic with comparative data from Guatemala, Swaziland, and Guinea-Bissau', *The History of the Family*, **6**, 271–99.

Bolton, B. and J. Thompson (2000), *Entrepreneurs: Talent, Temperament, Technique*, Oxford: Butterworth-Heinemann.

Boren, T. (2003), 'What are friends for? Rationales of informal exchange in Russian everyday life', in K. Arnstberg and T. Boren (eds), *Everyday Economy in Russia, Poland and Latvia*, Stockholm: Almqvist and Wiksell International.

Boris, E. and E. Prugl (1996), 'Introduction', in E. Boris and E. Prugl (eds), *Homeworkers in Global Perspective: Invisible No More*, London: Routledge.

Bornstein, D. (1996), *The Price of a Dream*, New York: Simon and Schuster.

Borocz, J. (1989), 'Mapping the class structures of state socialism in East-Central Europe', *Research in Social Stratification and Mobility*, **8**(2), 279–309.

Bourdieu, P. (2001), 'The forms of capital', in N. Woolsey Biggart (ed.), *Readings in Economic Sociology*, Oxford: Blackwell.

Bower, T. (2001), *Branson*, London: Fourth Estate.

Brockhaus, R.H. (1980), 'Risk-taking propensity of entrepreneurs', *Academy of Management Journal*, **23**(3), 509–20.

Brockhaus, R.H. and P.S. Horowitz (1986), 'The psychology of the entrepreneur', *Entrepreneurship Theory and Practice*, **23**(2), 29–45.

Browne, K.E. (2004), *Creole Economics: Caribbean Cunning Under the French Flag*, Austin: University of Texas.

Bunker, N. and C. Dewberry (1984), 'Unemployment behind closed doors', *Journal of Community Education*, **2**(4), 31–3.

Bunting, M. (2004), *Willing Slaves: How the Overwork Culture is Ruling our Lives*, London: HarperCollins.

Burawoy, M. and J. Lukacs (1985), 'Mythologies of work: a comparison of firms in state socialism and advanced capitalism', *American Sociological Review*, **50**(2), 723–37.

Burbach, R., O. Núñez and B. Kagarlitsky (1997), *Globalization and its Discontents: The Rise of Postmodern Socialism*, London: Pluto.

Burns, P. (2001), *Entrepreneurship and Small Business*, Basingstoke: Palgrave.

Button, K. (1984), 'Regional variations in the irregular economy: a study of possible trends', *Regional Studies*, **18**(2), 385–92.

Caianiello, D. and I. Voltura (2003), 'Proposal for a service bureau', Rome: Comitato per l'emersione del lavoro no regolare, accessed at www.emersionelavororegolare.it/catania/index.php.

Cancedda, A. (2001), *Employment in Household Services*, Dublin: European Foundation for the Improvement of Living and Working Conditions.

Cannon, T. (1991), *Enterprise: Creation, Development and Growth*, Oxford: Butterworth-Heinemann.

Capital Economics Ltd (2003), *VAT and the Construction Industry*, London: Capital Economics Ltd.

Cappechi, V. (1989), 'The informal economy and the development of flexible specialisation in Emilia Romagna', in A. Portes, M. Castells and L.A. Benton (eds), *The Informal Economy: Studies in Advanced and Less Developing Countries*, Baltimore: Johns Hopkins University Press.

Caridi, P. and P. Passerini (2001), 'The underground economy, the demand for currency approach and the analysis of discrepancies: some recent

European experience', *The Review of Income and Wealth*, **47**(2), 239–50.

Carr, P. (2002), 'Enterprise culture: understanding a misunderstood concept', in Beaver, G. (ed.), *Small Business, Entrepreneurship and Enterprise Development*, London: Prentice Hall.

Carrier, J.G. (ed.) (1997), *Meanings of the Market: The Free Market in Western Culture*, Oxford: Berg.

Carrier, J.G. (1998), 'Introduction', in J.G. Carrier and D. Miller (eds), *Virtualism: A New Political Economy*, Oxford: Berg.

Carter, M. (1984), 'Issues in the hidden economy: a survey', *Economic Record*, **60**(170), 209–21.

Castells, M. and A. Portes (1989), 'World underneath: the origins, dynamics and effects of the informal economy', in A. Portes, M. Castells and L.A. Benton (eds), *The Informal Economy: Studies in Advanced and Less Developing Countries*, Baltimore: Johns Hopkins University Press.

Castree, N., N.M. Coe, K. Ward and M. Samers (2004), *Spaces of Work: Global Capitalism and the Geographies of Labour*, London: Sage.

CENSIS (1976), 'L'occupazione occultra-carratteristiche della partecipazione al lavoro in Italia', cited in B.S. Frey and W.W. Pommerehne (1984), 'The hidden economy: state and prospects for measurement', *Review of Income and Wealth*, **30**(1), 1–23.

Chatterjee, S., K. Chaudhury and F. Schneider (2002), 'The size and development of the Indian shadow economy and a comparison with 18 Asian countries: an empirical investigation', University of Linz Department of Economics discussion paper, Linz.

Chavdarova, T. (2002), 'The informal economy in Bulgaria: historical background and present situation', in R. Neef and M. Stanuclescu (eds), *The Social Impact of Informal Economies in Eastern Europe*, Aldershot: Ashgate.

Chell, E., J. Haworth and S. Brearly (1991), *The Entrepreneurial Personality: Concepts, Cases and Categories*, London: Routledge.

Chittenden, F., S. Kauser and P. Poutzouris (2002), 'Regulatory burdens of small business: a literature review', accessed at www.sbs.gov.uk/content/analytical/research/regulation-report.pdf.

Chittenden, F., S. Kauser and P. Poutzouris (2003), 'Tax regulation and small business in the USA, UK, Australia and New Zealand', *International Small Business Journal*, **21**(1), 93–115.

Cicero, F.R. and A. Pfadt (2002), 'Investigation of a reinforcement-based toilet training procedure for children with autism', *Research in Developmental Disabilities*, **23**(5), 319–31.

Clark, M. and T. Hustom (1992), *1992 Directory of US Micro-Enterprise Programs*, Washington DC: Aspen Institute.

Clark, P. and A. Kays with L. Zandiapour, E. Soto and K. Doyle (1999), *Microenterprise and the Poor: Findings from the Self-employment Learning Project Five Year Study of Microentrepreneurs*, Washington DC: Aspen Institute.

Clinton, H.R. (1999), 'Transcript of remarks by First Lady at presidential awards for microenterprise event', Washington DC: White House Press Office, 5 February

Cocco, M.R. and Santos, E. (1984), 'A economia subterranea: contributos para a sua analisee quanticacao no caso Portugues', *Buletin Trimestral do Banco de Portugal*, **6**(1), 5–15.

Cole, A.H. (1969), 'Definition of entrepreneurship', in J. Komives (ed.), *Karl A. Bostrum Seminar in the Study of Enterprise*, Milwaukee, WI: Centre for Venture Management.

Collard, S., E. Kempson and C. Whyley (2001), *Tackling Financial Exclusion: An Area-based Approach*, Bristol: Policy Press.

Collins, O.F., D.G. Moore and D.B. Unwalla (1964), *The Enterprising Man*, East Lansing, MI: Bureau of Business and Economic Research, Michigan State University.

Comitato per l'emersione del lavoro no regolare (2003a), 'The network of business consortia founded and/or supported by the National Committee for the Surfacing of Undeclared Work', Rome: Comitato per l'emersione del lavoro no regolare, accessed at www.emersionelavororegolare.it/catania/index.php.

Comitato per l'emersione del lavoro no regolare (2003b), 'The surfacing network: how the system "national committee-local commissions-tutors" works and why we believe it is good practice for the EU', Rome: Comitato per l'emersione del lavoro no regolare, accessed at www.emersionelavororegolare.it/catania/index.php.

Comitato per l'emersione del lavoro no regolare (2003c), 'The figure of the national committee, the provincial and regional commissions, and the tutors for the surfacing of undeclared work', Rome: Comitato per l'emersione del lavoro no regolare, accessed at www.emersionelavororegolare.it/catania/index.php.

Community Economies Collective (2001), 'Imagining and enacting noncapitalist futures', *Socialist Review*, **28**(1), 93–135.

Conroy, P. (1996), 'Equal opportunities for all', Brussels: European Social Policy Forum working paper I, DG V, European Commission.

Contini, B. (1982), 'The second economy in Italy', in V.V. Tanzi (ed.), *The Underground Economy in the United States and Abroad*, Lexington, MA: Lexington Books.

Cook, D. (1989), *Rich Law, Poor Law: Different Responses to Tax and Supplementary Benefit Fraud*, Milton Keynes: Open University Press.

Cook, D. (1997), *Poverty, Crime and Punishment*, London: Child Poverty Action Group.

Copisarow, R. (2004), *Street UK – A Micro-finance Organisation: Lessons Learned from its First Three Years' Operations*, Birmingham: Street UK.

Copisarow, R. and A. Barbour (2004), *Self-Employed People in the Informal Economy: Cheats or Contributors?*, London: Community Links.

Cornelius, W.A. (1992), 'From sojourners to settlers: the changing profile of Mexican immigration to the United States', in J.A. Bustamante, C.W. Reynolds and R.A. Hinojosa Oseda (eds), *US-Mexico Relations: Labour Market Interdependence*, Stanford, CA: Stanford University Press.

Cornuel, D. and B. Duriez (1985), 'Local exchange and state intervention', in N. Redclift and E. Mingione (eds), *Beyond Employment: Household, Gender and Subsistence*, Oxford: Basil Blackwell.

Cornwall, J.R. (1998), 'The entrepreneur as a building block for community', *Journal of Developmental Entrepreneurship*, **3**(1), 141–8.

Counts, A. (1996), *Give Us Credit: How Muhammad Yunus's Micro-lending Revolution is Empowering Women from Bangladesh to Chicago*, New York: Random House.

Coyle, M., M. Houghton, C. Evans and J. Vindasius (1994), *Going Forward: The Peer Group Lending Exchange November 2–4 1993*, Toronto: CALMEADOW.

Creevey, L. (1996), *Changing Women's Lives and Work: An Analysis of the Impacts of Eight Microenterprise Projects*, London: IT Press.

Crewe, L. and N. Gregson (1998), 'Tales of the unexpected: exploring car boot sales as marginal spaces of contemporary consumption', *Transactions of the Institute of British Geographers*, **23**(1), 39–54.

Crnkovic-Pozaic, S. (1999), 'Measuring employment in the unofficial economy by using labor market data', in E.L. Feige and K. Ott (eds), *Underground Economies in Transition: Unrecorded Activity, Tax Evasion, Corruption and Organized Crime*, Aldershot: Ashgate.

Crompton, R., D. Gallie and K. Purcell (1996), 'Work, economic restructuring and social regulation', in R. Crompton, D. Gallie and K. Purcell (eds), *Changing Forms of Employment: Organisation, Skills and Gender*, London: Routledge.

Cross, J.C. (1997), 'Entrepreneurship and exploitation: measuring independence and dependence in the informal economy', *International Journal of Sociology and Social Policy*, **17**(3/4), 37–63.

Cross, J.C. (2000), 'Street vendors, modernity and postmodernity: conflict and compromise in the global economy', *International Journal of Sociology and Social Policy*, **20**(1), 29–51.

Cunningham J.B. and J. Lischeron (1991), 'Defining entrepreneurship', *Journal of Small Business Management*, **29**(1), 45–67.

Dagg, A. (1996), 'Organizing homeworkers into unions: the Homeworkers Association of Toronto, Canada', in E. Boris and E. Prugl (eds), *Homeworkers in Global Perspective: Invisible No More*, London: Routledge.

Das, K. (2003), 'Income and employment in informal manufacturing: a case study', in in R. Jhabvala, R.M. Sudarshan and J. Unni (eds), *Informal Economy Centrestage: New Structures of Employment*, London: Sage.

Dawes, L. (1993), *Long-Term Unemployment and Labour Market Flexibility*, Leicester: Centre for Labour Market Studies, University of Leicester.

De Bono, E. (1985), *Tactics: The Art of Science and Success*, London: Pion.

De Grazia, R. (1982), 'Clandestine employment: a problem for our time', in V. Tanzi (ed.), *The Underground Economy in the United States and Abroad*, Lexington MA: Lexington Books.

De Soto, H. (1989), *The Other Path: The Economic Answer to Terrorism*, London: Harper and Row.

De Soto, H. (2001), *The Mystery of Capital: Why Capitalism Triumphs in the West and Fails Everywhere Else*, London: Black Swan.

De Sutter, T. (2000), *Het Plaatselijk Werkgelegenheidsagentschap: regelgeving en praktijk*, Leuven: HIVA.

Deakin, S. and Wilkinson, F. (1991/2), 'Social policy and economic efficiency: the deregulation of labour markets in Britain', *Critical Social Policy*, **33**(1), 40–51.

Del Boca, D. and Forte, F. (1982), 'Recent empirical surveys and theoretical interpretations of the parallel economy', in V. Tanzi (ed.), *The Underground Economy in the United States and Abroad*, Lexington, MA: Lexington Books.

Delmar, F. (2000), 'The psychology of the entrepreneur', in S. Carter and D. Jones-Evans (eds), *Enterprise and Small Business*, London: Pearson.

Denison, E. (1982), 'Is US growth understated because of the underground economy? Employment ratios suggest not', *Review of Income and Wealth*, **28**(1), 1–16.

Department for Work and Pensions (2003a), *Tackling Benefit Fraud*, London: The Stationery Office.

Department for Work and Pensions (2003b), *Departmental Report 2003*, London: Department for Work and Pensions.

Department for Work and Pensions (2003c), 'Keeping in touch with the labour market: qualitative evaluation of the back to work bonus', Research Report No. 96, London: Department for Work and Pensions.

Department for Work and Pensions (2003d), 'Prospects of part-time work: the impact of the back to work bonus' Department for Work and Pensions research report no. 115, London. .

Department for Work and Pensions (2004a), *Departmental Report 2004*, London: Department for Work and Pensions.

Department for Work and Pensions (2004b), *Fraud and Error in Income Support and Jobseeker's Allowance from April 2002 to March 2003*, London: Department for Work and Pensions.

Department for Work and Pensions (2004c), *UK National Action Plan for Employment*, London: Department for Work and Pensions.

Derrida, J. (1967), *Of Grammatology*, Baltimore: Johns Hopkins University Press.

Desai, M. (2002), 'Transnational solidarity: women's agency, structural adjustment and globalization', in N. Naples and M. Desai (eds), *Women's Activism and Globalization*, New York: Routledge.

Deutschmann, C. (2001), 'Capitalism as religion? An unorthodox analysis of entrepreneurship', *European Journal of Sociology*, **44**(3), 387–403.

Dilnot, A. (1992), 'Social security and labour market policy', in I.E. McLaughlin (ed.), *Understanding Employment*, London: Routledge.

Dilnot, A. and C.N. Morris (1981), 'What do we know about the black economy?', *Fiscal Studies*, **2**(1), 58–73.

DILTI (2002), *Plaquette de presentation de la DILTI*, accessed at www.travail.gouv.fr/ministere/dilti.html.

DILTI (2004a), *Commission Nationale de Lutte Contre le Travail Illégal*, Paris: Ministere de l'Emploi , du Travail et de la Cohesion Sociale

DILTI (2004b), *3eme Comité National de Lutte contre le Travail Illégal*, Paris: Ministere de l'Emploi, du Travail et de la Cohesion Sociale.

Dixon H. (1999), 'Controversy: on the use of the "hidden economy" estimates', *The Economic Journal*, **109**(456), 335–7.

Doane, D., D. Srikajon and R. Ofrenco (2003), 'Social protection for informal workers in the garment industry', in F. Lund and J. Nicholson (eds), *Chains of Production, Ladders of Protection: Social Protection for Workers in the Informal Economy*, Durban: School of Development Studies, University of Natal.

DTI (1998), *Our Competitive Future: Building the Knowledge Driven Economy*, cmnd 4176, London: HM Stationery Office.

Du Gay, P. (2005), 'The values of bureaucracy: an introduction', in P. du Gay (ed.), *The Values of Bureaucracy*, Oxford: Oxford University Press.

Du Gay, P. and G. Salaman (1998), 'The cult[ure] of the customer', in C. Mabey, G. Salaman and J. Storey (eds), *Strategic Human Resource Management: A Reader*, London: Sage.

Dugmore, D. (2004), *The Inter-Departmental Business Register: Its Future Potential*, London: Demographic Decisions Ltd.

Duncan, C.M. (1992), 'Persistent poverty in Appalachia: scarce work and rigid stratification', in C. Duncan (ed.), *Rural Poverty in America*, New York: Auburn House.

Economist Intelligence Unit (1982), *Coping with Unemployment: The Effects on the Unemployed Themselves*, London: Economist Intelligence Unit.

Edgcomb, E., J. Klein and P. Clark (1996), *The Practice of Microenterprise in the US: Strategies, Costs and Effectiveness*, Washington DC: Aspen Institute.

Edwards, P. (1979), *Contested Terrain: The Transformation of the Workplace in the Twentieth Century*, London: Heinemann.

Edwards, P., M. Ram and J. Black (2003), *The Impact of Employment Legislation on Small Firms: A Case Study Analysis*, research series no. 20, London: DTI Employment Relations.

Edwards, P., M. Ram and J. Black (2004), 'Why does employment legislation not damage small firms?', *Journal of Law and Society*, **31**(2), 245–65.

Ehlers, T. and Main, K. (1998), 'Women and the false promise of microenterprise', *Gender and Society*, **12**, 424–40.

Elkin, T. and D. McLaren (1991), *Reviving the City: Towards Sustainable Urban Development*, London: Friends of the Earth.

Engbersen, G., K. Schuyt, J. Timmer and F. van Waarden (1993), *Cultures of Unemployment: A Comparative Look at Long-term Unemployment and Urban Poverty*, San Francisco: Westview.

Espenshade, J. (2004), *Monitoring Sweatshops: Workers, Consumers and the Global Apparel Industry*, Philadelphia: Temple University Press.

Esping-Andersen, G. (1996), 'After the golden age? Welfare state dilemmas in a global economy', in G. Esping-Anderson (ed.), *Welfare States in Transition: National Adaptations in Global Economies*, London: Sage.

European Commission (1990), *Underground Economy and Irregular Forms of Employment*, Luxembourg: Office for Official Publications of the European Communities.

European Commission (1996a), *Employment in Europe 1996*, Luxembourg: European Commission DG for Employment, Industrial Relations and Social Affairs.

European Commission (1996b), *For a Europe of Civic and Social Rights: Report by the Comite des Sages*, Luxembourg: European Commission DG for Employment, Industrial Relations and Social Affairs.

European Commission (1998), 'Communication of the Commission on undeclared work', accessed at www.europa.eu.int/comm/employment_ social/empl_esf/docs/com98–219_en.pdf.

European Commission (2000a), *Report on the Commission Communication on Undeclared Work, A5–0220/2000, rapporteur: A-K.Glase*, Brussels: Committee on Employment and Social Affairs.

European Commission (2000b), *The Social Situation in the European Union 2000*, Brussels: European Commission.

European Commission (2000c), *Employment in Europe 2000*, Brussels: European Commission.

European Commission (2002), 'Commission calls on governments to do more to fight the shadow economy', press release IP/02/339, European Commission, Brussels.

European Commission (2003a), 'European Commission proposes 10 priorities for employment reform', press release 0311, European Commission, Brussels.

European Commission (2003b), 'Council decision on guidelines for the employment policies of the Member States', *Official Journal of the European Union*, 22 July 2003, L.197/13.

European Commission (2003c), 'Council resolution on transforming undeclared work into regular employment', *Official Journal of the European Union*, 29 October, C260, accessed at www.europa.eu.int/eur-lex/en/archive/index.html.

European Commission (2004), 'Action plan: the European agenda for entrepreneurship', accessed at www.europa.eu.int/comm/entreprenruship/promoting_entreprenruship/doc/com_70_en.pdf.

Evans, M., S. Syrett and C.C. Williams (2004), *The Informal Economy and Deprived Neighbourhoods: A Systematic Review*, London: Office of the Deputy Prime Minister.

Evason, E. and R. Woods (1995), 'Poverty, deregulation of the labour market and benefit fraud', *Social Policy and Administration*, **29**(1), 40–55.

Fainstein, N. (1996), 'A note on interpreting American poverty', in E. Mingione (ed.), *Urban Poverty and the Underclass*, Oxford: Basil Blackwell.

Falkinger, J. (1988), 'Tax evasion and equity: a theoretical analysis', *Public Finance*, **43**(2), 388–95.

Feige, E.L. (1979), 'How big is the irregular economy?', *Challenge*, **November/ December**, 5–13.

Feige, E.L. (1990), 'Defining and estimating underground and informal economies', *World Development*, **18**(7), 989–1002.

Feige, E.L. (1999), 'Underground economies in transition: non-compliance and institutional change', in E.L. Feige and K. Ott (eds), *Underground Economies in Transition: Unrecorded Activity, Tax Evasion, Corruption and Organized Crime*, Aldershot: Ashgate.

Feige, E.L. and K. Ott (1999), 'Introduction', in E.L. Feige and K. Ott (eds), *Underground Economies in Transition: Unrecorded Activity, Tax Evasion, Corruption and Organized Crime*, Aldershot: Ashgate.

Fernandez-Kelly, M.P. and A.M. Garcia (1989), 'Informalisation at the core: Hispanic women, homework, and the advanced capitalist state', *Environment and Planning D*, **8**(3), 459–83.

Finger, D. (1997), *Service Cheques in Europe: A Model for Germany?*, Berlin: Wissenschaftszentrum.

Fortin, B., G. Garneau, G. Lacroix, T. Lemieux and C. Montmarquette (1996), *L'Economie Souterraine au Quebec: mythes et realites*, Laval: Presses de l'Universite Laval.

Fortin, G. and G. Lacroix (2006), 'Informal work in Canada', in E. Marcelli and C.C. Williams (eds), *Informal Work in Developed Nations*, Ann Arbor, MI: University of Michigan Press.

Foudi, R., F. Stankiewicz and N. Vanecloo (1982), *Chomeurs et Economie Informelle*, Paris: Cahiers de l'observation du changement social et culturel, no. 17.

Fournier, V. (1998), 'Stories of development and exploitation: militant voices in an enterprise culture', *Organization*, **61**(1), 107–28.

Frank, A.G. (1996), 'The underdevelopment of development', in S.C. Chew and R.A. Denemark (eds), *The Underdevelopment of Development*, London: Sage.

Franks, J.R. (1994), 'Macroeconomic policy and the informal economy', in C.A. Rakowski (ed.), *Contrapunto: The Informal Sector Debate in Latin America*, New York: State University of New York Press.

Freeman, G. and N. Ogelman (2000), 'State regulatory regimes and immigrants' informal economic activity', in J. Rath (ed.), *Immigrant Businesses: The Economic, Political and Social Environment*, London: Macmillan.

Freud, D. (1979), 'A guide to underground economics', *Financial Times*, 9 April, 16.

Frey, B.S. and H. Weck (1983), 'What produces a hidden economy? An international cross-section analysis', *Southern Economic Journal*, **49**(4), 822–32.

Frey, B.S., H. Weck and W.W. Pommerhne (1982), 'Has the shadow economy grown in Germany? An exploratory study', *Weltwirtschaftliches Archiv*, **118**, 499–524.

Friedman, E., S. Johnson, D. Kaufmann and P. Zoido (2000), 'Dodging the grabbing hand: the determinants of unofficial activity in 69 countries', *Journal of Public Economics*, **76**(3), 459–93.

Fries, S., T. Lysenko and S. Polanec (2003) 'The 2002 business environment and enterprise performance survey: results from a survey of 6,100 firms',

EBRD working paper no. 84, accessed at www.ebrd.com/pubs/find/index. html.

Friman, H.R. (2004), 'The great escape? Globalization, immigrant entrepreneurship and the criminal economy', *Review of International Political Economy*, **11**(1), 98–131.

Gabor, I.R. (1988), 'Second economy and socialism: the Hungarian experience', in E.L. Feige (ed.), *The Underground Economies*, Cambridge: Cambridge University Press.

Gadea, M.D. and J.M. Serrano-Sanz (2002), 'The hidden economy in Spain: a monetary estimation, 1964–1998', *Empirical Economics*, **27**(3), 499–527.

Gallin, D. (2001), 'Propositions on trade unions and informal employment in time of globalisation', *Antipode*, **19**(4), 531–49.

Geeroms, H. and J. Mont (1987), 'Evaluation de l'importance de l'economie souterraine en Belgique: application de la methode monetaire', in V. Ginsburgh and P. Pestieau (eds.), *L'Economie Informelle*, Bruxelles: Editions Labor.

Geertz, C. (1963), *Peddlers and Princes: Social Change and Economic Modernization in Two Indonesian Towns*, Chicago: University of Chicago Press.

General Accounting Office (1994), 'Tax administration: IRS can better pursue noncompliant sole proprietors', 2 Aug, GAO/GGD-94–175, Washington DC: General Accounting Office.

General Accounting Office (1998), *IRS Tax Year 1994 EIC Compliance Study*, GAO/GGD-98–150, Washington DC: General Accounting Office.

General Accounting Office (1999), 'IRS audits: weakness in selecting and conducting correspondence audits', GGD-99–48 March 31, Washington DC: General Accounting Office.

Gerschlager, C. (2005), 'Introduction', in C. Gerschlager (ed.), *Deception in Markets: An Economic Analysis*, Basingstoke: Palgrave Macmillan.

Gerxhani, K. (2004), 'The informal sector in developed and less developed countries: a literature survey', *Public Choice*, **120**(2), 267–300.

Ghezzi, S. (2006), 'The fallacy of the formal and informal divide: lessons from a post-Fordist regional economy', in E. Marcelli and C.C. Williams (eds), *Informal Work in Developed Nations*, Ann Arbor, MI: University of Michigan Press.

Gibb, A.A. (1987), 'Enterprise culture: its meaning and implications for education and training', *Journal of European Industrial Training*, **11**(2), 21–2.

Gibson-Graham, J.K. (1996), *The End of Capitalism as We Knew It?: A Feminist Critique of Political Economy*, Oxford: Blackwell.

Gilbert, A. (1994), 'Third world cities: poverty, unemployment, gender roles and the environment during a time of restructuring', *Urban Studies*, **31**(4/5), 605–33.

Gilder, G. (1981), *Wealth and Poverty*, New York: Basic Books.

Giles, D. (1999a), 'Measuring the hidden economy: implications for econometric modelling', *The Economic Journal*, **109**(456), 370–80.

Giles, D. (1999b), *Modelling the Hidden Economy in the Tax Gap in New Zealand*, Victoria: Department of Economics, University of Victoria.

Giles, D. and Tedds, L. (2002), 'Taxes and the Canadian underground economy', Canadian tax paper no. 106, Toronto: Canadian Tax Foundation.

Gilman, M., P. Edwards, M. Ram and J. Arrowsmith (2002), 'Pay determination in small firms in the UK: the case of the national minimum wage', *Industrial Relations Journal*, **33**(1), 52–67.

Glatzer, W. and R. Berger (1988), 'Household composition, social networks and household production in Germany', in R.E. Pahl (ed.), *On Work: Historical, Comparative and Theoretical Approaches*, Oxford: Basil Blackwell.

Glautier, S. (2004), 'Measures and models of nicotine dependence: positive reinforcement', *Addiction*, **99**(1), 30–50.

Global Employment Forum (2001), 'Informal economy: formalizing the hidden potential and raising standards', session III-C, Global Employment Forum 1–3 November 2001, Geneva: ILO, accessed at www.oracle02.ilo.org/public/english/employment/geforum/shadow.htm.

Goodin, R.E., B. Heady, R. Muffels and H-J. Dirven (1999), *The Real Worlds of Welfare Capitalism*, Cambridge: Cambridge University Press.

Grabiner Lord (2000), *The Informal Economy*, London: HM Treasury.

Gregg, P. and J. Wadsworth (1996), 'It takes two: employment polarisation in the OECD', discussion paper no. 304, Centre for Economic Performance London School of Economics, London.

Grossman, G. (1989), 'Informal personal incomes and outlays of the Soviet urban population', in A. Portes, M. Castells, and L.A. Benton (eds), *The Informal Economy: Studies in Advanced and Less Developing Countries*, Baltimore, MD: Johns Hopkins University Press.

Guest, D. (1987), 'Human resource management and industrial relations', *Journal of Management Studies*, **27**(4), 377–97.

Guimiot, A. and S. Adjerad (2003), *Le Titre Emploi Service: en mal de success*, Paris: DARES Premiers.

Gutmann, P.M. (1977), 'The subterranean economy', *Financial Analysts Journal*, **34**(11), 26–7.

Gutmann, P.M. (1978), 'Are the unemployed, unemployed?', *Financial Analysts Journal*, **34**(1), 26–9.

Hadjimichalis, C. and D. Vaiou (1989), 'Whose flexibility?: the politics of informalisation in Southern Europe', paper presented to the IAAD/SCG Study Groups of the IBG conference on Industrial Restructuring and Social Change: the Dawning of a New Era of Flexible Accumulation?, Durham.

Hansford, A., J. Hasseldine and C. Howorth (2003), 'Factors affecting the costs of UK VAT compliance for small and medium-sized enterprises', *Environment and Planning C*, **21**(4), 479–92.

Hansson, I. (1982), 'The underground economy in Sweden', in V. Tanzi (ed.), *The Underground Economy in the United States and Abroad*, Lexington, MA: Lexington Books.

Hansson, I. (1984), *Sveriges svarta sector. Berakning av skatteundandragandet I Sverige*, Stockholm: RSV.

Hapke, L. (2004), *Sweatshop: The History of an American Idea*, New Brunswick, NJ: Rutgers University Press.

Harding, P. and R. Jenkins (1989), *The Myth of the Hidden Economy: Towards a New Understanding of Informal Economic Activity*, Milton Keynes: Open University Press.

Harris, L. (2002), 'Small firm responses to employment regulation', *Journal of Small Business and Enterprise Development*, **9**(3), 296–306.

Hart, K. (1973), 'Informal income opportunities and urban employment in Ghana', *Journal of Modern African Studies*, **11**(1), 61–89.

Hart, K. (1990), 'The idea of economy: six modern dissenters', in R. Friedland and A.F. Robertson (eds), *Beyond the Marketplace: Rethinking Economy and Society*, New York: Aldine de Gruyter.

Hart, M., R. Blackburn and J. Kitching (2005), *The Impact of Regulation on Small Business Growth: An Outline Research Programme*, London: Small Business Research Centre, Kingston University.

Hasseldine, J. and L. Zhuhong (1999), 'More tax evasion research required in new millennium', *Crime, Law and Social Change*, **31**(1), 91–104.

Haughton, G., S. Johnson, L. Murphy and K. Thomas (1993), *Local Geographies of Unemployment: Long-term unemployment in Areas of Local Deprivation*, Aldershot: Avebury.

Hellberger, C. and J. Schwarze (1986), *Umfang und struktur der nebenerwerbstatigkeit in der Bundesrepublik Deutschland*, Berlin: Mitteilungen aus der Arbeits-market- und Berufsforschung.

Hellberger, C. and J. Schwarze (1987), 'Nebenerwerbstatigkeit: ein indikator fur arbeitsmarkt-flexibilitat oder schattenwirtschaft', *Wirtschaftsdienst*, **2**(1), 83–90.

Henry, J. (1976), 'Calling in the big bills', *Washington Monthly*, **5**, 6.

Henry, S. (1978), *The Hidden Economy*, London: Martin Robertson.

Herrold, M. (2003), 'Cranes and conflicts: NGO programs to improve people-park relations in Russia and China', PhD thesis, Berkeley: University of California.

Hill, R. (2002), 'The underground economy in Canada: boom or bust?', *Canadian Tax Journal*, **50**(5), 1641–54.

Himes, C. and L. Servon (1998), *Measuring Client Success: An Evaluation of ACCION's Impact on Microenterprises in the US*, Washington DC: ACCION International.

HM Customs and Excise (2003), 'Our fight against smuggling, tax fraud and crime', accessed at www.hmce.gov.uk.

Hofstede, G. (1981), *Cultures and Organisation: Software of the Mind*, London: HarperCollins.

Holmstrom, M. (1993), 'Flexible specialisation in India', *Economic and Political Weekly*, **28**(35), 25–47.

Home Office (2003a), 'Tackling benefit fraud', report no. 31, London: HMSO.

Home Office (2003b), *Prevention of Illegal Working: Proposed Changes to Document List Under Section 8 of the Asylum and Immigration Act 1996, Consultation from the Immigration and Nationality Directorate of the Home Office*, London: Home Office.

Hondagneu-Sotelo, P. (2001), *Domestica: Immigrant Workers Cleaning and Caring in the Shadows of Affluence*, Berkeley and Los Angeles, CA: University of California Press.

Houghton, D. (1979), 'The futility of taxation menaces', in A. Seldon (ed.), *Tax Avoision*, London: Institute of Economic Affairs.

Howe, L. (1988), 'Unemployment, doing the double and local labour markets in Belfast', in C. Cartin and T. Wilson (eds), *Ireland from Below: Social Change and Local Communities in Modern Ireland*, Dublin: Gill and Macmillan.

Howe, L. (1990), *Being Unemployed in Northern Ireland: An Ethnographic Study*, Cambridge: Cambridge University Press.

Howells, L. (2000), 'The dimensions of microenterprise: a critical look at microenterprise as a tool to alleviate poverty', *Journal of Affordable Housing and Community Development*, **9**(1), 161–82.

Hull, D., J.J. Bosley and G.G. Udell (1980), 'Renewing the hunt for the heffalump: identifying potential entrepreneurs by personality characteristics', *Journal of Small Business*, **18**(1), 11–18.

Hulme, D. and P. Mosley (1996), *Finance Against Poverty*, London: Routledge.

Husband, J. and B. Jerrard (2001), 'Formal aid in an informal sector: institutional support for ethnic minority enterprise in local clothing and textiles industries', *Journal of Ethnic and Migration Studies*, **27**(1), 115–31.

Hutton, W. (1995), *The State We're In*, London: Vintage.

Illie, S. (2002), 'Formal and informal incomes of the Romanian households', in R. Neef and M. Stanuclescu (eds), *The Social Impact of Informal Economies in Eastern Europe*, Aldershot: Ashgate.

International Labour Office (1996), *World Employment 1996/97: National Policies in a Global Context*, Geneva: International Labour Office.

International Labour Office (2002), *Decent Work and the Informal Economy*, Geneva, International Labour Office.

International Labour Office (2004), 'Local employment offices (ALE) (Agences locales pour l'emploi)', accessed at www.logos-net/ilo/150_base/en/init/bel_7.htm.

Isachsen, A.J. and S. Strom (1985), 'The size and growth of the hidden economy in Norway', *Review of Income and Wealth*, **31**(1), 21–38.

Isachsen, A.J., J.T. Klovland and S. Strom (1982), 'The hidden economy in Norway', in V. Tanzi (ed.), *The Underground Economy in the United States and Abroad*, Lexington, KY: D.C. Heath.

Itzigsohn, J. (2000), *Developing Poverty: The State, Labor Market Deregulation and the Informal Economy in Costa Rica and the Dominican Republic*, University Park, PA: Pennsylvania State University Press.

Jensen, L., G.T. Cornwell and J.L. Findeis (1995), 'Informal work in nonmetropolitan Pennsylvania', *Rural Sociology*, **60**(1), 91–107.

Jessen, J., W. Siebel, C. Siebel-Rebell, U. Walther and I. Weyrather (1987), 'The informal work of industrial workers', paper presented at 6th Urban Change and Conflict Conference, University of Kent at Canterbury, September.

Jhabvala, R. (2003), 'Bringing informal workers centrestage', in R. Jhabvala, R.M. Sudarshan and J. Unni (eds), *Informal Economy Centrestage: New Structures of Employment*, London: Sage.

Johnson, S. (1998), 'Policy arena: microfinancing North and South: contrasting current debates', *Journal of International Development*, **10**(3), 799–809.

Jones, C. and A. Spicer (2005), 'The sublime object of entrepreneurship', *Organization*, **12**(2), 223–46.

Jones, C. and A. Spicer (2006), 'Outline of a genealogy of the value of the entrepreneur', in G. Erreygers and G. Jacobs (eds), *Language, Communication and the Economy*, Amsterdam: John Benjamins.

Jones, T., M. Ram and P. Edwards (2004), 'Illegal immigrants and the informal economy: worker and employer experiences in the Asian underground economy', *International Journal of Economic Development*, **6**(1), 92–106.

Jönsson, H. (2001), 'Undeclared work in Sweden: results and recommendations', paper presented at the European Scientific Workshop on The Shadow Economy: Empirical Evidence and New Policy Issues at the European Level, Ragusa, Sicily, 20–21 September.

Jordan, B. and A. Travers (1998), 'The informal economy: a case study in unrestrained competition', *Social Policy and Administration*, **32**(3), 292–306.

Jurik, N.C. (2005), *Bootstrap Dreams: US Microenterprise Development in an Era of Welfare Reform*, Ithaca, NY: Cornell University Press.

Kanter, R.M. (1983), *The Change Masters*, New York; Simon and Schuster.

Kaufmann, D. and A. Kaliberda (1996), 'Integrating the unofficial economy into the dynamics of post-socialist economies: a framework for analyses and evidence', in B. Kaminski (ed.), *Economic Transition in Russia and the New States of Eurasia*, London: M.E. Sharpe.

Kellard, K., K. Legge and K. Ashworth (2002), 'Self-employment as a route off benefit', research report no. 177, London: Department of Work and Pensions.

Kempson, E. (1996), *Life on a Low Income*, York: York Publishing Services.

Kempson, E. and C. Whyley (1999), *Kept Out or Opted Out: Understanding and Combating Financial Exclusion*, Bristol: Policy Press.

Kesteloot, C. and H. Meert (1999), 'Informal spaces: the geography of informal economic activities in Brussels', *International Journal of Urban and Regional Research*, **23**(2), 232–51.

Keter, V. (2004), 'Small firms: red tape', House of Commons Library research paper 04/52, London.

Kets de Vries, M.F.R. (1977), 'The entrepreneurial personality: a person at the crossroads', *Journal of Management Studies*, **14**, 34–58.

Kidder, T. (1998), 'Microfinance experiences in rural central America: issues of food security and gender relations', paper presented at Latin American Studies Association meeting, Chicago, September.

Kinsey, K. (1992), 'Deterrence and alienation effects of IRS enforcement: an analysis of survey data', in J. Slemrod (ed.), *Why People Pay Taxes*, Ann Arbor, MI: University of Michigan Press.

Kitchen, R. and N. Tate (2001), *Conducting Research in Human Geography: Theory, Practice and Methodology*, London: Prentice Hall.

Klovland, J.T. (1980), *In Search of the Hidden Economy: Tax Evasion and the Demand for Currency in Norway and Sweden*, Bergen: Norwegian School of Economics and Business Administration.

Kochan, T. and P. Osterman (1998), 'The mutual gains enterprise', in C. Mabey, Salaman and J. Story (eds), *Strategic Human Resource Management: A Reader*, London: Sage.

Kochan, T. and P. Osterman (2003), 'The mutual gains enterprise', in C. Mabey, G. Salaman and J. Storey (eds), *Strategic Human Resource Management: A Reader*, London: Sage.

Koopmans, C.C. (1989), *Informele Arbeid: vraag, aanbod, participanten, prijzen*, Amsterdam: Proefschrift Universitiet van Amsterdam.

Labruyere, C. (1997), *Services for Persons at Home: Issues of Professionalization*, Paris: Centre d'Etudes et de Recherches sur les Qualifications.

Lacko, M. (1999), 'Electricity intensity and the unrecorded economy in post-socialist countries', in E.L. Feige and K. Ott (eds), *Underground Economies in Transition: Unrecorded Activity, Tax Evasion, Corruption and Organized Crime*, Aldershot: Ashgate.

Lagos, R.A. (1995), 'Formalising the informal sector: barriers and costs', *Development and Change*, **26**(1), 110–31.

Langfelt, E. (1989), 'The underground economy in the Federal Republic of Germany: a preliminary assessment', in E.L. Feige (ed.), *The Underground Economies: Tax Evasion and Information Distortion*, Cambridge: Cambridge University Press.

Latouche, S. (1993), *In the Wake of Affluent Society: An Exploration of Post-development*, London: Zed.

Lazaridis, G. and M. Koumandraki (2003), 'Ethnic entrepreneurship in Greece: a mosaic of informal and formal business activities', *Sociological Research On Line*, **8**, 2.

Le Feuvre, N. (2000), *Employment, Family and Community Activities: A New Balance for Men and Women – Summary of the French National Report*, Dublin: European Foundation for the Improvement of Living and Working Conditions.

Legge, K. (1989), 'Human resource management: a critical analysis', in J. Storey (ed.), *New Perspectives in Human Resource Management*, London: Routledge.

Legge, K. (1995), *Human Resource Management: Rhetorics and Realities*, London: Macmillan.

Legrain, C. (1982), 'L'economie informelle a Grand Failly', *Cahiers de l'OCS*, **7**, Paris: CNRS.

Lemieux, T., B. Fortin and P. Frechette (1994), 'The effect of taxes on labor supply in the underground economy', *American Economic Review*, **84**(1), 231–54.

Leonard, M. (1994), *Informal Economic Activity in Belfast*, Aldershot: Avebury.

Leonard, M. (1998a), 'The long-term unemployed, informal economic activity and the underclass in Belfast: rejecting or reinstating the work ethic', *International Journal of Urban and Regional Research*, **22**(1), 42–59.

Leonard, M. (1998b), *Invisible Work, Invisible Workers: The Informal Economy in Europe and the US*, London: Macmillan.

Levitan, L. and S. Feldman (1991), 'For love or money: non-monetary economic arrangements among rural households in central New York', *Research in Rural Sociology and Development*, **5**(1), 149–72.

Lewis, A.W. (1954), 'Economic development with unlimited supplies of labor', *Manchester School of Economics and Social Studies*, **22**(1), 139–91.

Leyshon, A. and N.J. Thrift (1994), 'Geographies of financial exclusion: financial abandonment in Britain and the United States', *Transactions of the Institute of British Geographers*, **20**(2), 312–41.

Light, I. and M. Pham (1998), 'Beyond credit-worthy: microcredit and informal credit in the US', *Journal of Developmental Entrepreneurship*, **3**(1), 35–51.

Lin, J. (1995), 'Polarized development and urban change in New York's Chinatown', *Urban Affairs Review*, **30**(3), 332–54.

Lindbeck, A. (1981), *Work Disincentives in the Welfare State*, Stockholm: Institute for International Economic Studies, University of Stockholm.

Little, P.D. (2003), *Somalia: Economy without State*, Bloomington, IN: Indiana University Press.

Lobo, F.M. (1990a), 'Irregular work in Spain', in *Underground Economy and Irregular Forms of Employment, Final Synthesis Report*, Brussels: Office for Official Publications of the European Communities.

Lobo, F.M. (1990b), 'Irregular work in Portugal', in *Underground Economy and Irregular Forms of Employment, Final Synthesis Report*, Brussels: Office for Official Publications of the European Communities.

Lomnitz, L.A. (1988), 'Informal exchange networks in formal systems: a theoretical model', *American Anthropologist*, **90**(1), 42–55.

LópezLaborda, J. and F. Rodrigo (2003), 'Tax amnesties and income tax compliance: the case of Spain', *Fiscal Studies*, **24**(1), 73–96.

Lozano, B. (1989), *The Invisible Workforce: Transforming American Business with Outside and Home-based Workers*, New York: Free Press.

Luiselli, J., R.F. Putnam and M. Sunderland (2002), 'Longitudinal evaluation of behaviour support intervention in a public middle school', *Journal of Positive Behaviour Interventions*, **4**(3), 184–91.

Lund, F. (2003), 'Introduction: a new approach to social protection', in F. Lund and J. Nicholson (eds), *Chains of Production, Ladders of Protection: Social Protection for Workers in the Informal Economy*, Durban: School of Development Studies, University of Natal.

Lysestol, P.M. (1995), '"The other economy" and its influences on job-seeking behaviour for the long term unemployed', paper presented at the Euroconference on Social Policy in an Environment of Insecurity, Lisbon, November.

Macafee, K. (1980), 'A glimpse of the hidden economy in the national accounts', *Economic Trends*, **2**(1), 81–7.

MacDonald, R. (1994), 'Fiddly jobs, undeclared working and the something for nothing society', *Work, Employment and Society*, **8**(4), 507–30.

MacGillivray, A., P. Conaty and C. Wadhams (2001), *Low Flying Heroes: Micro-social Enterprise Below the Radar Screen*, London: New Economics Foundation.

Maguire, K. (1993), 'Fraud, extortion and racketeering: the black economy in Northern Ireland', *Crime, Law and Social Change*, **20**(2), 273–92.

Mahadea, D. (2001), 'Similarities and differences between male and female entrepreneurial attributes in manufacturing firms in the informal sector in the Transkei', *Development in Southern Africa*, **18**(2), 189–99.

Maldonado, C. (1995), 'The informal sector: legalization or laissez-faire?', *International Labour Review*, **134**(6), 705–28.

Marcelli, E.A., M. Pastor and P.M. Joassart (1999), 'Estimating the effects of informal economic activity: evidence from Los Angeles County', *Journal of Economic Issues*, **33**(3), 579–607.

Marchese, M. (2002), *Beyond Laissez-Faire: How the State Relates to Different Patterns of the Irregular Economy*, Rome: Comitato per l'emersione del lavoro no regolare, accessed at www.emersionelavororegolare.it/catania/index.php.

Marie, C-V. (1999), 'Emploi des etrangers sans titre, travail illegal, regularisations: des debates en trompe-l'oeil', in P. Dewitte (ed.), *Immigration et Integration l'Etat des Savoirs*, Paris: Harmattan.

Marie, C-V. (2000), 'Measures taken to combat the employment of undocumented foreign workers in France: their place in the campaign against illegal employment and their results', in OECD (ed.), *Combating the Illegal Employment of Foreign Workers*, Paris: OECD.

Martino, A. (1981), 'Measuring Italy's underground economy', *Policy Review*, **16**, 87–106.

Mateman, S. and P.H. Renooy (2001), *Undeclared Labour in Europe: Towards an Integrated Approach of Combating Undeclared Labour*, Amsterdam: Regioplan.

Mattera, P. (1980), 'Small is not beautiful: decentralised production and the underground economy in Italy', *Radical America*, **14**(5), 67–76.

Mattera, P. (1985), *Off the Books: The Rise of the Underground Economy*, New York: St Martin's Press.

Matthews, K. (1982), 'The demand for currency and the black economy in the UK', *Journal of Economic Studies*, **9**(2), 3–22.

Matthews, K. (1983), 'National income and the black economy', *Journal of Economic Affairs*, **3**(4), 261–7.

Matthews, K. and J. Lloyd-Williams (2001), 'The VAT evading firm and VAT evasion: an empirical analysis', *International Journal of the Economics of Business*, **6**(1), 39–50.

Matthews, K. and A. Rastogi (1985), 'Little mo and the moonlighters: another look at the black economy', *Quarterly Economic Bulletin*, **6**(1), 21–4.

McClelland, D. (1961), *The Achieving Society*, Princeton, NJ: Van Nostrand.

McCrohan, K., J.D. Smith and T.K. Adams (1991), 'Consumer purchases in informal markets: estimates for the 1980s, prospects for the 1990s', *Journal of Retailing*, **67**(1), 22–50.

McLaughlin, E. (1994), *Flexibility in Work and Benefits*, London: Institute of Public Policy Research.

Meadows, T.C. and J.A. Pihera (1981), 'A regional perspective on the underground economy', *Review of Regional Studies*, **11**(1), 83–91.

Meager, N., P. Bates and M. Cowling (2001), *Long-Term Evaluation of Self Employment Assistance Provided by the Prince's Trust*, Sheffield: DfES.

Meldolesi, L. (2003), 'Policy for the regulation of the underground economy and employment', *Review of Economic Conditions in Italy*, **1**(1), 89–116.

Meldolesi, L. and S. Ruvolo (2003), *A Project for Formalisation*, Rome: Comitato per l'emersione del lavoro no regolare, accessed at www.emersionelavororegolare.it/catania/index.php.

Mezzera, J. (1992), 'Subordinación y complementaridad: el sector informal urbano en América Latina', *Crítica and Comunicación*, **9**, Lima: organización Internacional del trabajo.

Michaelis, C., K. Smith and S. Richards (2001), 'Regular survey of small businesses' opinions: first survey – final report', accessed at www.sbs.gov.uk/content/analytical/research/omnibussurvey1.pdf.

Microcredit Summit (1997), 'Declaration and plan for action', accessed at www.microcreditsummit.org/declaration.htm.

Milliron, V. and D. Toy (1988), 'Tax compliance: an investigation of key features', *The Journal of the American Tax Association*, **9**(1), 84–104.

Minc, A. (1980), 'Le chomage et l'economie souterraine', *Le Debat*, **2**, 3–14.

Minc, A. (1982), *L'Apres-Crise a Commence*, Paris: Gallimard.

Mingione, E. (1990), 'The case of Greece', in *Underground Economy and Irregular Forms of Employment, Final Synthesis Report*, Brussels: Office for Official Publications of the European Communities.

Mingione, E. (1991), *Fragmented Societies: A Sociology of Economic Life Beyond the Market Paradigm*, Oxford: Basil Blackwell.

Mingione, E. and M. Magatti (1995), 'Social Europe follow up to the white paper: the informal sector', DGV supplement 3/95, Brussels: European Commission.

Mingione, E. and E. Morlicchio (1993), 'New forms of urban poverty in Italy: risk path models in the North and South', *International Journal of Urban and Regional Research*, **17**(3), 413–27.

Mirus, R. and R.S. Smith (1989), 'Canada's underground economy', in E.L. Feige (ed.), *The Underground Economies: Tax Evasion and Information Distortion*, Cambridge: Cambridge University Press.

Mogensen, G.V. (1985), *Sort Arbejde i Danmark*, Copenhagen: Institut for Nationalokonomi.

Mogensen, G.V. (1990), 'Black markets and welfare in Scandinavia: some methodological and empirical issues', in M. Estellie Smith (ed.), *Perspectives on the Informal Economy*, New York: University Press of America.

Mordoch, J. (1999), 'The microfinance promise', *Journal of Economic Literature*, **37**, 1569–614.

Mordoch, J. (2000), 'The microfinance schism', *World Development*, **28**, 617–29.

Morris, L. (1994), 'Informal aspects of social divisions', *International Journal of Urban and Regional Research*, **18**(1), 112–26.

Mueller, S.L. and A.S. Thomas (2001), 'Culture and entrepreneurial potential: a nine-country study of locus of control and innovativeness', *Journal of Business Venturing*, **16**(1), 51–75.

Myles, J. (1996), 'When markets fail: social welfare in Canada and the US', in G. Esping-Anderson (ed.), *Welfare States in Transition: National Adaptations in Global Economies*, London: Sage.

Neef, R. (2002), 'Observations on the concept and forms of the informal economy in Eastern Europe', in R. Neef and M. Stanuclescu (eds), *The Social Impact of Informal Economies in Eastern Europe*, Aldershot: Ashgate.

Nelson, M.K. and J. Smith (1999), *Working Hard and Making Do: Surviving in Small Town America*, Los Angeles: University of California Press.

O'Higgins, M. (1981), 'Tax evasion and the self-employed', *British Tax Review*, **26**, 367–78.

Observatory of European SMEs (2004), *Highlights from the 2003 Observatory*, no. 8, accessed at www.europa.eu.int/comm/enterprise/enterprise_policy/analysis/doc/smes_observatory_2003_report8_en.pdf.

OECD (1989), 'Towards an "enterprising" culture: a challenge for education and training', *OECD/CERI Educational Monograph*, **4**, 6–7.

244 *The hidden enterprise culture*

OECD (1993), *Employment Outlook*, Paris: OECD.
OECD (1994), *Jobs Study: Part 2*, Paris: OECD.
OECD (1997), *Framework for the Measurement of Unrecorded Economic Activities in Transition Economies*, OECD/GDE (97), 177, Paris: OECD.
OECD (2000a), *Reducing the Risk of Policy Failure: Challenges for Regulatory Compliance*, Paris: OECD.
OECD (2000b), *Tax Avoidance and Evasion*, Paris: OECD.
OECD (2002), *Measuring the Non-Observed Economy*, Paris: OECD.
OECD (2003), *From Red Tape to Smart Tape: Administrative Simplification in OECD Countries*, accessed at www.oecd.org/topic/0,2686,en_2649_37421_1_1_1_1_37421,00.html.
OECD (2004), *OECD Employment Outlook 2004*, Paris: OECD.
Office of National Statistics (2005), *Identifying Data Sources on Entrepreneurship and the Informal Economy*, London: Office of National Statistics.
Office of the Deputy Prime Minister (2000), *Index of Multiple Deprivation*, London: Department of Local Government, Transport and the Regions.
Okun, A.M. (1975), *Equality and Efficiency: The Big Trade-off*, Washington DC: Brookings Institute.
Oladimeji, S.I. and R.A. Ajisafe (2003), 'Informal sector, micro-credit delivery and entreprenurial development in Nigeria', *Indian Journal of Economics*, **LXXXIII** (330), 377–89.
Otero, M. (1994), 'The role of governments and private institutions in addressing the informal sector in Latin America', in C.A. Rakowski (ed.), *Contrapunto: The Informal Sector Debate in Latin America*, New York: State University of New York Press.
Paglin, M. (1994), 'The underground economy: new estimates from household income and expenditure surveys', *The Yale Law Journal*, **103**(8), 2239–57.
Pahl, R.E. (1984), *Divisions of Labour*, Oxford: Blackwell.
Pahl, R.E. (1988), 'Some remarks on informal work, social polarization and the social structure', *International Journal of Urban and Regional Research*, **12**(2), 247–67.
Park, T. (1979), *Reconciliation Between Personal Income and Taxable Income (1947–1977)*, Washington DC: Bureau of Economic Analysis.
Parra-Medina, D., A. D'Antonio, S.M. Smith, S. Levin, G. Kirkner and E. Mayer-Davis (2004), 'Successful recruitment and retention strategies for a randomized weight management trial for people with diabetes living in rural, medically underserved counties of South Carolina: the POWER study', *Journal of the American Dietetic Association*, **104**(1), 7–75.

Peberdy, S. (2000), 'Mobile entrepreneurship: informal sector cross-border trade and street trade in South Africa', *Development in Southern Africa*, **17**(2), 201–19.

Peck, J. (1996a), *Work-Place: The Social Regulation of Labour Markets*, London: Guilford Press.

Peck, J. (1996b), 'The geo-politics of the workfare state', paper presented at CUDEM Seminar, Leeds Metropolitan University, October.

Pedersen, S. (1998), 'The shadow economy in Western Europe: measurement and results for selected countries', Rockwool Foundation Research Unit, study no. 5. Copenhagen.

Pedersen, S. (2003), *The Shadow Economy in Germany, Great Britain and Scandinavia: A Measurement Based on Questionnaire Surveys*, Copenhagen: The Rockwool Foundation Research Unit.

Pérez Sáinz, J.P. (1989), *Respuestas silenciosas: proletarización urbana y reproducción de la fuerzade trabajo en América Latina*, Caracas: Editorial Nueva Sociedad.

Pestieau, P. (1983), 'Belgium's irregular economy', paper presented to the International Conference on the Economics of the Shadow Economy, University of Bielefeld, West Germany, 10–14 October.

Pestieau, P. (1985), 'Belgium's irregular economy', in W. Gaeartner and A. Wenig (eds), *The Economics of the Shadow Economy*, Berlin: Springer Verlag.

Pfau-Effinger, B. (2003), 'Development of informal work in Europe', paper presented to the EU Workshop Informal/Undeclared Work: Research on its Changing Nature and Policy Strategies in an Enlarged Europe; DG Research/DG Employment and Social Affairs, Brussels, 21 May 2003, accessed at www.cordis.lu/improving/socio-economic/conf_work.htm.

Pfau-Effinger, B. (2006), 'Informal employment in the work-welfare arrangement of Germany', in E. Marcelli and C.C. Williams (eds), *Informal Work in Developed Nations*, Ann Arbor, MI: University of Michigan Press.

Phizacklea, A. and C. Wolkowitz (1995), *Homeworking Women: Gender, Racism and Class at Work*, London: Sage.

Pinch, S. (1994), 'Social polarization: a comparison of evidence from Britain and the United States', *Environment and Planning A*, **25**(6), 779–95.

Platzer, E. (2002), 'Domestic services and the division of labour: the example of the Danish Home Service Scheme', accessed at www.hum.vxu.se/publ/humanetten/nummer10/art0207.html.

Polanyi, K. (1944), *The Great Transformation*, Boston: Beacon Press.

Porter, R.D. and A.S. Bayer (1989), 'Monetary perspective on underground economic activity in the United States', in E.L. Feige (ed.), *The*

246   *The hidden enterprise culture*

Underground Economies: Tax Evasion and Information Distortion,
Cambridge: Cambridge University Press.

Portes, A. (1994), 'The informal economy and its paradoxes', in N.J. Smelser
and R. Swedberg (eds), *The Handbook of Economic Sociology*, Princeton,
NJ: Princeton University Press.

Portes, A. (1997), 'Neoliberalism and the sociology of development:
emerging trends and unanticipated facts', *Population and Development
Review*, **23**, 229–59.

Portes, A. and Sassen-Koob, S. (1987), 'Making it underground: comparative
material on the informal sector in Western market economies', *American
Journal of Sociology*, **93**(1), 30–61.

Portes, A. and Walton, J. (1981), *Labor, Class and the International System*,
New York: Academic Press.

Potter, D. (1998), 'Entrepreneurship: Psion and Europe', *Business Strategy
Review*, **9**(1), 15–20.

Prewitt, V. (2003), 'Leadership development of learning organisations',
Leadership and Organization Development Journal, **24**(2), 58–61.

Raijman, R. (2001), 'Mexican immigrants and informal self-employment
in Chicago', *Human Organization*, **60**(1), 47–55

Rakowski, C. (1994), 'The informal sector debate, part II: 1984–1993', in
C.A. Rakowski (ed.), *Contrapunto: The Informal Sector Debate in Latin
America*, New York: State University of New York Press.

Ram, M., P. Edwards, M. Gilman and J. Arrowsmith (2001), 'The dynamics
of informality: employment relations in small firms and the effects of
regulatory change', *Work, Employment and Society*, **15**(4), 845–61.

Ram, M., P. Edwards and T. Jones (2002a), *Employers and Illegal Migrant
Workers in the Clothing and Restaurant Sectors*, London: DTI Central
Unit Research.

Ram, M., T. Jones, T. Abbas and B. Sanghera (2002b), 'Ethnic minority
enterprise in its urban context: South Asian restaurants in Birmingham',
International Journal of Urban and Regional Research, **26**(1), 24–40.

Ram, M., M. Gilman, J. Arrowsmith and P. Edwards (2003), 'Once more
into the sunset? Asian clothing firms after the National Minimum Wage',
Environment and Planning C: Government and Policy, **71**(3), 238–261.

Ranis, G. (1989), 'Labor surplus economies', in J. Eatwell, M. Millgate and
P. Newman (eds), *The New Palgrave: Economic Development*, London:
Macmillan.

Recio, A. (1988), *El Trabajo Precario en Catalunya : la industria textilanera
des valles Occidental*, Barcelona: Commission Obrera Nacional de
Catalunya.

Reed, M. (2005), 'Beyond the iron cage? Bureaucracy and democracy in the knowledge economy and society', in P. du Gay (ed.), *The Values of Bureaucracy*, Oxford: Oxford University Press.

Remenyi, J. and B. Quiñones (eds) (2000), *Microfinance and Poverty Alleviation: Case Studies from Asia and the Pacific*, London: Pinter.

Renooy, P. (1990), 'The informal economy: meaning, measurement and social significance', Netherlands Geographical Studies no. 115, Amsterdam.

Renooy, P., S. Ivarsson, O. van der Wusten-Gritsai and R. Meijer (2004), *Undeclared Work in an Enlarged Union: An Analysis of Shadow work – an In-depth Study of Specific Items*, Brussels: European Commission.

Riksskatteverket – Swedish National Tax Board (RSV) (2000), *Tax Yearbook of Sweden 2000*, Stockholm: RSV.

Roberts, B. (1991), 'Household coping strategies and urban poverty in a comparative perspective', in M. Gottdiener and C.G. Pickvance (eds), *Urban Life In Transition*, London: Sage.

Robinson, J. (1985), *The Risk Takers*, London: Pion.

Robinson, J, (1990), *The Risk Takers: Five Years On*, London: Pion.

Robson, B.T. (1988), *Those Inner Cities: Reconciling the Social and Economic Aims of Urban Policy*, Oxford: Clarendon.

Rogaly, B. (1996), 'Micro-finance evangelism, "destitute women" and the hard selling of a new anti-poverty formula', *Development in Practice*, 6(1), 100–12.

Romero, J. and B.H. Kleiner (2000), 'Global trends in motivating employees', *Management Research News*, 23(78), 14–17.

Rosanvallon, P. (1980), 'Le developpement de l'economie souterraine et l'avenir des societe industrielles', *Le Debat*, 2, 8–23.

Rose, K. (1996), 'SEWA: women in movement', in N. Visvanathan, L. Duggan, L. Nisonoff and N. Wiegerasma (eds), *The Women, Gender and Development Reader*, London: Zed.

Ross, A. (2004), *Low Pay High Profile: The Global Push for Fair Labor*, London: The New Press.

Ross, I. (1978), 'Why the underground economy is booming', *Fortune*, 9 October: 92–198.

Ross, R. (2001), 'The new sweatshops in the United States: how new, how real, how many and why?', in G. Gereffi, D. Spener and J. Bair (eds), *Globalisation and Regionalism: NAFTA and the New Geography of the North American Apparel Industry*, Philadelphia, PA: Temple University Press.

Ross, R.J.S. (2004), *Slaves to Fashion: Poverty and Abuse in the New Sweatshops*, Ann Arbor, MI: University of Michigan Press.

Rotter, J. (1966), 'Generalised expectancies for internal versus external control of reinforcement', *Psychological Monographs*, 80(1), 1–27.

Rubbrecht, I. and I. Nicaise (2003), *Service Vouchers to Create 25 000 Legal Jobs*, Brussels: European Employment Observatory.

Rubery, J. (1996), 'The labour market outlook and the outlook for labour market analysis', in R. Crompton, D. Gallie and K. Purcell (eds), *Changing Forms of Employment: Organisation, Skills and Gender*, London: Routledge.

RVA (2001), *De Plaatselijke Werkgelegenheidsagentschappen. Beschrijvende analyse van 1995–1999*, Brussels: RVA.

Salmi, A-M. (1996), 'Finland is another world: the gendered time of homework', in E. Boris and E. Prugl (eds), *Homeworkers in Global Perspective: Invisible No More*, London: Routledge.

Salmi, A-M. (2003), 'Neighbours and the everyday economy', in K. Arnstberg and T. Boren (eds), *Everyday Economy in Russia, Poland and Latvia*, Stockholm: Almqvist and Wiksell International.

Sandford, C. (1999), 'Policies dealing with tax evasion', in E. Feige and K. Ott (eds), *Underground Economies in Transition: Unrecorded Activity, Tax Evasion, Corruption and Organized Crime*, Aldershot: Ashgate.

Santos, J.A. (1983), *A Economia Subterranea*, Lisbon: Minietrio do trabalho e seguranca social, Coleccao estudos, serie A, no. 4.

Sassen, S. (1989), 'New York city's informal economy', in A. Portes, M. Castells and L. Benton (eds), *The Informal Economy: Studies in Advanced and Less Developed Countries*, Baltimore, MD: Johns Hopkins University Press.

Sassen, S. (1991), *The Global City: New York, London, Tokyo*, Princeton, NJ: Princeton University Press.

Sassen, S. (1994a), *Cities in a World Economy*, Thousand Oaks, CA: Pine Forge/Sage.

Sassen, S. (1994b), 'The informal economy: between new developments and old regulations', *Yale Law Journal*, **103**(8), 2289–304.

Sassen, S. (1996), 'Service employment regimes and the new inequality', in E. Mingione (ed.), *Urban Poverty and the Underclass*, Oxford: Basil Blackwell.

Sassen, S. (1997), 'Informalisation in advanced market economies', International Labour Office, Issues in Development discussion paper 20, Geneva.

Sassen, S. and R.C. Smith (1992), 'Post-industrial growth and economic reorganisation: their impact on immigrant employment', in J. Bustamante, C.W. Reynolds and R.A. Hinojosa (eds), *US-Mexico Relations: Labour Markets Interdependence*, Stanford, CA: Stanford University Press.

Sauvy, A. (1984), *Le Travail Noir et l'Economie de Demain*, Paris: Calmann-Levy.

Schneider F. (2001), 'What do we know about the shadow economy? Evidence from 21 OECD countries', *World Economics*, **2**(4), 19–32.

Schneider, F. (2003), 'The shadow economy', in C.K. Rowley and F. Schneider (eds), *Encyclopedia of Public Choice*, Dordrecht: Kluwer.

Schneider, F. and D.H. Enste (2002), *The Shadow Economy: An International Survey*, Cambridge: Cambridge University Press.

Schneider, F. and R. Klinglmair (2004), 'Shadow economies around the world: what do we know?', Department of Economics discussion paper, University of Linz, Linz.

Schreiner, M. (1999), 'Self-employment, microenterprise and the poorest of the poor in the US', *Social Service Review*, **73**(2), 496–523.

Schumpeter, J.A. (1996), *The Theory of Economic Development*, Piscataway, NJ: Transaction Publishers.

Seabrook, J. (2003), *The No-Nonsense Guide to World Poverty*, London: Verso.

Seldon, R. (1991), 'The rhetoric of enterprise', in R. Keat and N. Abercrombie (eds), *Enterprise Culture*, London: Routledge.

Select Committee on Environment, Food and Rural Affairs (2004), *Eighth Report*, London: HM Stationery Office, accessed at www.publications. parliament.uk/pa.cm200304/cmselect/cmenvfru/455/45506.htm.

Select Committee on Public Accounts (2003), *Minutes of Evidence: Supplementary Memorandum Submitted by the DWP*, London: HM Stationery Office, accessed at www.publications.parliament.uk/pa/ cm200203/cmselect/cmpubacc/488/303031.htm.

Select Committee on Public Accounts (2004), *House of Commons – Public Accounts – First Report*, London: HM Stationery Office.

Servon, L. (1999), 'Credit and social capital: the community development potential of US microenterprise programs', *Housing Policy Debate*, **9**(1), 115–49.

Shaver, K.G. and L.R. Scott (1991), 'Person, process, choice: the psychology of new venture creation', *Entrepreneurship Theory and Practice*, **16**(2), 23–45.

Sik, E. (1993), 'From the second economy to the informal economy', *Journal of Public Policy*, **12**(1), 153–75.

Sik, E. (1994), 'From the multicoloured to the black and white economy: the Hungarian second economy and the transformation', *Urban Studies*, **31**(1), 47–70.

Slater, D. and F. Tonkiss (2001), *Market Society: Markets and Modern Social Theory*, Cambridge: Polity.

Small Business Council (2004), *Small Business in the Informal Economy: Making the Transition to the Formal Economy*, London: Small Business Council.

Small Business Service (2003), *New Drive for Better Enforcement of Regulations Launched*, London: Small Business Service.

Smets, J. (2003), 'Alle hens aan dek voor werk', Wergelegenheidconferentie, 19 September.

Smith, A. (2002), 'Culture/economy and spaces of economic practice: positioning households in post-communism', *Transactions of the Institute of British Geographers*, **27**(2), 232–50.

Smith, A. (2006), 'Informal work and the diverse economies of post-socialist Europe', in E. Marcelli and C.C. Williams (eds), *Informal Work in Developed Nations*, Ann Arbor, MI: University of Michigan Press.

Smith, J.D. (1985), 'Market motives in the informal economy', in W. Gaertner and A. Wenig (eds), *The Economics of the Shadow Economy*, Berlin: Springer-Verlag.

Smith, K. (1992), 'Reciprocity and fairness: positive incentives for tax compliance', in J. Slemrod (ed.), *Why People Pay Taxes*, Ann Arbor, MI: University of Michigan Press.

Smith, R.S. (2002), 'The underground economy: guidance for policy makers?' *Canadian Tax Journal*, **50**(5), 1655–61.

Smith, S. (1986), *Britain's Shadow Economy*, Oxford: Clarendon.

Smithies, E. (1984), *The Black Economy in England since 1914*, Dublin: Gill and Macmillan.

Snyder, K. (2003), 'Working "Off the Books": patterns of informal market participation within New York's East Village', *Sociological Inquiry*, **73**(2), 284–308.

Snyder, K.A. (2004), 'Routes to the informal economy in New York's East village: crisis, economics and identity', *Sociological Perspectives*, **47**(2), 215–40.

Sole, C. (1998), 'Irregular employment amongst immigrants in Spanish cities', *Journal of Ethnic and Migration Studies*, **24**(2), 333–46.

Staudt, K. (1998), *Free Trade? Informal Economies at the US-Mexico Border*, Philadelphia, PA: Temple University Press.

Stebbins, R.A. (2004), 'Serious leisure, volunteerism and quality of life', in J.T. Haworth and A.J. Veal (eds), *Work and Leisure*, London: Routledge.

Stoleru, L. (1982), *La France a Deux Vitesses*, Paris: Flammarion.

Storey, D.J. and N. Sykes (1996), 'Uncertainty, innovation and management', in P. Burns and J. Dewhurst (eds), *Small Business and Entrepreneurship*, London: Macmillan.

Sundbo, J. (1997), 'The creation of service markets to solve political-sociological problems: the Danish Home Service', *The Service Industries Journal*, **17**(4), 580–602.

Tabak, F. (2000), 'Introduction: informalization and the long term', in F. Tabak and M.A. Crichlow (eds), *Informalization: Process and Structure*, Baltimore, MD: Johns Hopkins University Press.

Tanzi, V. (1980), 'The underground economy in the United States: estimates and implications', *Banco Nazionale del Lavoro*, **135**, 427–53.

Tanzi, V. (ed.) (1982), *The Underground Economy in the United States and Abroad*, Lexington, MA: Lexington Books.

Tanzi V. (1999), 'Uses and abuses of estimates of the underground economy', *The Economic Journal*, **109**(456), 338–47.

Tengblad, A. (1994), *Berakning av svart ekonomi och skatteundandragandet I Sverige 1980–1991*, Stockholm: Arhundradets Skattereform.

Thomas, J.J. (1988), 'The politics of the black economy', *Work, Employment and Society*, **2**(2), 169–90.

Thomas, J.J. (1992), *Informal Economic Activity*, Hemel Hempstead: Harvester Wheatsheaf.

Thomas, J.J. (1999), 'Quantifying the black economy: "measurement with theory" yet again', *Economic Journal*, **109**, 381–9.

Thomas, J.J. (2000), 'The black economy: benefit frauds or tax evaders?', *World Economics*, **1**(1), 167–75.

Thomas, R., N. Pettigrew, D. Cotton and P. Tovey (1999), 'Keeping in touch with the labour market: a qualitative evaluation of the back to work bonus', Department of Social Security research report no. 96, London.

Thompson, P. and M. Alvesson (2005), 'Bureaucracy at work: misunderstandings and mixed blessings', in P. du Gay (ed.), *The Values of Bureaucracy*, Oxford: Oxford University Press.

Thurman, Q.C., C. St. John and L. Riggs (1984), 'Neutralisation and tax evasion: how effective would a moral appeal be in improving compliance to tax laws?', *Law and Policy*, **6**(3), 309–27.

Tickamyer, A.R. and T.A. Wood (1998), 'Identifying participation in the informal economy using survey research methods', *Rural Sociology*, **63**(2), 323–39.

Tievant, S. (1982), *Vivre autrement: echanges et sociabilite en ville nouvelle*, Paris: Cahiers de l'OCS vol 6, CNRS.

Timmons, J. (1994), *New Venture Creation*, Boston: Irwin.

Tokman, V.E. (1989a), 'Economic development and labor market segmentation in the Latin American periphery', *Journal of Inter-American Studies and World Affairs*, **31**(1), 23–47.

Tokman, V.E. (1989b), 'Policies of heterogeneous informal sector in Latin America', *World Development*, **17**, 1067–76.

Torgler, B. (2003), 'Tax morale in transition countries', *Post-Communist Economies*, **15**(3), 357–82.

Travers, A. (2002), 'Prospects for enterprise: an investigation into the motivations of workers in the informal economy', Community Links evidence paper no. 2, London.

Trinci, S. (2005), 'Underground work, immigrants and networks: some preliminary findings', *International Journal of Economic Development*, 7(1), 126–51.

Trundle, J.M. (1982), 'Recent changes in the use of cash', *Bank of England Quarterly Bulletin*, **22**, 519–29.

Turner, R., A.M. Bostyn and D. Wight (1985), 'The work ethic in a Scottish town with declining employment', in B. Roberts, R. Finnegan and D. Gallie (eds), *New Approaches to Economic Life: Economic Restructuring, Unemployment and the Social Division of Labour*, Manchester: Manchester University Press.

Unai, J. and U. Rani (2003), 'Employment and income in the informal economy: a micro-perspective', in R. Jhabvala, R.M. Sudarshan and J. Unni (eds), *Informal Economy Centrestage: New Structures of Employment*, London: Sage.

US Congress Joint Economic Committee (1983), *Growth of the Underground Economy 1950–81*, Washington DC: Government Printing Office.

US General Accounting Office (1989), *Sweatshops in New York City: A Local Example of a Nationwide Problem*, Washington DC: US General Accounting Office.

Vaknin, S. (2000), 'The blessings of the informal economy', *Central Europe Review*, **2**(40), 20 November.

Valenzuela, A. (2003), 'Day labor work', *Annual Review of Sociology*, **29**, 307–33.

Van Eck, R. and B. Kazemeier (1985), *Swarte Inkomsten uit Arbeid: resultaten van in 1983 gehouden experimentele*, Den Haag: CBS-Statistische Katernen nr 3, Central Bureau of Statistics.

Van Geuns, R., J. Mevissen and P. Renooy (1987), 'The spatial and sectoral diversity of the informal economy', *Tijdschrift voor Economische en Sociale Geografie*, **78**(5), 389–98.

Van Ours, J. (1991), 'Self-service activities and formal or informal market services', *Journal of Applied Economics*, **23**(3), 505–15.

VanderBeken, T. (2004), 'Risky business: a risk-based methodology to measure organized crime', *Crime, Law and Social Change*, **41**(5), 471–516.

Vanduyne, P.C. (1993), 'Organized-crime and business-crime enterprises in the Netherlands', *Crime, Law and Social Change*, **19**(2), 103–42.

Vinay, P. (1987), 'Women, family and work: symptoms of crisis in the informal economy of Central Italy', proceedings of the Sames 3rd international seminar, University of Thessaloniki, Thessaloniki, Greece.

Wahid, A.N.M. (1993), 'The growth and progress of the Grammen Bank', in A.N.M. Wahid (ed.), *The Grameen Bank: Poverty Relief in Bangladesh*, Boulder, CO: Westview.

Waldinger, R. and M. Lapp (1993), 'Back to the sweatshop or ahead to the informal sector', *International Journal of Urban and Regional Research*, **17**(1), 6–29.

Wallace, C. (2002), 'Household strategies: their conceptual relevance and analytical scope in social research', *Sociology*, **36**, 275–92.

Wallace, C. and C. Haerpfer (2002), 'Patterns of participation in the informal economy in East-Central Europe, 1991–1998', in R. Neef and M. Stanuclescu (eds), *The Social Impact of Informal Economies in Eastern Europe*, Aldershot: Ashgate.

Warde, A. (1990), 'Household work strategies and forms of labour: conceptual and empirical issues', *Work, Employment and Society*, **4**(4), 495–515.

Warren, M.R. (1994), 'Exploitation or co-operation? The political basis of regional variation in the Italian informal economy', *Politics and Society*, **22**(1), 89–115.

Watson, T.J. (2003), *Sociology, Work and Industry* (4th edition), London: Routledge.

Weck-Hanneman, H. and B.S. Frey (1985), 'Measuring the shadow economy: the case of Switzerland', in W. Gaertner and A. Wenig (eds), *The Economics of the Shadow Economy*, Berlin: Springer-Verlag.

Wenig, A. (1990), 'The shadow economy in the Federal Republic of Germany', in *Underground Economy and Irregular Forms of Employment, Final Synthesis Report*, Brussels: Office for Official Publications of the European Communities.

Westall, A., P. Ramsden and J. Foley (2000), *Micro-entrepreneurs: Creating Enterprising Communities*, London: New Economics Foundation and IPPR.

Wheen, F. (2004), *How Mumbo-Jumbo Conquered the World*, London: Harper Perennial.

White, J.B. (2001), *Money Makes Us Relatives: Women's Labour in Urban Turkey*, London: Routledge.

Wilkinson, A. and H. Willmott (1995), 'Introduction', in A. Wilkinson and H. Willmott (eds), *Making Quality Critical: New Perspectives on Organisational Change*, London: Routledge.

Williams, C.C. (2001a), 'Does work pay? Spatial variations in the benefits of employment and coping abilities of the unemployed', *Geoforum*, **32**(2), 199–214.

Williams, C.C. (2001b), 'Tackling the participation of the unemployed in paid informal work: a critical evaluation of the deterrence approach', *Environment and Planning C*, **19**(5), 729–49.

Williams, C.C. (2002a), 'A critical evaluation of the commodification thesis', *The Sociological Review*, **50**(4), 525–42.

Williams, C.C. (2002b), 'Beyond the commodity economy: the persistence of informal economic activity in rural England', *Geografiska Annaler B*, **83**(4), 221–33.

Williams, C.C. (2003), 'Evaluating the penetration of the commodity economy', *Futures*, **35**(8), 857–68.

Williams, C.C. (2004a), *Cash-in-Hand Work: The Underground Sector and the Hidden Economy of Favours*, Basingstoke: Palgrave Macmillan.

Williams, C.C. (2004b), 'Evaluating the architecture of governance in the UK for tackling undeclared work', *Local Governance*, **30**(4), 167–77.

Williams, C.C. (2004c), 'Beyond deterrence: rethinking the UK public policy approach towards undeclared work', *Public Policy and Administration*, **19**(1), 15–30.

Williams, C.C. (2004d), 'Harnessing enterprise and entrepreneurship in the underground economy', *International Journal of Economic Development*, **6**(1), 23–53.

Williams, C.C. (2004e), 'Geographical variations in the nature of undeclared work', *Geografiska Annaler B*, **86**(3), 187–200.

Williams, C.C. (2004f), 'Rethinking the "economy" and uneven development: spatial disparities in household coping capabilities in contemporary England', *Regional Studies*, **38**(5), 507–18.

Williams, C.C. (2004g), 'The myth of marketization: an evaluation of the persistence of non-market activities in advanced economies', *International Sociology*, **19**(4), 437–49.

Williams, C.C. (2005a), *Small Business in the Informal Economy: Making the Transition to the Formal Economy – the Evidence Base*, London: Small Business Service.

Williams, C.C. (2005b), 'The undeclared sector, self-employment and public policy', *International Journal of Entrepreneurial Behaviour and Research*, **11**(4), 244–57.

Williams, C.C. (2005c), 'Fostering community engagement and tackling undeclared work: the case for an evidence-based "joined up" public policy approach', *Regional Studies*, **39**(8), 1145–55.

Williams, C.C. (2005d), 'Unraveling the meanings of underground work', *Review of Social Economy*, **63**(1), 1–18.

Williams, C.C. (2005e), 'Formalising the informal economy: the case for local initiatives', *Local Government Studies*, **31**(3), 337–51.

Williams, C.C. (2005f), *A Commodified World? Mapping the Limits of Capitalism*, London: Zed.

Williams, C.C. (2006a), 'How much for cash? Tackling the cash-in-hand ethos in the household services sector', *The Service Industries Journal*, **26**(5).

Williams, C.C. (2006b), 'What is to be done about undeclared work? An evaluation of the policy options', *Policy and Politics*, **34**(1), 76–98.

Williams, C.C. (2006c), 'Beyond market-orientated readings of paid informal work: some lessons from rural England', *The American Journal of Economics and Sociology*, **65**.

Williams, C.C. and R. Thomas (1996), 'Paid informal work in the Leeds hospitality industry: regulated or unregulated work?', in G. Haughton and C.C. Williams (eds), *Corporate City?: Partnership, Participation and Partition in Urban Development in Leeds*, Aldershot: Avebury.

Williams, C.C. and J. Windebank (1993), 'Social and spatial inequalities in informal economic activity: some evidence from the European Community', *Area*, **25**(4), 358–64.

Williams, C.C. and J. Windebank (1994), 'Spatial variations in the informal sector: a review of evidence from the European Union', *Regional Studies*, **28**(8), 819–25.

Williams, C.C. and J. Windebank (1995a), 'Black market work in the European Community: peripheral work for peripheral localities?', *International Journal of Urban and Regional Research*, **19**(1), 22–39.

Williams, C.C. and J. Windebank (1995b), 'Social polarisation of households in contemporary Britain: a "whole economy" perspective', *Regional Studies*, **29**(8), 727–32.

Williams, C.C. and J. Windebank (1998), *Informal Employment in the Advanced Economies: Implications for Work and Welfare*, London: Routledge.

Williams, C.C. and J. Windebank (1999a), 'The formalisation of work thesis: a critical evaluation', *Futures*, **31**(6), 547–58.

Williams, C.C. and J. Windebank (1999b), 'Reconceptualising paid informal work and its implications for policy: some lessons from a case study of Southampton', *Policy Studies*, **20**(4), 221–33.

Williams, C.C. and J. Windebank (2001a), *Revitalising Deprived Urban Neighbourhoods: An Assisted Self-help Approach*, Aldershot: Ashgate.

Williams, C.C. and J. Windebank (2001b), 'Reconceptualising paid informal exchange: some lessons from English cities', *Environment and Planning A*, **33**(1), 121–40.

Williams, C.C. and J. Windebank (2001c), 'Beyond profit-motivated exchange: some lessons from the study of paid informal work', *European Urban and Regional Studies*, **8**(1), 49–61.

Williams, C.C. and J. Windebank (2001d), 'Paid informal work in deprived urban neighbourhoods: exploitative employment or co-operative self-help?', *Growth and Change*, **32**(4), 562–71.

Williams, C.C. and J. Windebank (2001e), 'Paid informal work: a barrier to social inclusion?', *Transfer: Journal of the European Trade Union Institute*, **7**(1), 25–40.

Williams, C.C. and J. Windebank (2002a), 'The uneven geographies of informal economic activities: a case study of two British cities', *Work, Employment and Society*, **16**(2), 231–50.

Williams, C.C. and J. Windebank (2002b), 'Why do people engage in paid informal work? A comparison of affluent suburbs and deprived urban neighbourhoods in Britain', *Community, Work and Family*, **5**(1), 67–83.

Williams, C.C. and J. Windebank (2003a), *Poverty and the Third Way*, London: Routledge.

Williams, C.C. and J. Windebank (2003b), 'The slow advance and uneven penetration of commodification', *International Journal of Urban and Regional Research*, **27**(2), 250–64.

Wintrobe, R. (2001), 'Tax evasion and trust', Department of Economics working papers 2001–11, University of Western Ontario.

Wood, G.D. and I.A. Sharif (1997), *Who Needs Credit? Poverty and Finance in Bangladesh*, London: Zed.

World Bank (2004), 'Doing business in 2004: understanding regulation', accessed at www.rru.worldbank.org/DoingBusiness/main/DoingBusiness2004.aspx.

Ybarra, J.-A. (1989), 'Informalisation in the Valencian economy: a model for underdevelopment', in A. Portes, M. Castells, and L.A. Benton (eds), *The Informal Economy: Studies in Advanced and Less Developing Countries*, Baltimore, MD: Johns Hopkins University Press.

Index